TRS-80® Assembly Language Made Simple

by

Earles L. McCaul

Howard W. Sams & Co., Inc.
4300 WEST 62ND ST. INDIANAPOLIS, INDIANA 46268 USA

FIRST EDITION
FIRST PRINTING—1981

International Standard Book Number: 0-672-21851-8
Library of Congress Catalog Card Number: 81-84281

Edited by: *Bob Manville*
Illustrated by: *D. B. Clemens*

Printed in the United States of America.

Preface

The Radio Shack TRS-80® Model I microcomputer is a truly remarkable machine that offers high-level computing power far beyond its affordable, low-level price. Since its introduction in the fall of 1977, more than 300,000 of these "personal" computers have been sold, making the TRS-80 the "world's most popular computer."

This book is written for the TRS-80 Model I user who is interested in writing short assembly-language programs, but is not necessarily interested in learning assembly-language programming. The goal of this book is to show you how to *use* assembly-language programming, not how to become an assembly-language programmer. Instead of stressing the academics of theory, flowcharting, and the tedious writing of routines that someone has already written, this book emphasizes the use of the existing Level II BASIC ROM subroutines. Why struggle with writing your own subroutines when you can use the existing ROM subroutines by simply calling them? You put the operands in the proper registers and memory locations, call the appropriate ROM subroutine, and the Level II BASIC ROMs do the rest. Your assembly-language programming task is simplified to little more than moving the operands into the proper locations and retrieving the results.

To use the information presented in this book, you must either have, or have access to, a Model I TRS-80 with Level II BASIC and 16K RAM and a copy of T-BUG. You do not need to know anything about assembly-language programming, but it is assumed that you have an understanding of how to program in BASIC. Although this book is written primarily for the TRS-80 user who has no experience in assembly-language programming, it contains information of interest to both the novice and advanced programmer.

In eight chapters, you are shown how to plan, write, and "hand-assemble" short assembly-language programs directly in memory using the machine-language monitor T-BUG and the Level II BASIC ROM subroutines. Chapter 1 discusses some of the reasons for using assembly language, such as its speed, efficient use of memory, and special-purpose applications. Chapter 2 discusses the "heart" of the TRS-80, the Z-80 microprocessor and its instruction set. Chapter 3 covers the Radio Shack machine-language monitor T-BUG, its commands and their uses, with numerous examples. In Chapter 4, you are introduced to the memory map of the TRS-80 and the Level II BASIC ROMs. Chapter 5 discusses the use of ROM subroutines to perform data formatting, moving, and conversion. The use of ROM subroutines to perform arithmetic and mathematic functions are discussed in Chapter 6. Chapter 7 covers the cassette, printer, and port I/Os. You are shown how to write your own read/write programs using ROM subroutines, how to send the contents of the video display to the printer, and how to use the Z-80's I/O ports. Chapter 8 brings everything together with a discussion of program planning and coding, and covers the use of jump-relative instructions to write relocatable programs as well as the actual relocation of programs in memory. Also discussed are some of the problem-areas that you are likely to encounter, such as the use of the stack, what to do when there aren't enough registers, real-time timing considerations, and linking assembly-language programs with BASIC programs.

This book was written with the aid of a TRS-80 Model I computer equipped with Level II BASIC and 16K RAM, a Centronics 730 printer with Radio Shack Printer Interface Cable (26-1411), an Exatron *Stringy Floppy* and Duncan Pittman's *Type Right Secretary* word-processing program.

I would like to acknowledge the many people whose assistance has helped to make this book possible. First, I would like to thank Dr. Christopher Titus, my editor, for his patience and guidance through the course of bringing this book from an outline to a reality. I must also thank Jill Montney and Ken Mroczek for their photography work used in Chapter 1, Richard Richardson for his permission to use *JKL LPRINT*, and Mostek's Jim Gaspard for his help in obtaining permission to excerpt the Z-80 instruction set tables used in Chapter 2. And, finally, I want to thank my family, Cathy my wife, Paul my son, and Connie and Renée my daughters, for their patience through it all. And, yes, Renée, there really is a Daddy.

EARLES L. MCCAUL

Dedicated to my father
Vincent Fremont McCaul
who started it all
by getting me interested in electronics

Contents

CHAPTER 6

CHAPTER 7

CHAPTER 8

APPENDIX A

APPENDIX B

APPENDIX C

APPENDIX D

APPENDIX E

APPENDIX F

APPENDIX G

CHAPTER 1

Why Assembly Language?

INTRODUCTION

All computer programming languages can be divided into three general classifications: *high-level, assembly-level,* and *machine-level.* Machine-level programming involves the coding of programs and data in the computer's native language—ONEs and ZEROs. Assembly-language programming utilizes symbolic codes to represent the actual coding of programs, *mnemonics* replace computer instructions and *labels* replace addresses and data variables. High-level programming incorporates "English-like" words and phrases using precisely defined structures and syntax. Fig. 1-1 shows a computer-language tree that illustrates the overall relationship of the three general classifications of computer programming languages.

Each of the three general classifications offers a distinct combination of advantages and disadvantages. High-level languages are easy to learn and use, are generally compatible between different computers, and relieve the programmer of the need for knowledge about the computer's processor or its instructions. At the same time, they are less efficient in terms of memory utilization and speed of execution, and are rather inflexible due to their "standardizations." Assembly-level languages offer a compromise between the "isolation" of high-level languages and the "intimate complexity" of machine-level languages. However, they are machine dependent and require a knowledge of the processor's instruction codes. Machine-level languages execute fastest, are the most memory-efficient, and offer the most flexibility. They are also the most difficult to learn and complex to use, and require a thorough knowledge of both the processor's operation and its instruction codes.

The specific requirements of the task to be programmed will determine which level of programming language the programmer actually uses, but generally high-level languages are better suited to applications requiring computer-to-computer compatibility and ease of debugging and modification, while assembly- or machine-level languages are used when efficient use of memory and maximum speed of execution are important.

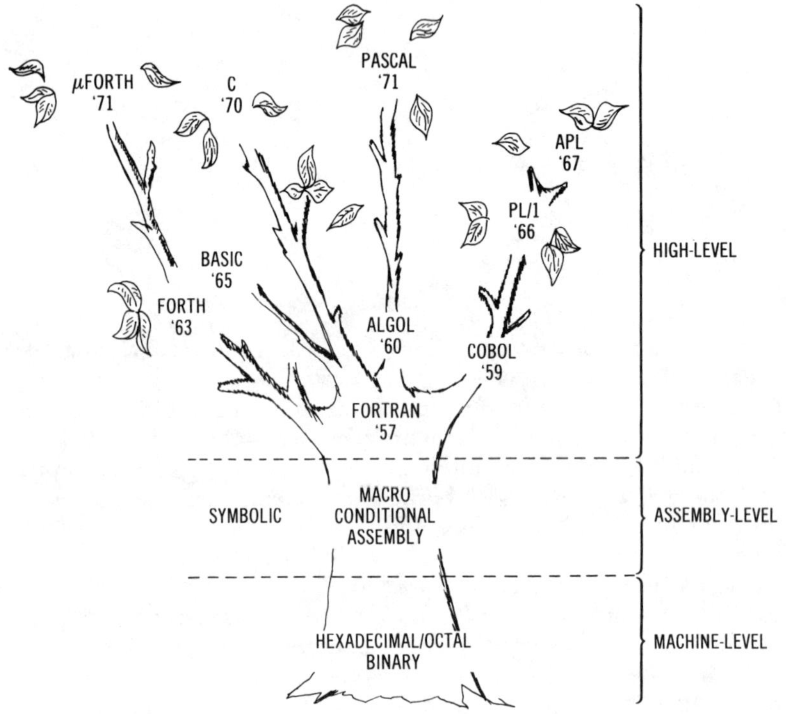

Fig. 1-1. Computer language tree.

MACHINE LANGUAGE

Because digital computers work only with ONEs and ZEROs, machine language is the most direct and efficient method of programming a computer, but it is also the most difficult and error-prone method of programming. Program instructions and data are entered as numbers, usually *binary* (0–1), although some computers are designed to accept *octal* (0–7), or *hexadecimal* (0–F). The program sequence must be translated into the proper combination of computer processor instruction codes by the programmer. This requires that the programmer possess a thorough knowledge not only of the computer's hardware and processor, but also of the processor's instruction codes. With some processors having more than 700 individual instructions (Z-80), this method of programming becomes tedious and time-consuming for all but the shortest of programs.

Fig. 1-2 shows three typical microcomputers, the Altair 8800, the Heath H8, and the KIM-1, which are, respectively, programmed in binary, octal, and hexadecimal machine language. Note the "front-panel" switches on the Altair 8800 that are used to enter either a ONE or ZERO into each bit of each byte of a program. Special "key-pads" enable the direct entry of octal and hexadecimal numbers which special electronic circuits must then convert into the binary numbers actually used by the processor. The TRS-80 has no such provision for direct entry of either binary, octal, or hexadecimal information and thus cannot be programmed directly in machine language. It can, however, be programmed in assembly language, the next step up from machine language.

ASSEMBLY LANGUAGE

With assembly language, programming is accomplished using *symbolic codes* rather than ONEs and ZEROs as with machine language. These symbolic codes consist of memory-assisting combinations of letters and abbreviations, called *mnemonics,* which represent the processor's instructions, and descriptive names, called *labels,* which suggest the use of data variables and memory addresses. Computers cannot directly "understand" the mnemonics and the instructions or data that they represent—they must be translated, or *assembled,* into binary coding before they can be run. The symbolic coding written by the programmer is called *source code,* and the assembled binary coding is called the *object code.* Only object code is understood and used by the computer's processor—computers work only with ONEs and ZEROs, not symbols.

Mnemonics

Mnemonics are a combination of letters and abbreviations that help the programmer to understand and remember the processor's instruction codes. Mnemonics simplify and condense the cumbersome binary of machine language into descriptive operation codes, or *op-codes,* and *operands* which are much easier for the programmer to use and read once written in program form. For example, the Z-80 machine language instruction, 11001110, becomes *ADC A,n* in assembly language, where *ADC A* is the mnemonic and *n* is the operand representing a one-byte variable. The mnemonic *ADC A,n* stands for: *AD*d with *C*arry to *A*ccumulator the byte *n,* which is

(A) Altair 8800 microcomputer programmed in binary.

(B) Heath H8 microcomputer programmed in octal. (*Courtesy Heath Co.*)

(C) KIM-1 microcomputer programmed in hexadecimal.

Fig. 1-2. Typical microcomputers.

certainly more meaningful and much easier to use and remember than the binary number 11001110.

Labels

Labels are programmer-assigned names, such as ITEM1 or SUMB, which replace the actual numerical values of addresses or data variables. The use of labels relieves the programmer of having to keep track of addresses or the actual numerical value of data and constants, especially when using the "stack." Instead, special routines within the assembler program perform these address and value-assignment tasks for the programmer. The use of labels for

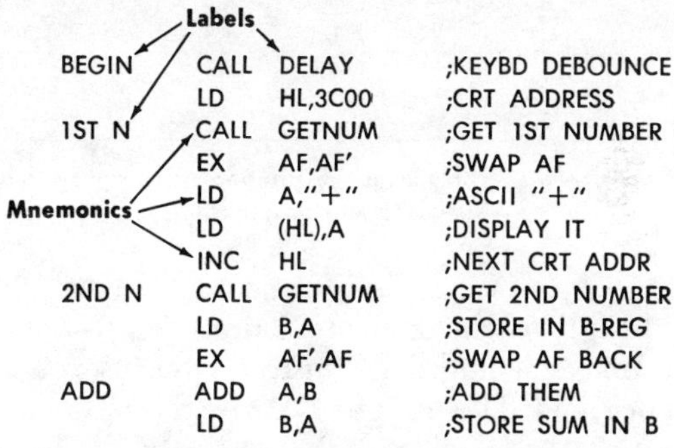

Labels
Mnemonics
BEGIN CALL DELAY ;KEYBD DEBOUNCE
LD HL,3C00 ;CRT ADDRESS
1ST N CALL GETNUM ;GET 1ST NUMBER
EX AF,AF' ;SWAP AF
LD A,"+" ;ASCII "+"
LD (HL),A ;DISPLAY IT
INC HL ;NEXT CRT ADDR
2ND N CALL GETNUM ;GET 2ND NUMBER
LD B,A ;STORE IN B-REG
EX AF',AF ;SWAP AF BACK
ADD ADD A,B ;ADD THEM
LD B,A ;STORE SUM IN B

Fig. 1-3. Assembly language mnemonics and labels.

addresses and data is shown in Fig. 1-3. Labels are only an aid for the programmer, they do not occur in the object code after being assembled. They are only used as reference points to aid the programmer during writing of the source code, and are "removed" during the assembly of the program.

Op-Codes

Operation codes, shortened to op-codes, are *numeric* representations of the *symbolic* mnemonics and labels, and are usually given in either octal or hexadecimal. Op-codes and operands may be generated in either of two ways: by the computer itself during the process of "assembling" the source code into object code, or manually by the programmer translating each instruction with the aid of a table that cross-references op-codes and machine language codes. Once the op-codes and operands have been generated, they may be used as-is and manually entered as machine code using a master control program called a *monitor*. This method of programming is referred to as "hand-assembly" and is the method described and discussed in this book. The list of op-codes and operands, whether manually or computer generated, is essentially an octal or hexa-

Machine Language (Object Code)				Assembly Language (Source Code)			
Addr	**Op-Code**			**Label**	**Mnemonic/Operand**		**Remarks**
5000	CD	00	70	BEGIN	CALL	DELAY	;KEYBD DEBOUNCE
5003	21	00	3C		LD	HL,3C00	;CRT ADDRESS
5006	CD	00	60	1ST N	CALL	GETNUM	;GET 1ST NUMBER
5009	08				EX	AF,AF'	;SWAP AF
500A	3E	2B			LD	A,"+"	;ASCII "+"
500C	77				LD	(HL),A	;DISPLAY IT
500D	23				INC	HL	;NEXT CRT ADDR
500E	CD	00	60	2ND N	CALL	GETNUM	;GET 2ND NUMBER
5011	47				LD	B,A	;STORE IN B-REG
5012	08				EX	AF',AF	;SWAP AF BACK
5013	80			ADD	ADD	A,B	;ADD THEM
5014	47				LD	B,A	;STORE SUM IN B
.	.				.	.	.
.	.				.	.	.

Fig. 1-4. Sample assembly-language program showing mnemonics, op-codes and operands.

decimal version of the binary object code. Appendix B provides a hexadecimal listing of the Z-80 op-codes. Fig. 1-4 is an example of a program object listing and illustrates the use of a mnemonic, op-code, and operand. The use of REMARKS is optional, but greatly enhances program readability and understanding by providing a rationale for each operation.

Compatibility

Unlike high-level languages, assembly-language programs are not usually capable of being run on computers having different processors. Thus, while a BASIC program written on a Z-80-based computer, such as the TRS-80, can usually be run on any other

Microprocessor	Response
Z80	LD A,n—Move immediate data byte n into accumulator.
6502	ROL —Rotate Left through the Carry bit.
6800	WAI —Wait for Interrupt/implied.

Figure 1-5. Three popular microprocessors response to the binary number 11001110.

computer regardless of its processor, a Z-80 assembly-language program will only work on another Z-80-based computer. This occurs because different processors respond differently to the same binary number. Fig. 1-5 illustrates how three popular microprocessors (the Z-80, 6502, and 6800) respond to the same binary number, 11001110. What this means is that each microprocessor has its *own* assembly- and machine-level languages! Knowing how to program the Z-80 does not necessarily guarantee an ability to program either a 6502 or 6800 microprocessor. The one exception is the 8080/Z-80 family of microprocessors where the 8080 instructions are a subset of the Z-80 instructions. Programs written on the 8080 will generally run on a Z-80, but not necessarily the other way around.

ASSEMBLY LANGUAGE BENEFITS

Why program the TRS-80 in assembly language, when such excellent high-level languages as Level II BASIC, FORTRAN, COBOL, and Pascal are so readily available? The answer is simply that assembly language offers a unique combination of advantages that the high-level languages cannot match. Specifically:

- Low cost of implementation.
- Direct microprocessor control.
- Maximum program execution speed.
- Minimum program memory requirement.
- Special-purpose programs and routines.

Assembly language offers the opportunity to go beyond BASIC and try something new without the need for additional hardware or peripherals. It allows the Z-80 within the TRS-80 to be programmed in its native code, and provides access to, and direct control over, the microprocessor's operation, its registers and input/output ports, and the contents of memory. It is fast, typically 100–300 times faster than an equivalent program written in BASIC. This is an important factor when you are processing data as it occurs, called *real-time* processing, or when sorting large arrays. It is also very thrifty with memory, typically using less than one-fifth the memory required for an equivalent BASIC program. Also assembly language enables the programmer to create special-purpose programs and routines suited specifically to the programmer's needs. Best of all is the fact that learning to program the TRS-80 in assembly language is not as difficult as it might seem. Rather than learn to write programs and routines that someone has already written (and probably written better), this book instead stresses the immediate use of the existing Level II ROM subroutines. Emphasis is placed upon learning how to move data to and from the memory addresses and microprocessor registers used by the ROM subroutines. Appendix D lists some of the Level II BASIC ROM subroutines and their addresses. Look them over at this time as they will greatly simplify programming in assembly language.

Low Cost of Implementation

Assembly language is very inexpensive to implement. With the TRS-80, the use of high-level languages beyond the resident Level

II BASIC requires at least one mini-disk (which means the Expansion Interface, too) and additional memory, usually a minimum of 32K of user read/write (RAM) memory, before actual programming may be done. But, with assembly language, all that is required is a monitor, such as T-BUG, and programming may commence immediately. There is nothing else, except possibly this book, to buy.

No additional memory is needed with assembly language because 4K of user memory programmed in assembly language is equivalent to about 20–24K of BASIC! This makes the typical 16K TRS-80 capable of almost 80–96K worth of equivalent BASIC programming when it is programmed in assembly language.

The only real expense with assembly language is the price of the monitor program which can cost anywhere from $10 to over $100, depending upon the options incorporated. All the "bells" and "whistles" on the fancier monitors are useful only IF they are actually utilized, otherwise, they simply occupy memory. Those monitor functions that are truly necessary are:

- Inspect and change memory contents.
- Display register contents.
- Set/remove breakpoints.
- Jump to start address.
- Save assembly programs.

Anything beyond these five functions is extra. Everything can be accomplished using just these five functions, although many other useful functions are available. The T-BUG monitor and its functions will be covered more fully in Chapter 3.

Direct Microprocessor Control

Assembly language enables *direct* communication with the Z-80 microprocessor in the TRS-80. This direct communication provides control over exactly what the microprocessor does and when it is done. With a high-level language, the programmer seldom thinks about what the microprocessor does because the language takes care of everything. The programmer communicates to the high-level language and *it* in turn tells the microprocessor what to do. When a program is entered, special routines within the language's interpreter or compiler determine which combination of microprocessor instructions should be used to perform the program. The high-level language "isolates" the programmer from the control of what the microprocessor actually does.

With assembly language, however, the programmer must plan and direct each and every operation the microprocessor performs. Why? Simply, because *assembly language IS microprocessor operation.* Thus, writing a program in assembly language consists of se-

```
BASIC                                    Assembly Language
10  IF A=B THEN GOTO 200        5000  7E               LD A,(HL)
 .                              5003  23               INC HL
 .                              5004  BE               CP (HL)
 .                              5007  C2  C8  00       JP NZ,00C8H
                                 .
                                 .
                                 .
```

Figure 1-6. BASIC IF-THEN conditional branch vs. assembly language equivalent.

lecting from the microprocessor's instructions that sequence of op-codes which, when executed, will (hopefully) produce the intended results. To do this, the programmer must know something about both how and why the computer's microprocessor works.

Fig. 1-6 compares a simple BASIC IF-THEN conditional branch statement with its assembly-language counterpart. In the BASIC program, the programmer simply enters the line number and then the statement, and the BASIC's interpreter takes care of the rest. In the assembly language version, the programmer must define exactly what the microprocessor is to do each step of the way. The BASIC statement performed a single *multipurpose* operation: IF (condition) THEN (execution). The assembly-language routine accomplishes the same result using four separate, *specific* Z-80 instructions:

- LD A (HL)—A *load* instruction which tells the microprocessor to put the variable found at memory location (HL) into the "accumulator," or A register.
- INC HL—An *increment* instruction which tells the microprocessor to go to the *next* memory location (HL+1) where the second variable is to be found.
- CP (HL)—a *compare* instruction which tells the microprocessor to see if the first and second variable are the same.
- JP NZ,nn—A *jump* instruction which directs the microprocessor to loop back to the compare instructions at address "nn" *if* the first variable is NOT the same as the second variable.

Only four instructions and two variable addresses, for a total of 11 bytes of memory, are required with the assembly-language routine. In contrast, the BASIC statement needs 13 bytes just for the line number and the IF-THEN statement, plus 725 bytes for the actual ROM subroutine, for a total of 738 bytes. That's about a 60-to-1 better memory utilization for the assembly-language routine. Also, by changing *just one* instruction (JP NZ,nn), the conditions of not-equal (≠), greater-than (>), or less-than (<) could have just as easily been tested.

Using the block-move capabilities of the Z-80 makes it possible to move data, *or programs*, from memory locations where conflicts occur to free memory. No such feature exists in BASIC. Why move data or programs? Sometimes there is no other alternative, such as when the T-BUG resides in the same portion of memory as the many available special-purpose "utility" routines. Obviously, one must be moved, and this can be easily accomplished using a short assembly-language routine. Block moves will be discussed later in greater detail.

Maximum Program Execution Speed

Assembly-language programs typically execute between 100 and 300 times faster than their BASIC counterparts. Freed of the task of having to "interpret" each line and statement before executing its purpose, the Z-80 assembly-language program can zip along at close to clock speed, which for the Model I TRS-80 is approximately 1.77 MHz.

Fig. 1-7 compares a simple BASIC FOR-NEXT loop with an assembly-language equivalent. Note the use of an integer counter (I%) in the BASIC statement to help reduce execution time. The PRINT"*" statement executes only once to indicate when the loop is done, and contributes very little to the overall timing.

The BASIC loop takes about 38.7 seconds to complete 32,767 loops (remember, the loop started from 0, not 1). If the total time is divided by the number of loops, the time required to complete a single loop can be approximated, about 1.18 milliseconds in this case.

The assembly-language counterpart executes the same 32,767 loops too fast to be clocked using a stopwatch. However, some idea of the time required for each loop may be *roughly* determined as follows:

- One clock cycle at 1.77 MHz lasts 0.565 microsecond.
- A *typical* Z-80 instruction requires 7 clock cycles.
- Multiplying the 7 clock cycles-per-instruction times the time of 0.565 microsecond-per-clock cycle yields an average instruction time of about 4 microseconds.

BASIC

```
10 FOR I%=0 TO 32766:NEXT:PRINT"*"
.
.
.
```

Assembly Language

```
5000  11  FF  7F    LD DE,7FFFH
5003  1B            DEC DE
5004  C2  03  50    JP NZ,5003H
5007  21  00  3C    LD HL,3C00H
500A  3E  2A        LD A,2AH
500C  77            LD (HL),A
  .
  .
  .
```

Figure 1-7. BASIC IF-THEN loop vs. assembly language equivalent.

Thus, the assembly language routine takes only about 260 milliseconds to execute the same 32,767 loops. That is 150 times faster than the equivalent BASIC program. Stated another way, the BASIC program will execute only 2096 statements in roughly the same time that an assembly language routine will execute 314,400 instructions.

Because of its speed, assembly language is sometimes the *only* alternative, such as real-time processing of data, performing lengthy iterations or repeated operations, and sorting large arrays of data. A rule-of-thumb for determining when to use assembly language is, "If money can't buy it, use assembly- or machine-level language." Loosely translated, this means that when *time* or *extra* memory beyond what's available is needed, the only alternative is to utilize either assembly- or machine language. Why? Because money cannot buy time, nor can it buy 2097 bytes of memory for a 2096 byte memory computer.

Minimum Program Memory Requirement

Assembly language is very frugal with memory, typically using less than one-fifth as much as an equivalent BASIC program. Returning to the comparisons shown in Figs. 1-6 and 1-7, it can be determined using the "?MEM" command before and after entering each BASIC line number and statement, that the BASIC IF-THEN example needed 13 bytes of memory for the line number and statement alone, and the BASIC FOR-NEXT statement needed 23 bytes. However, when the lengths of the BASIC ROM subroutines are included, which are respectively 725 and 44 bytes, the total memory requirement becomes 738 bytes for the IF-THEN statement and 67 bytes for the FOR-NEXT statement. Compared to the assembly language requirements of only 11 and 12 bytes, respectively, it becomes quite clear that assembly language requires much less memory than BASIC.

The actual length of an assembly-language program depends largely upon the skill of the programmer. Generally speaking, the more familiar the programmer is with the particular microprocessor in use and its instruction set, the "tighter" the programs are. This results from the programmer being aware of the "tricks" and idiosyncrasies of the microprocessor which can be made to work "for" as well as against the programmer.

Special-Purpose Programs and Routines

Assembly language allows the programmer to write programs and routines to answer specialized needs and applications. After loading such programs into a "protected" section of memory, they can execute as though they were an original feature of the resident programming language. Examples of specialized routines are Radio Shack's Keyboard Debounce program and the Operating Systems used with mass-storage devices such as Exatron's *Stringy-Floppy* and JPC's *Poor Man's Floppy*. Once loaded, these operating systems appear invisible to normal BASIC programs and function without further attention from the programmer; their operation is automatic.

Another method of using specialized assembly-language programs and routines is to embed them within BASIC programs and have them execute only upon demand, using the USR(X) command in BASIC. The Level II BASIC even permits the "passing" of a 2-byte signed integer variable between the BASIC program and the assembly-language routine. Although this technique will be covered later, you might also wish to read over pages 8/8 through 8/12 of the *Radio Shack Level II BASIC Reference Manual*, 2nd Edition.[1]

An excellent example of a special-purpose assembly-language program is the "JKL" LPRINT program, found in Robert Richardson's *Disassembled Handbook for TRS-80, Volume 2*.[2] This program provides, in just 70 bytes, the ability to print out the content of the video display to a line-printer, initiated by the simultaneous pressing of the J, K, and L keys. The assembly-language program resides quietly in memory until called into action by pressing the "JKL" keys and then returns to dormancy when done. This program will be discussed again later.

Can YOU think of some special program or routine that you'd like to have? Of course you can, and before you finish this book, you will be able to write it yourself.

REFERENCES

1. *Radio Shack Level II Basic Reference Manual*, 2nd Edition, 1979, pp. 8/8-8/12.

2. Richardson, Robert, *Disassembled Handbook for TRS-80, Volume 2*, pp. 113-114.

REVIEW QUESTIONS

1. What are the three general classifications of computer programming languages?

2. Machine-level programming involves the coding of programs and data in ____________'s and ____________'s.

3. Assembly-level programming utilizes ______________-codes to represent actual coding of programs.

4. High-level programming incorporates ______________-like words and phrases using precisely defined structure and syntax.

5. In assembly-language programming, ________________ replace computer instructions, and ____________ replace addresses and data variables.

6. The most "efficient" method of programming is:
A. Computer-wise: ____________________________.
B. Programmer-wise: ___________________________.

7. In assembly language, the programmer writes the program using mnemonics and labels; the program is also called __________________.

8. The purpose of an "assembler" is to translate ______________-code written by the programmer into ____________-code understood by the computer.

9. *Numeric codes* which represent the microprocessor's actual instructions are called ____________________.

10. How are mnemonics and labels related to op-codes and operands?

11. Explain why it is said that assembly language *IS* microprocessor operation.

12. Typically, BASIC programming uses single _________________ operations, while assembly language uses multiple _________________ instructions.

13. The typical Z-80 instruction executes in about _________________ clock cycles.

14. For the TRS-80, a typical Z-80 instruction executes in about ______________ microseconds.

15. Name the two criteria which make machine- or assembly-level programming a "must."

CHAPTER 2

The Z-80 Microprocessor

In the first chapter, we discussed a few of the reasons for using assembly language on the TRS-80. In this chapter, we will discuss the device that makes it all possible, the Z-80 microprocessor. This device is the single most important piece of microcircuitry in the TRS-80 because it is the central processing unit (CPU) or "heart" of the computer. Without it, the TRS-80 could not function, and probably would not even exist. It is the device that controls everything that the TRS-80 does. For this reason, and because our goal is to do assembly-language programming using *object code* directly, it is important that we understand both how and why the Z-80 functions. An understanding of the registers and flags contained in the Z-80 provides insight into how it works and an understanding of its instructions explains why it does what it does.

These following aspects of the Z-80 microprocessor will be discussed:

- General Description.
- 8080/Z-80 Family of Microprocessors.
- The Z-80 Registers.
- The Z-80 Flags.
- The Z-80 Instruction Set.

The purpose of this chapter is to provide a functional overview and description of the Z-80 microprocessor.

GENERAL DESCRIPTION

The Z-80 is an 8-bit, general purpose, digital microprocessor designed by Zilog, Inc., as an enhancement of the popular 8080 microprocessor. The Z-80 is fabricated on a single, large-scale integrated (LSI) chip using NMOS technology, and is housed in a 40 pin DIP (Dual Inline Package). The pinout of the Z-80 is shown in Fig. 2-1. The Z-80 has 16 address pins (A0 through A15), eight data pins (D0 through D7), along with a number of other pins that are used to indicate what the Z-80 is doing, or are used by the Z-80 to control external devices.

Thus, the Z-80 has three buses: an 8-bit *data bus* that carries data to and from the Z-80; a 16-bit *address bus* that is used to address memory and peripherals; and a *control bus* consisting of 13 signals that the Z-80 uses to direct and coordinate all operations. Since all of the address pins can assume either a logic one or logic zero state, there are 2^{16}, or 65,536 different memory locations that the Z-80 can address. During the execution of I/O instructions, up to 256 input devices, and 256 output devices, can be addressed. Of these 512 possible peripherals, one, *port 255*, is contained within the TRS-80, and is used to control the cassette and a portion of the video display logic.

The address bus is also used when the Z-80 refreshes dynamic read/write memory (RAM). Thus, the Z-80 can be used with either *static* or *dynamic* memory, and virtually no external logic is required for dynamic memories to be refreshed. The CPU-generated refresh is completely transparent to the user. The refresh address is only on the address bus for a short period of time, after an instruction op-code is read from memory.

Because of the sophistication of the Z-80, it operates from a single +5-volt power supply, and needs only an externally generated, non-TTL compatible clock for operation. All of the other inputs and outputs of the CPU chip *are* TTL compatible. The address, data, and control buses can also be put into a high-impedance, or "third state," enabling other devices to share access to these buses. Generally, high speed, direct memory access (DMA) devices use the buses in this manner.

As a result of its 8080-based origin, the Z-80 can execute all 78 instructions that the 8080 can execute, along with 80 new instructions. Thus, the Z-80 has a total of 158 different instruction *types*. If all possible permutations of the instructions are considered, the Z-80 actually has over 700 individual instructions, making it one of the most powerful microprocessors around. Included on the chips are two interrupts to provide external devices with access to the CPU even though it may be busy executing instructions.

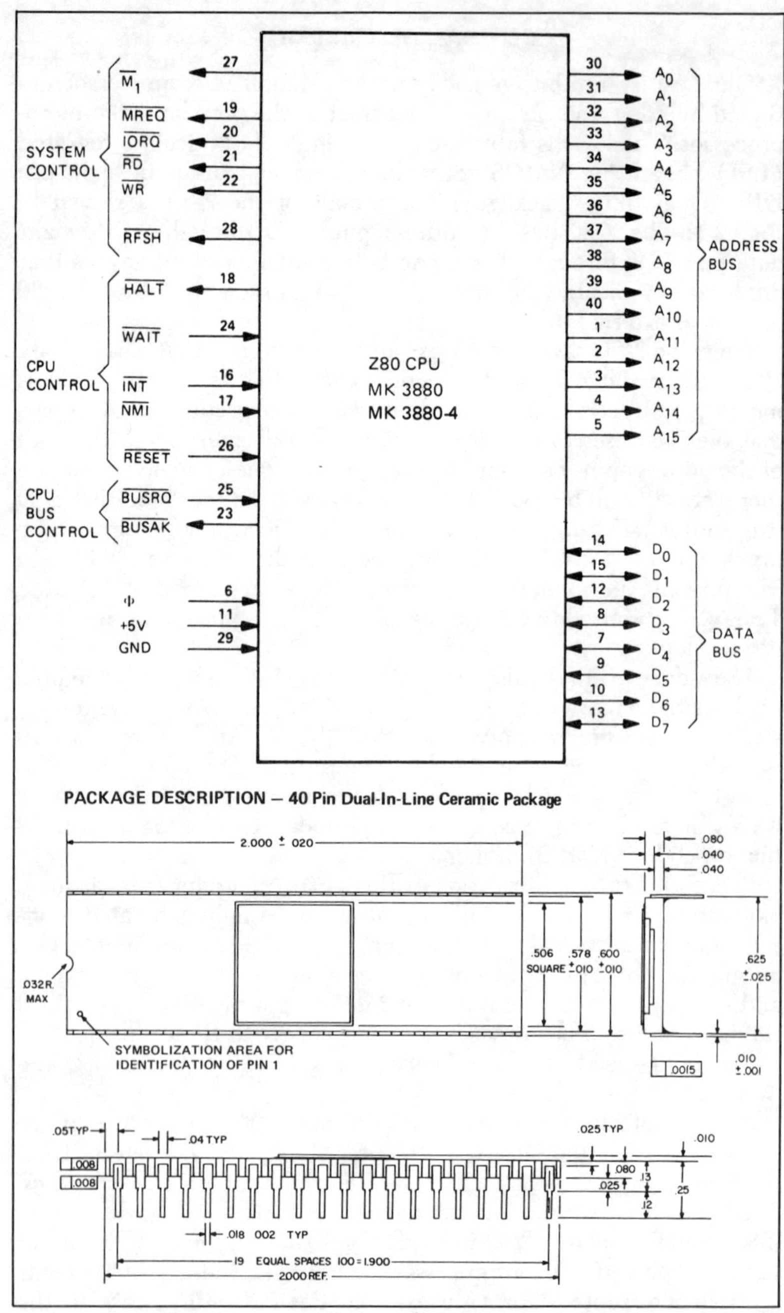

Fig. 2-1. Z-80 pinout and package configuration. (*Courtesy Mostek Corp.*)

8080/Z-80 FAMILY

The Zilog Z-80 is a third-generation microprocessor, being the descendant of the Intel 8080 (second generation) and the earlier Intel 8008 (first generation). Because of this "family" background, the Z-80 exhibits certain traits that the programmer should know about.

When the Z-80 was designed, its instruction set purposely included all 78 of the earlier 8080 instructions to ensure software compatibility with existing 8080 programs. However, the 80 new Z-80 instructions prohibit Z-80 software from being compatible with the 8080. This successive incorporating of instruction sets culminates with 8080 software being *upward compatible* with Z-80 software, but not the other way around. Software compatibility within the 8080/Z-80 "family" is illustrated in Fig. 2-2.

The 8080 is not very sophisticated by today's standards, however the experience and knowledge gained from its use paved the way for the success of the Z-80. It is interesting to note that rather than design a "better" 8-bit Z-80, the electronics industry turned instead to 16-bit CPUs, a silent commentary on the power of the Z-80. The Z-80 microprocessor is truly a remarkable device. In fact, a complete microcomputer system is formed when the Z-80 microprocessor is interfaced with I/O devices and memory.

THE Z-80 REGISTERS

The Z-80 has more than twice as many internal registers as the 8080, 22 *vs* 10! What are registers? They are *temporary* storage locations built into the microprocessor chip; some are accessible to the programmer, others are not. They enable the Z-80 to perform some operations much faster than some other processors, because less time is required to access a value in a register than to access a value stored in memory. Each register is one-byte (8-bits) wide, the same as read/write memory (RAM) and read-only memory (ROM). The Z-80 is referred to as a "register-oriented" CPU in contrast to such CPUs as the 6502 and 6800 which are "memory-oriented."

In addition to the 10 registers that the 8080 has—the program counter (PC), stack pointer (SP), accumulator (A), status or "flag" register (F), and six general-purpose registers (B, C, D, E, H, and L)—the Z-80 has a second, *alternate* bank of 8-bit general-purpose registers and four special-purpose registers. The 8080 and Z-80 registers are depicted in Fig. 2-3.

Two of the four new special-purpose Z-80 registers are 16-bits wide (the Index registers, IX and IY) and two are 8-bits wide, the

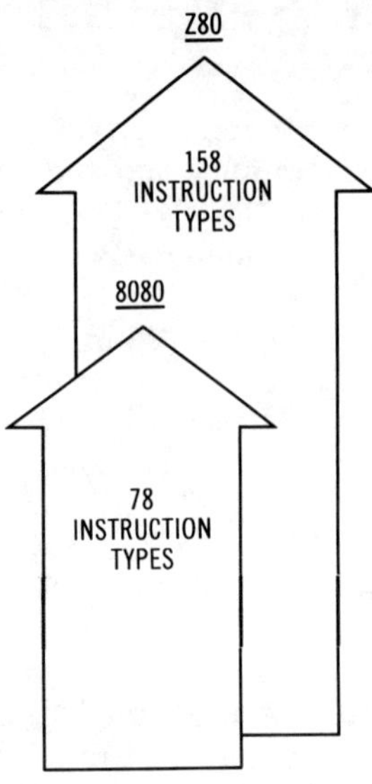

Fig. 2-2. 8080/Z-80 software compatibility.

Interrupt Vector (I) and Memory Refresh (R) registers. Neither the I register nor the R register is general-purpose, their use being reserved by the CPU.

The 16 general-purpose registers and 6 special-purpose registers of the Z-80 are shown in Fig. 2-4. Note that the A and F registers are treated separately.

Arithmetic Logic Unit

The arithmetic logic unit (ALU) is the most important register in the Z-80, because this is where the *arithmetic* and *logic* operations are actually performed on data. The specific operation or test performed within the ALU is determined by the instructions (opcode) supplied by the programmer. Although the ALU is only an 8-bit (one-byte) register, it requires *two* 8-bit values. The first value *always* comes from the accumulator, or A register, and the second value or *operand* comes either from one of the internal general-purpose registers (A-E, H, or L), or from an external memory location. The result of an arithmetic or logic operation is stored in the A register, overwriting or destroying the original contents. While the ALU is not directly accessible to the programmer, its operations are implicitly controlled through the programmer's selection of program instructions.

Because the ALU is an 8-bit register, it can only operate on 8-bit words. However, special instructions and programming techniques enable the Z-80 to handle 16-bit data words simply as two contiguous 8-bit bytes.

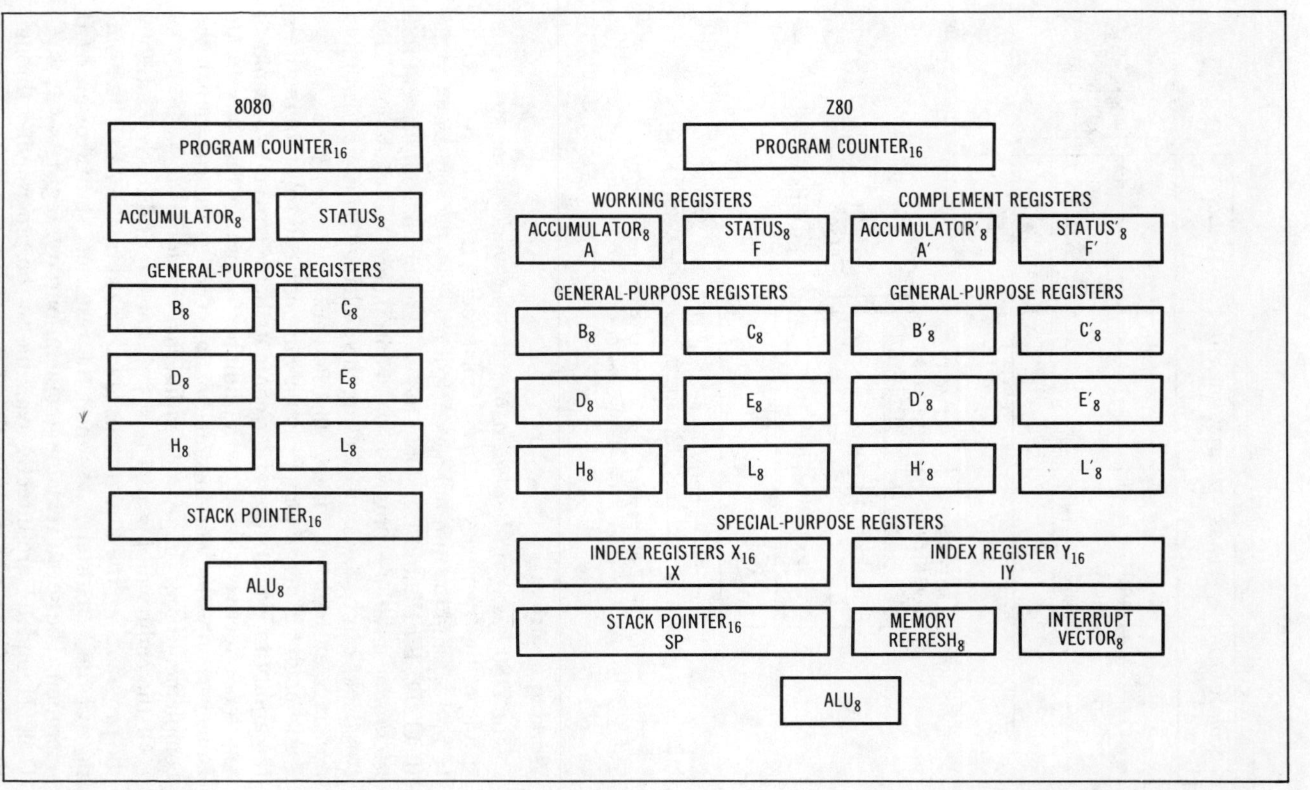

Fig. 2-3. 8080 versus Z-80 registers.

MAIN REG SET		ALTERNATE REG SET		
ACCUMULATOR A	FLAGS F	ACCUMULATOR A′	FLAGS F′	
B	C	B′	C′	GENERAL PURPOSE REGISTERS
D	E	D′	E′	
H	L	H′	L′	

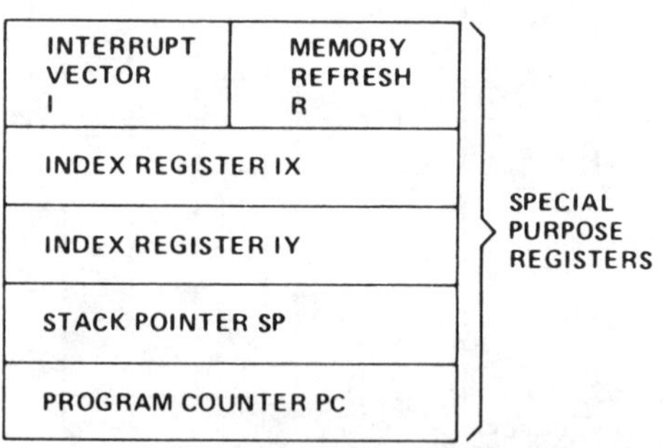

Fig. 2-4. Z-80 general-purpose and special-purpose registers. (*Courtesy Mostek Corp.*)

Working Registers

The Z-80 has two *identical* banks of 8-bit working registers, consisting of the "working" or *operational* registers (A, F, B, C, D, E, H, and L) and the internal memory or *complement* registers (A′, F′, B′, C′, D′, E′, H′, and L′). Only the working or noncomplement registers are under the programmer's control, but the contents of the two banks can be "swapped" using the exchange registers (EX) and exchange all registers (EXX) instructions.

Although the programmer can only *directly* control eight registers, the ability to exchange register contents between the two banks of registers effectively doubles the number of usable registers to 16. However, only the working registers are "active" or functional, the complement bank simply acts as *internal memory*.

Of the eight working registers, only seven are directly usable by the programmer, the F register is always used by the ALU. The purpose of the F register is to report the result or "status" of an ALU operation. The seven remaining general-purpose registers (A, B, C, D, E, H, and L) are directly available to the programmer through the instruction set of the Z-80. Six of these 8-bit registers can also be "paired" to produce an equivalent, single, 16-bit (*two*-byte) register:

- B register + C register = 16-bit, BC register pair.
- D register + E register = 16-bit, DE register pair.
- H register + L register = 16-bit, HL register pair.

When paired, these registers can be used for double-precision arithmetic or as *pointers* to memory locations. When used as pointers, the name of the *register pair* is enclosed in parentheses, for example, (HL), indicating that the CPU is "to use the contents" of the memory location "pointed to" or *addressed* by register pair HL.

In the first 8-bit microprocessor, the 8008, only the HL register pair could be used in this manner, which accounts for their H and L names. The H register held the *high-byte* of the memory address and the L register held the *low-byte* of the memory address. This method of specifying a memory address is called *indirect addressing* and is denoted by the use of the parentheses.

Special-Purpose Registers

Four 16-bit and two 8-bit registers comprise the special-purpose registers in the Z-80. The four 16-bit registers are strictly *address* registers, because they always contain memory addresses. The two 8-bit registers are reserved for CPU use and are not normally used by the programmer. The six Z-80 special-purpose registers are the program counter (PC), stack pointer (SP), index (IX and IY), interrupt vector (I), and memory refresh (R).

The program counter (PC) is a 16-bit register controlled by the CPU (and *some* instructions) and always contains the address of the *next* instruction the CPU is supposed to execute. When the CPU executes a "fetch," or "get-instruction" operation, the contents of the PC register are placed on the address bus, causing the contents of the selected memory location to be read back into the CPU over the data bus. This register is not directly available to the programmer and cannot perform arithmetic or logic operations or be used to temporarily store data. Its job is to point to, or address, the next instruction to be executed. During certain operations, notably jumps, branches, calls, and interrupts, the contents of the PC register are automatically "saved" in the stack area of memory. Execution of these instructions also causes the PC register to be "loaded" with a new address.

The stack pointer (SP) is a 16-bit register used by the CPU to address the *last* entry in the *stack area* (or, simply the *stack*), which is in read/write memory. The stack is a specific portion of read/write memory designated by the programmer for use by the CPU for temporary storage of data and register contents. Because of the way the SP was designed, the *l*ast item *i*n the stack will be *f*irst item *o*ut of the stack (LIFO), and the stack grows *downward* (the SP is decremented) as new items are added to it. Conversely, the stack grows *upward* (the SP is incremented) as items are removed from it.

The index registers (IX and IY) are 16-bit registers used by the programmer to hold a "base" address to which an "offset," or *displacement* value is automatically added to create an *indexed,* indirect memory address. This method of specifying an address for the CPU is called *indexed addressing* and enables the Z-80 to access any word stored anywhere in memory. By using one index register as a "source" pointer and the other index register as a "destination" pointer, blocks of data can be easily moved between memory locations. These registers can also be utilized by the programmer for temporary 16-bit storage when not otherwise used.

The interrupt vector (I) register is an 8-bit register used by the CPU during *interrupts* to store the *high*-byte of an indirect address, also called a *vector.* The *low*-byte of the address is supplied by the device generating the interrupt. Up to 128 devices may be referenced in this manner. Only 128 devices can be addressed because the least-significant bit (lsb) of the low-byte must be zero. The I register is not a general-purpose register, but it can be loaded with a value, and the value stored in the I register can be read into the A register, or accumulator.

The memory refresh (R) register is an 8-bit register which the CPU continually increments from 00000000 through 11111111 to provide the refresh address required by the dynamic read/write memory chips used in the TRS-80. The BASIC interpreter uses the contents of the R register to "reseed" the RANDOM number generator.

The Z-80 Flags

Another important register in the Z-80 is the status or "flag" register (F). While the ALU actually performs the arithmetic and logic operations, it is the F register that indicates the results of those operations. This register enables the Z-80 to make decisions, using the *conditional* instructions.

Six of the eight bits in the F register are set or reset depending upon the results of the many different arithmetic and logic operations performed in the ALU upon data. The flags in the F register are shown in Fig. 2-5. Because the condition or state of the flags affects so many of the Z-80 instructions, they deserve further attention.

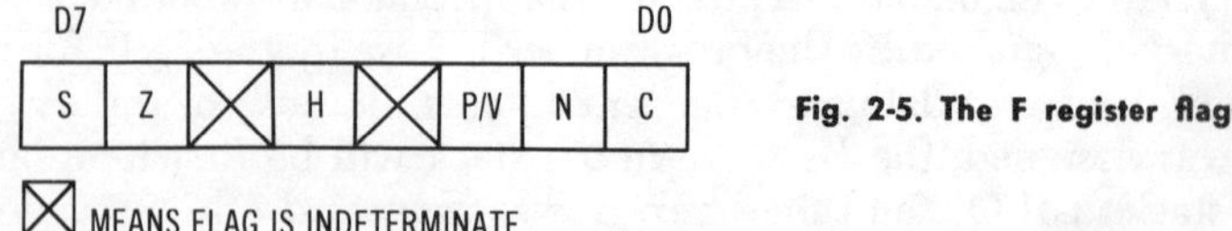

Fig. 2-5. The F register flags.

The carry (C) flag indicates the generation of an *overflow* or "carry" or an *underflow* or "borrow" during arithmetic and logic operations. Arithmetic operations cause this bit to be either set (1) or reset (0) depending upon the result in the ALU. Logical operations (AND, OR, and exclusive-OR) cause this bit to be reset or "zeroed." Those instructions that affect the C flag are listed in Appendix C. This flag may be tested (1? or 0?) and *conditioned* (set to logical one or reset to logical zero) by the programmer using the bit manipulation instructions that the Z-80 has.

The negative (N) flag is used by the CPU during binary-coded decimal (BCD) operations to indicate addition (N = O) or subtraction (N = 1). This flag cannot be tested with decision-making instructions, nor can it be directly set or reset.

The parity/overflow (P/V) flag is a dual-function flag. During arithmetic operations, this flag indicates an "accidental" sign change resulting when two numbers that have the same sign are added or subtracted using two's complement arithmetic. During most other arithmetic and logic operations, the P/V flag indicates the "odd" or "even" count (parity) of the bits in the result. The P/V flag is a logic one (P = 1) when there is an *odd* number of bits (1, 3, 5, or 7) in the result, and the flag is a logic zero (P = 0) when the number of bits is *even* (2, 4, 6, or 8). This bit may be tested and can be conditioned by the programmer.

The half-carry (H) flag indicates a carry or borrow between the *low*-order (D0-D3) *nibble* (4-bits) and the *high*-order (D4-D7) nibble in the ALU during BCD arithmetic operations. The H flag is a logic one (H = 1) if a carry or borrow occurs, and is a logic zero (H = 0) when no carry or borrow occurs. Like the negative (N) flag, this flag cannot be tested, set, or reset.

The zero (Z) flag indicates whether or not the result of an arithmetic or logic operation is zero, or whether a "match" between the contents of two registers has occurred. Note that the Z flag is *set* to a logic one (Z = 1) when the result is zero or when a match occurs, and is *reset* to a logic zero (Z = 0) when a nonzero result, or difference, occurs. The state of the Z flag is also used to indicate the state of a bit (set = 1 and reset = 0) during the bit manipulation operations. This flag is probably the most important flag available to the programmer. It can be tested by the decision-making instructions.

The sign (S) flag indicates the value of the most-significant bit (msb) of an arithmetic or logical result. If the sign flag is a logic zero (S = 0), it indicates a *positive* number, if the sign flag is a logic one (S = 1), it indicates a *negative* number. The S flag may be tested by the decision-making instructions and can be conditioned by the programmer.

The state of four of the flags in the F register (C, Z, S, and P/V) can be tested by the Z-80, using decision-making instructions such as call or carry (CALL C) or jump if nonzero (JP NZ). However, only *one* flag at a time can be tested with these instructions. Some instructions have no effect on the state of the flags, others have specific effects, and still others have an indeterminate or random effect. The effect each Z-80 instruction has upon the individual flags is given in Appendix C.

THE Z-80 INSTRUCTION SET

The Z-80 instruction set consists of 158 different instruction types, the 78 instructions from the 8080, plus 80 new instructions. However, individually, there are over 700 different instructions that are actually available. We will discuss only the most important and most often used instructions, although Appendix B lists the complete Z-80 instruction set.

Included in the 80 new instructions are instructions for 4, 8, and 16 bit operations; indexed and relative addressing; bit manipulation and checking; and memory-to-memory block transfer and search. The 158 instruction types are grouped together as follows:

- 8-bit Load.
- 16-bit Load.
- Exchange, Block Transfer, and Search.
- 8-bit Arithmetic and Logic.
- 16-bit Arithmetic.
- General-Purpose Arithmetic and CPU Control.
- Shift and Rotate.
- Bit Manipulation.
- Jump.
- Call and Return.
- Input and Output.

Z-80 Terminology

Before discussing the individual instructions, a short review of the conventions (rules) and terminology used with the Z-80 instructions, along with its addressing modes, is in order. Some rules are based on the 8080, others are unique to the Z-80, thus some rules will be familiar to you and others will be new.

The terminology used with the Z-80 instructions is based upon the actual function performed, and so is generally self-explanatory. The terminology used with the Z-80 instruction set is summarized in Chart 2-1.

Due to the convention established by Intel with the 8080, all two-byte words are stored with the last-significant byte (LSB) preced-

Chart 2-1. Z-80 Conventions and Terminology

b = BIT value of any 8-bit register or memory address.
cc = CONDITION CODE of the flags:

NZ = nonzero	Z = zero
NC = noncarry	C = carry
PO = parity odd/no overflow	PE = parity even /overflow
P = positive sign (+)	M = (minus) negative sign (−)

d = DISPLACEMENT, an 8-bit **signed** two's complement number used with indexed addressing.
e = EXTENSION, an 8-bit **signed** two's complement number used with relative jumps.
L = Call LOCATION in Page Zero; 8 special locations at decimal addresses 0, 8, 16, 24, 32, 40, 48, and 56.
n = NUMBER, any 8-bit binary number.
nn = NUMBER, any 16-bit binary number.
r = REGISTER, any 8-bit general-purpose register (A, B, C, D, E, H, or L).
( ) = Use the CONTENTS OF as a "pointer" to memory location or I/O port number.
msb = Most-significant BIT.
lsb = Least-significant BIT.
MSB = Most-significant BYTE.
LSB = Least-significant BYTE.

ing the most-significant byte (MSB). For example, the instruction jump to address 1A19H (JP nn) is stored as C3 19 1A in memory (JP nn = C3H). The H after a number means that the number is hexadecimal.

ADDRESSING MODES

The Z-80 provides 10 different addressing modes, or methods, of addressing a memory location, some of which can also be used to address registers. Each mode has its own special use and application, but some are more useful than others. Some are one-byte instructions, while others may consist of two, three, or four bytes. Which instruction to use, and when to use it, depends upon the programmer's knowledge of the different addressing modes available and the task to be performed.

The 10 Z-80 addressing modes available to the programmer include *implied addressing,* which is also called *implicit* or "no-address" addressing. If this type of addressing is used, the instruction specifies the *operation* to be performed as well as the *operand* or operator. Some one-byte instructions related to CPU control (NOP, HALT, etc.), and some two-byte (LD SP,IY etc.) instructions, use this addressing mode.

Register addressing, also called register-to-register addressing, is found in one-byte instructions that specify the operation (op-code)

D7	OP-CODE	D0

D7	OP-CODE	D0
D7	OP-CODE	D0

and both the *destination-* and *source-operands* within the instruction. The operands are specified by three-bit *fields* (D0-D2 = source register, REG_s; D3-D5 = destination register, REG_d).

(binary) REG = 000 = B register
001 = C register
010 = D register
011 = E register
100 = H register
101 = L register
111 = A register

OP	REG_d	REG_s

Example: LD A,B ...meaning, load the A register with a copy of the content of the B register. The content of the B register remains unchanged.

Register indirect addressing is similar to register addressing, except one of the operands is used as a *pointer* to the memory location where the actual operand resides (or is to reside). The second operand is a register. The *pointer register* is denoted with the use of parentheses, for example, (BC). Either the source or the destination operand may be addressed using register indirect addressing. However, both operands *cannot* use register indirect addressing, thus LD (BC),(HL) is not a valid instruction.

Example: LD A,(BC) ...meaning, load the A register with a copy of the content of the memory location pointed to or addressed by the BC register pair.

OP	REG_d	(REG_{ss})

Example: LD (BC),A ...meaning, load the memory location pointed to by the BC register pair with a copy of the content of the A register.

OP	(REG_{dd})	REG_s

Immediate addressing is often used in two-byte instructions where the *operation* and *destination operand* are contained in the first byte and an 8-bit *literal,* or "constant," is contained in the second or *immediate* byte. In effect, the instruction tells the CPU to, "use the following data. . . ."

Example: LD A,3FH ...meaning, load the A register with the 8-bit immediate data, 3FH.

OP	REG_d	OP
8-BIT DATA		

Immediate extended addressing is similar to immediate addressing, except 16-bit literals or data words are used, and is used to load

16-bit values into one of the register pairs (BC, DE, or HL), the stack pointer (SP), or one of the index registers (IX and IY).

OP	REG_d	OP
16-BIT DATA		(LSB)
		(MSB)

Example: LD BC,ABCDH ... meaning, load the 16-bit immediate data, ABCDH, into the BC register pair. Remember, with 16 bits (two bytes) of information, the LSB precedes the MSB.

Extended addressing is sometimes called direct addressing. The first one or two bytes contain the operation code and define one operand while the remaining two bytes are used as a 16-bit pointer to the memory location(s) where the second operand resides. Both 8-bit and 16-bit values can be accessed using direct addressing.

Example: LD A,(nn) ...which loads an 8-bit data value from the memory address pointed to by the address nn. And, LD (nn), A, which loads the content of the A register into the memory address pointed to by the address nn.

Example: LD BC,(nn) ...meaning, load the BC register pair with a copy of the contents of memory location nn and nn+1, where the value at nn is loaded into the C register, and the value at nn+1 is loaded into the B register.

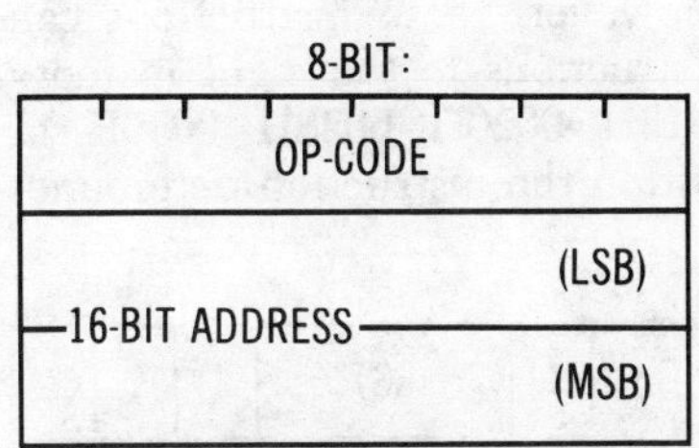

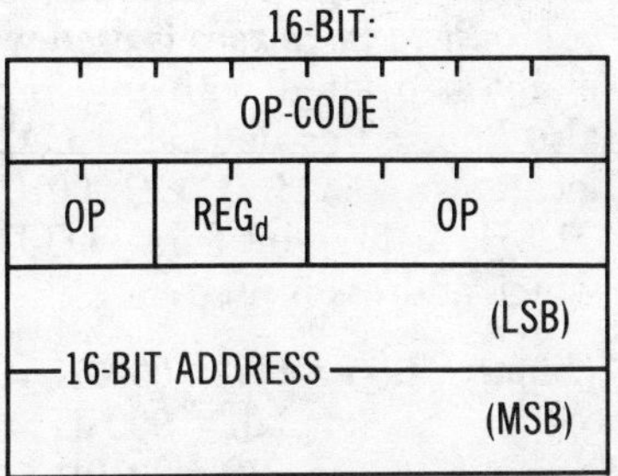

Indexed addressing is similar to register indirect addressing except a *signed* 8-bit *displacement*, or "extension," is used to select any memory location between IX+127 and IX−128 (either the IX *or* IY register may be used). A *negative displacement* is formed using two's complement math and is denoted as e^{-2}.

Example: IX+7FH = IX+127
IX+7EH = IX+126
.
IX+01H = IX+1
IX+00H = IX
IX+FFH = IX−1
.

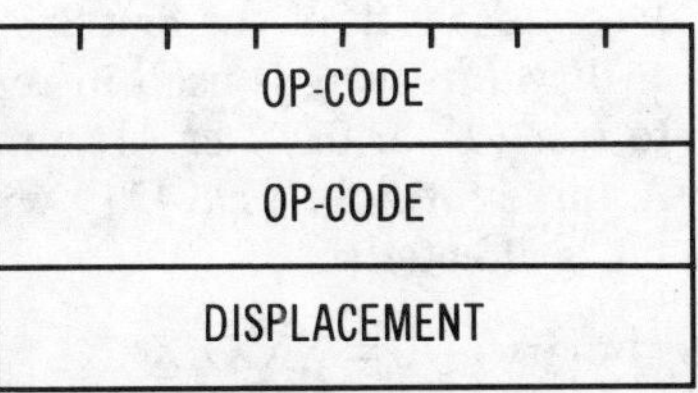

IX+81H = IX−127
IX+80H = IX−128

Relative addressing is only used with *jump relative* instructions. Relative addressing permits us to reference, or jump to, memory locations *ahead* or *behind* the current location, locations "relative" to the current location addressed by the program counter (PC). The displacement ahead or behind the PC address is determined in the same manner as displacements for indexed addressing using two's complement values. With this addressing mode, jumps of between 2 and 129 memory locations forward, and 1 to 126 memory locations backward, are possible. Thus, the *minimum forward jump* is 2 and the *minimum backward jump* is 1. This addressing mode permits *relocatable* code to be written, that is, code or programs that operate anywhere in memory without regard to absolute addresses.

Example: 5000H JR NZ,64H ... meaning, program execution will jump ahead 100_{10} memory locations, to address 5064H, and proceed if the result of the last mathematical or logic operation is nonzero (NZ).

OP-CODE
DISPLACEMENT

Modified page zero is used with one-byte instructions that are normally associated with interrupts. However, these instructions can also be used as dedicated CALL instructions to the eight memory locations: 0000H, 0008H, 0010H, 0018H, 0020H, 0028H, 0030H, or 0038H. A three-bit field (D3-D5) within the instruction determines which address is used:

(binary) RST = 000 = 0000H = 0
001 = 0008H = 8
010 = 0010H = 16
011 = 0018H = 24
100 = 0020H = 32
101 = 0028H = 40
110 = 0030H = 48
111 = 0038H = 56

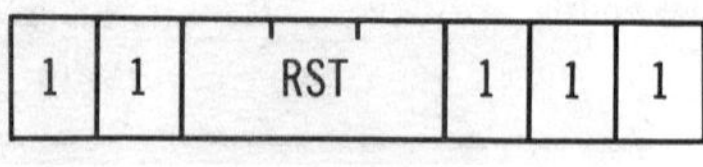

Page Zero is 2^8 or the first 256 8-bit memory locations.

Bit addressing is used in conjunction with other addressing modes to *test* (1? or 0?), *set* (1) or *reset* (0) any bit in an 8-bit operand. A three-bit field (D3-D5) within the instruction determines which bit is affected:

(binary) D0 = XXXXXXX1 = 000
D1 = XXXXXX1X = 001

D2 = XXXXX1XX = 010
D3 = XXXX1XXX = 011
D4 = XXX1XXXX = 100
D5 = XX1XXXXX = 101
D6 = X1XXXXXX = 110
D7 = 1XXXXXXX = 111

OP-CODE		
OP	BIT	OP/REG

These instructions are also called *bit manipulation* instructions.

Typically, the programmer seldom worries about which addressing mode to use (except the relative addressing mode) and simply uses the instruction(s) that suit the particular task at hand. This is the approach taken in this book. But, the programmer must be aware that the different addressing modes are available. This same approach will be used when discussing the many different Z-80 instructions.

THE 8-BIT LOAD (LD) INSTRUCTIONS

The Z-80 provides 111 different 8-bit Load (LD) instructions (Fig. 2-6). Approximately half of these instructions move data from one CPU register to another. The remaining load instructions load 8-bit immediate data into CPU registers or memory locations, store the contents of CPU registers into memory locations, or simply transfer

SOURCE

			IMPLIED		REGISTER							REG INDIRECT			INDEXED		EXT. ADDR.	IMME.
			I	R	A	B	C	D	E	H	L	(HL)	(BC)	(DE)	(IX + d)	(IY + d)	(nn)	n
		A	ED 57	ED 5F	7F	78	79	7A	7B	7C	7D	7E	0A	1A	DD 7E d	FD 7E d	3A n n	3E n
		B			47	40	41	42	43	44	45	46			DD 46 d	FD 46 d		06 n
		C			4F	48	49	4A	4B	4C	4D	4E			DD 4E d	FD 4E d		0E n
	REGISTER	D			57	50	51	52	53	54	55	56			DD 56 d	FD 56 d		16 n
		E			5F	58	59	5A	5B	5C	5D	5E			DD 5E d	FD 5E d		1E n
		H			67	60	61	62	63	64	65	66			DD 66 d	FD 66 d		26 n
		L			6F	68	69	6A	6B	6C	6D	6E			DD 6E d	FD 6E d		2E n
DESTINATION		(HL)			77	70	71	72	73	74	75							36 n
	REG INDIRECT	(BC)			02													
		(DE)			12													
	INDEXED	(IX+d)			DD 77 d	DD 70 d	DD 71 d	DD 72 d	DD 73 d	DD 74 d	DD 75 d							DD 36 d n
		(IY+d)			FD 77 d	FD 70 d	FD 71 d	FD 72 d	FD 73 d	FD 74 d	FD 75 d							FD 36 d n
	EXT. ADDR	(nn)			32 n n													
	IMPLIED	I			ED 47													
		R			ED 4F													

Fig. 2-6. The 8-bit load instructions. (*Courtesy Mostek Corp.*)

the contents of the I and R registers into the A register and *vice versa.*

THE 16-BIT (LD) INSTRUCTIONS

The Z-80 has 33 16-bit Load instructions, which are summarized in Fig. 2-7. Six immediate extended instructions permit any register pair, BC, DE, HL, SP, IX, or IY, to be loaded directly with 16-bit data. Six extended addressing instructions enable indirect loading of any register pair from any two consecutive memory locations. Six register indirect instructions allow the content of two consecutive memory locations addressed by the stack pointer (SP) to be loaded into any register pair. Six extended instructions transfer the contents of any register pair into two consecutive memory locations. The remaining instructions either PUSH or POP the register pairs AF, BC, DE, HL, or the index registers IX or IY, respectively, on to or off of the stack.

EXCHANGE, BLOCK TRANSFER, AND SEARCH INSTRUCTIONS

The Z-80 provides six exchange instructions along with four block transfer and four block search instructions. The exchange instructions (Fig. 2-8) let us swap the contents of the AF and AF′ registers using the exchange registers (EX) instruction, or swap the contents

SOURCE

		REGISTER							IMM. EXT.	EXT. ADDR.	REG. INDIR.
		AF	BC	DE	HL	SP	IX	IY	nn	(nn)	(SP)
DESTINATION REGISTER	AF										F1
	BC								01 n n	ED 4B n n	C1
	DE								11 n n	ED 5B n n	D1
	HL								21 n n	2A n n	E1
	SP				F9		DD F9	FD F9	31 n n	ED 7B n n	
	IX								DD 21 n n	DD 2A n n	DD E1
	IY								FD 21 n n	FD 2A n n	FD E1
EXT. ADDR.	(nn)		ED 43 n n	ED 53 n n	22 n n	ED 73 n n	DD 22 n n	FD 22 n n			
PUSH INSTRUCTIONS → REG. IND.	(SP)	F5	C5	D5	E5		DD E5	FD E5			

NOTE: The Push & Pop Instructions adjust the SP after every execution

↑ POP INSTRUCTIONS

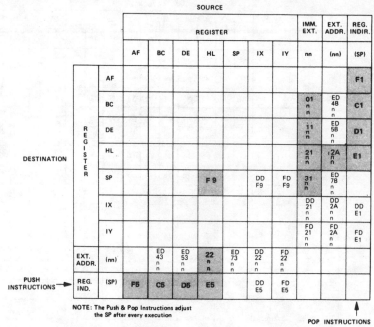

Fig. 2-7. The 16-bit load instructions. (*Courtesy Mostek Corp.*)

Fig. 2-8. Exchange instructions. (Courtesy Mostek Corp.)

		IMPLIED ADDRESSING				
		AF'	BC', DE' & HL'	HL	IX	IY
IMPLIED	AF	08				
	BC, DE & HL		D9			
	DE			EB		
REG. INDIR.	(SP)			E3	DD E3	FD E3

of the working and complement registers (B, C, D, E, H, and L and B′, C′, D′, E′, H′, and L′) using the exchange all registers (EXX) instruction. Also, the content of the HL, IX, or IY registers may be stored in any memory location pointed to by the SP register, and the DE register pair may be swapped with the HL register pair.

The four block transfer instructions (Fig. 2-9), LDI, LDIR, LDD, and LDDR, enable blocks (1 to 64K bytes) of data to be moved anywhere in memory. Before using these instructions in a program, the programmer must:

- Load BC register pair with the number of bytes to be transferred.

			SOURCE: REG. INDIR. (HL)	
DESTINATION	REG. INDIR.	(DE)	ED A0	'LDI' – Load (DE)←(HL) Inc HL & DE, Dec BC
			ED B0	'LDIR,' – Load (DE)←(HL) Inc HL & DE, Dec BC, Repeat until BC = 0
			ED A8	'LDD' – Load (DE)←(HL) Dec HL & DE, Dec BC
			ED B8	'LDDR' – Load (DE)←(HL) Dec HL & DE, Dec BC, Repeat until BC = 0

Reg HL points to source
Reg DE points to destination
Reg BC is byte counter

Fig. 2-9. Block transfer instructions. (Courtesy Mostek Corp.)

- Load HL register pair with the starting address of the source block.
- Load DE register pair with the starting address of the destination block.

The *Load* and *I*ncrement (LDI) and *Load* and *D*ecrement (LDD) instructions perform, respectively, block start-to-block end and block end-to-block start transfers. The LDI instruction increments the HL and DE register pairs and decrements the BC register pair. The LDD instruction decrements the HL and DE register pairs and decrements the BC register pair. These are "semi-automatic" instructions because only a single byte is moved each time the instruction is executed, and a separate instruction is needed to test the P/V flag to see if the entire block has been moved. When register pair BC is zero, the entire block will have been moved, so the P/V flag will be reset.

SEARCH LOCATION	
REG. INDIR.	
(HL)	
ED A1	'CPI' Inc HL, Dec BC
ED B1	'CPIR', Inc HL, Dec BC repeat until BC = 0 or find match
ED A9	'CPD' Dec HL & BC
ED B9	'CPDR' Dec HL & BC Repeat until BC = 0 or find match

HL points to location in memory to be compared with accumulator contents
BC is byte counter

Fig. 2-10. Block search instructions. *(Courtesy Mostek Corp.)*

The LDIR and LDDR instructions perform the same functions, but are "automatic" in operation, requiring no separate flag test instruction. Data bytes are moved until the content of the BC register pair reaches zero.

The four block search instructions (Fig. 2-10), CPI, CPIR, CPD, and CPDR, operate in the same fashion as the block transfer instructions, except that the content of each memory location is compared to a user-supplied, 8-bit value stored in the A register. As with the block transfer instructions, the CPI and CPD instructions require a separate flag test instruction to determine when the entire block has been searched. The CPIR and CPDR instructions are automatic, with execution continuing until one of two conditions is met: (1) register pair BC is decremented to zero, or (2) a comparison or "match" occurs between the content of the A register and a memory location.

8-BIT ARITHMETIC AND LOGIC INSTRUCTIONS

The Z-80 has 108 arithmetic and logic instructions (Fig. 2-11), including addition, subtraction, comparison, increment/decrement, and the logical operations, AND, OR, and XOR. Note that arithmetic and logic operations (except the increment, decrement, and compare) automatically use the A register as the destination register.

SOURCE

	REGISTER ADDRESSING							REG. INDIR.	INDEXED		IMMED.
	A	B	C	D	E	H	L	(HL)	(IX+d)	(IY+d)	n
'ADD'	87	80	81	82	83	84	85	86	DD 86 d	FD 86 d	C6 n
ADD w CARRY 'ADC'	8F	88	89	8A	8B	8C	8D	8E	DD 8E d	FD 8E d	CE n
SUBTRACT 'SUB'	97	90	91	92	93	94	95	96	DD 96 d	FD 96 d	D6 n
SUB w CARRY 'SBC'	9F	98	99	9A	9B	9C	9D	9E	DD 9E d	FD 9E d	DE n
'AND'	A7	A0	A1	A2	A3	A4	A5	A6	DD A6 d	FD A6 d	E6 n
'XOR'	AF	A8	A9	AA	AB	AC	AD	AE	DD AE d	FD AE d	EE n
'OR'	B7	B0	B1	B2	B3	B4	B5	B6	DD B6 d	FD B6 d	F6 n
COMPARE 'CP'	BF	B8	B9	BA	BB	BC	BD	BE	DD BE d	FD BE d	FE n
INCREMENT 'INC'	3C	04	0C	14	1C	24	2C	34	DD 34 d	FD 34 d	
DECREMENT 'DEC'	3D	05	0D	15	1D	25	2D	35	DD 35 d	FD 35 d	

Fig. 2-11. The 8-bit arithmetic and logic instructions. (*Courtesy Mostek Corp.*)

16-BIT ARITHMETIC INSTRUCTIONS

There are 32 instructions in the 16-bit arithmetic group, 12 register pair-to-register pair additions (ADD), four register pair-to-

			SOURCE					
			BC	DE	HL	SP	IX	IY
DESTINATION	'ADD'	HL	09	19	29	39		
		IX	DD 09	DD 19		DD 39	DD 29	
		IY	FD 09	FD 19		FD 39		FD 29
	ADD WITH CARRY AND SET FLAGS 'ADC'	HL	ED 4A	ED 5A	ED 6A	ED 7A		
	SUB WITH CARRY AND SET FLAGS 'SBC'	HL	ED 42	ED 52	ED 62	ED 72		
	INCREMENT 'INC.		03	13	23	33	DD 23	FD 23
	DECREMENT 'DEC'		0B	1B	2B	3B	DD 2B	FD 2B

Fig. 2-12. The 16-bit arithmetic instructions. (*Courtesy Mostek Corp.*)

register pair add-with-carry (ADC), four register pair-to-register pair subtract-with-carry (borrow) (SBC), and six increment (INC) and six decrement (DEC) instructions. Note that no 16-bit logic operations exist. The 16-bit arithmetic instructions are summarized in Fig. 2-12.

GENERAL-PURPOSE ARITHMETIC AND CPU CONTROL INSTRUCTIONS

The Z-80 has five general-purpose operations affecting the A and F registers, and seven miscellaneous CPU control operations. Note the difference between the complement accumulator (CPL) and negate accumulator (NEG) instructions:

- CPL . . . performs *one's complement* upon the contents of the accumulator (turns each 1 into 0 and *each 0 into a 1*).
- NEG . . . performs *two's complement* upon the contents of the accumulator (turns each 1 into 0 and *each 0 into a 1,* and adds 1 to the least-significant bit).

The general-purpose AF instructions are shown in Fig. 2-13.

The seven Z-80 miscellaneous CPU control instructions (Fig. 2-14) consist of two CPU control instructions, NOP and HALT, and five interrupt instructions: disable interrupt (DI), enable interrupt (EI), set interrupt mode 0 (IM 0), set interrupt mode 1 (IM 1),

Decimal Adjust Acc, 'DAA'	27
Complement Acc, 'CPL'	2F
Negate Acc, 'NEG' (2's complement)	ED 44
Complement Carry Flag, 'CCF'	3F
Set Carry Flag, 'SCF'	37

Fig. 2-13. General-purpose AF instructions. (*Courtesy Mostek Corp.*)

'NOP'	00	
'HALT'	76	
DISABLE INT '(DI)'	F3	
ENABLE INT '(EI)'	FB	
SET INT MODE 0 'IM0'	ED 46	8080A MODE
SET INT MODE 1 'IM1'	ED 56	CALL TO LOCATION 0038_H
SET INT MODE 2 'IM2'	ED 5E	INDIRECT CALL USING REGISTER I AND 8 BITS FROM INTERRUPTING DEVICE AS A POINTER.

Fig. 2-14. Miscellaneous CPU control instructions. (*Courtesy Mostek Corp.*)

Source and Destination

TYPE OF ROTATE OR SHIFT	A	B	C	D	E	H	L	(HL)	(IX + d)	(IY + d)
'RLC'	CB 07	CB 00	CB 01	CB 02	CB 03	CB 04	CB 05	CB 06	DD CB d 06	FD CB d 06
'RRC'	CB 0F	CB 08	CB 09	CB 0A	CB 0B	CB 0C	CB 0D	CB 0E	DD CB d 0E	FD CB d 0E
'RL'	CB 17	CB 10	CB 11	CB 12	CB 13	CB 14	CB 15	CB 16	DD CB d 16	FD CB d 16
'RR'	CB 1F	CB 18	CB 19	CB 1A	CB 1B	CB 1C	CB 1D	CB 1E	DD CB d 1E	FD CB d 1E
'SLA'	CB 27	CB 20	CB 21	CB 22	CB 23	CB 24	CB 25	CB 26	DD CB d 26	FD CB d 26
'SRA'	CB 2F	CB 28	CB 29	CB 2A	CB 2B	CB 2C	CB 2D	CB 2E	DD CB d 2E	FD CB d 2E
'SRL'	CB 3F	CB 38	CB 39	CB 3A	CB 3B	CB 3C	CB 3D	CB 3E	DD CB d 3E	FD CB d 3E
'RLD'								ED 6F		
'RRD'								ED 67		

	A
RLCA	07
RRCA	0F
RLA	17
RRA	1F

Fig. 2-15. Rotate and shift instructions. (*Courtesy Mostek Corp.*)

and set interrupt mode 2 (IM 2). Note the specific applications of the three different set interrupt mode instructions. Also, because of the way the TRS-80 was designed, the HALT instruction is no longer functional. Instead of simply suspending CPU execution, it now causes a complete system reset.

ROTATE AND SHIFT INSTRUCTIONS

These instructions (Fig. 2-15) provide the programmer with the ability to shift or rotate 8-bit values in registers or memory. The ability to move bits between adjacent positions within a register of

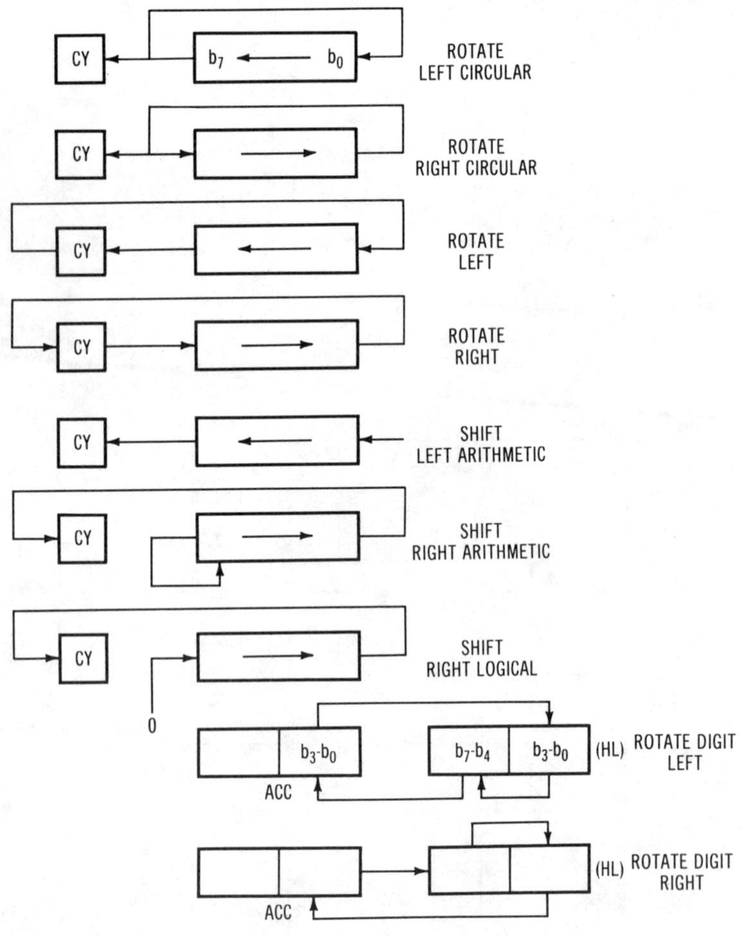

Fig. 2-16. Shifts and rotates.

		REGISTER ADDRESSING							REG. INDIR.	INDEXED	
	BIT	A	B	C	D	E	H	L	(HL)	(IX+d)	(IY+d)
TEST 'BIT'	0	CB 47	CB 40	CB 41	CB 42	CB 43	CB 44	CB 45	CB 46	DD CB d 46	FD CB d 46
	1	CB 4F	CB 48	CB 49	CB 4A	CB 4B	CB 4C	CB 4D	CB 4E	DD CB d 4E	FD CB d 4E
	2	CB 57	CB 50	CB 51	CB 52	CB 53	CB 54	CB 55	CB 56	DD CB d 56	FD CB d 56
	3	CB 5F	CB 58	CB 59	CB 5A	CB 5B	CB 5C	CB 5D	CB 5E	DD CB d 5E	FD CB d 5E
	4	CB 67	CB 60	CB 61	CB 62	CB 63	CB 64	CB 65	CB 66	DD CB d 66	FD CB d 66
	5	CB 6F	CB 68	CB 69	CB 6A	CB 6B	CB 6C	CB 6D	CB 6E	DD CB d 6E	FD CB d 6E
	6	CB 77	CB 70	CB 71	CB 72	CB 73	CB 74	GB 75	CB 76	DD CB d 76	FD CB d 76
	7	CB 7F	CB 78	CB 79	CB 7A	CB 7B	CB 7C	CB 7D	CB 7E	DD CB d 7E	FD CB d 7E
RESET BIT 'RES'	0	CB 87	CB 80	CB 81	CB 82	CB 83	CB 84	CB 85	CB 86	DD CB d 86	FD CB d 86
	1	CB 8F	CB 88	CB 89	CB 8A	CB 8B	CB 8C	CB 8D	CB 8E	DD CB d 8E	FD CB d 8E
	2	CB 97	CB 90	CB 91	CB 92	CB 93	CB 94	CB 95	CB 96	DD CB d 96	FD CB d 96
	3	CB 9F	CB 98	CB 99	CB 9A	CB 9B	CB 9C	CB 9D	CB 9E	DD CB d 9E	FD CB d 9E
	4	CB A7	CB A0	CB A1	CB A2	CB A3	CB A4	CB A5	CB A6	DD CB d A6	FD CB d A6
	5	CB AF	CB A8	CB A9	CB AA	CB AB	CB AC	CB AD	CB AE	DD CB d AE	FD CB d AE
	6	CB B7	CB B0	CB B1	CB B2	CB B3	CB B4	CB B5	CB B6	DD CB d B6	FD CB d B6
	7	CB BF	CB B8	CB B9	CB BA	CB BB	CB BC	CB BD	CB BE	DD CB d BE	FD CB d BE
SET BIT 'SET'	0	CB C7	CB C0	CB C1	CB C2	CB C3	CB C4	CB C5	CB C6	DD CB d C6	FD CB d C6
	1	CB CF	CB C8	CB C9	CB CA	CB CB	CB CC	CB CD	CB CE	DD CB d CE	FD CB d CE
	2	CB D7	CB D0	CB D1	CB D2	CB D3	CB D4	CB D5	CB D6	DD CB d D6	FD CB d D6
	3	CB DF	CB D8	CB D9	CB DA	CB DB	CB DC	CB DD	CB DE	DD CB d DE	FD CB d DE
	4	CB E7	CB E0	CB E1	CB E2	CB E3	CB E4	CB E5	CB E6	DD CB d E6	FD CB d E6
	5	CB EF	CB E8	CB E9	CB EA	CB EB	CB EC	CB ED	CB EE	DD CB d EE	FD CB d EE
	6	CB F7	CB F0	CB F1	CB F2	CB F3	CB F4	CB F5	CB F6	DD CB d F6	FD CB d F6
	7	CB FF	CB F8	CB F9	CB FA	CB FB	CB FC	CB FD	CB FE	DD CB d FE	FD CB d FE

Fig. 2-17. Bit manipulation instructions. (*Courtesy Mostek Corp.*)

memory location is a very powerful tool for the programmer. Most notably, the instructions enable multiplication and division to be performed, respectively, as simply successive *shift-left and add* or successive *shift-right and subtract* operations. Fig. 2-16 illustrates the results of various rotate and shift operations. Note that a *shift* is an "open-ended" movement of bits, either right or left, while a *rotate* is "closed" with all bits being preserved. Two instructions, RLD and RRD, are used during BCD operations to shift the contents of a memory location pointed to by the HL register pair, as shown in Fig. 2-16.

BIT MANIPULATION INSTRUCTIONS

Although there are only nine instruction types in this group (Fig. 2-17), there are actually 240 individual instructions available to the programmer. Any bit within any CPU register or memory location can be tested, set, or reset. The Z flag indicates the status of the bit. The bit being tested is a logic one when the Z flag is set (Z = 1), and is a logic zero when the Z flag is reset (Z = 0).

JUMP INSTRUCTIONS

The Z-80 has eight conditional, four conditional relative, and five unconditional jump instructions. During execution, the new address

			CONDITION									
			UN-COND.	CARRY	NON CARRY	ZERO	NON ZERO	PARITY EVEN	PARITY ODD	SIGN NEG	SIGN POS	REG B≠0
JUMP 'JP'	IMMED. EXT.	nn	C3 n n	DA n n	D2 n n	CA n n	C2 n n	EA n n	E2 n n	FA n n	F2 n n	
JUMP 'JR'	RELATIVE	PC+e	18 e-2	38 e-2	30 e-2	28 e-2	20 e-2					
JUMP 'JP'		(HL)	E9									
JUMP 'JP'	REG. INDIR.	(IX)	DD E9									
JUMP 'JP'		(IY)	FD E9									

NOTE—CERTAIN FLAGS HAVE MORE THAN ONE PURPOSE.

Fig. 2-18. Jump instructions. (*Courtesy Mostek Corp.*)

loaded into the PC register destroys the original PC contents. Fig. 2-18 summarizes the jump instructions as well as the flags that are tested by the conditional jump instructions.

CALL AND RETURN INSTRUCTIONS

The Z-80 has 20 call and return instructions (Fig. 2-19), of which eight are conditional calls, eight are conditional returns, and four are unconditional instructions. In contrast to the jump instructions, which load the PC register without first "saving" the current contents of the PC register, the call and return instructions use the stack to store the original contents of the PC. During the execution of a call

			CONDITION									
			UN-COND.	CARRY	NON CARRY	ZERO	NON ZERO	PARITY EVEN	PARITY ODD	SIGN NEG	SIGN POS	REG B≠0
'CALL'	IMMED. EXT.	nn	CD n n	DC n n	D4 n n	CC n n	C4 n n	EC n n	E4 n n	FC n n	F4 n n	
DECREMENT B, JUMP IF NON ZERO 'DJNZ'	RELATIVE	PC+e										10 e-2
RETURN 'RET'	REGISTER INDIR.	(SP) (SP+1)	C9	D8	D0	C8	C0	E8	E0	F8	F0	
RETURN FROM INT 'RETI'	REG. INDIR.	(SP) (SP+1)	ED 4D									
RETURN FROM NON MASKABLE INT 'RETN'	REG. INDIR.	(SP) (SP+1)	ED 45									

NOTE—CERTAIN FLAGS HAVE MORE THAN ONE PURPOSE.

Fig. 2-19. Call and return instructions. (*Courtesy Mostek Corp.*)

instruction, the PC contents are pushed onto the stack *before* the new address specified by the instruction is loaded into the PC. Upon execution of a return (RET) instruction, the original PC contents are popped off of the stack and are loaded back into the PC. These instructions provide the ability to access and use subroutines, including the Level II BASIC ROM subroutines, and then return to our own program upon completion.

INPUT AND OUTPUT (I/O) INSTRUCTIONS

In addition to being able to move 8-bit data values between any of the 512 possible *I/O ports* and any CPU register (Fig. 2-20), there are eight block input/output instructions that operate on data in the same fashion as the block-and-search transfer-and-search instructions. Their use enables the programmer to either input (load) or output (store) a block of data through any I/O port (the TRS-80 cassette and video display use output port 255 and input port 255). Notice that the C register is used as the pointer when using *register indirect* port addressing during both input and output operations. Only the A register is addressable via immediate, indirect addressing.

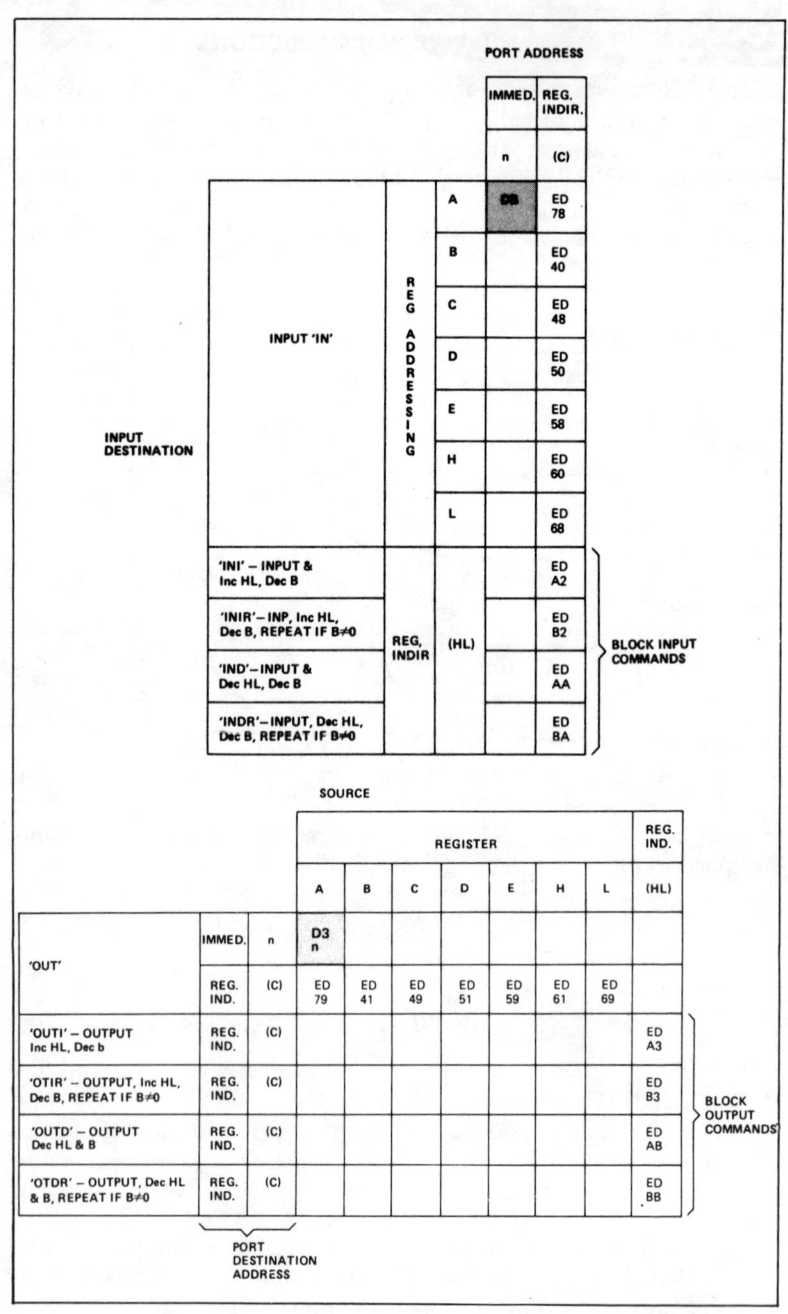

PORT ADDRESS

INPUT DESTINATION			IMMED. n	REG. INDIR. (C)
INPUT 'IN'	REG ADDRESSING	A	DB	ED 78
		B		ED 40
		C		ED 48
		D		ED 50
		E		ED 58
		H		ED 60
		L		ED 68
'INI' – INPUT & Inc HL, Dec B	REG, INDIR	(HL)		ED A2
'INIR'–INP, Inc HL, Dec B, REPEAT IF B≠0				ED B2
'IND'–INPUT & Dec HL, Dec B				ED AA
'INDR'–INPUT, Dec HL, Dec B, REPEAT IF B≠0				ED BA

BLOCK INPUT COMMANDS ('INI', 'INIR', 'IND', 'INDR')

SOURCE

			REGISTER							REG. IND.
			A	B	C	D	E	H	L	(HL)
'OUT'	IMMED.	n	D3 n							
'OUT'	REG. IND.	(C)	ED 79	ED 41	ED 49	ED 51	ED 59	ED 61	ED 69	
'OUTI' – OUTPUT Inc HL, Dec b	REG. IND.	(C)								ED A3
'OTIR' – OUTPUT, Inc HL, Dec B, REPEAT IF B≠0	REG. IND.	(C)								ED B3
'OUTD' – OUTPUT Dec HL & B	REG. IND.	(C)								ED AB
'OTDR' – OUTPUT, Dec HL & B, REPEAT IF B≠0	REG. IND.	(C)								ED BB

BLOCK OUTPUT COMMANDS ('OUTI', 'OTIR', 'OUTD', 'OTDR')

PORT DESTINATION ADDRESS (IMMED. / REG. IND. columns)

Fig. 2-20. Input and output (I/O) instructions. (*Courtesy Mostek Corp.*)

REVIEW QUESTIONS

1. The single most important piece of microcircuitry in a microcomputer is?
2. The Zilog Z-80 is what kind of microprocessor?
3. Memory chips that require periodic "refresh" are?
4. What constitutes a microcomputer?
5. What are the Z-80's three buses?
6. How many I/O ports can the Z-80 address?
7. How many interrupts does the Z-80 provide?
8. Which are the working general-purpose registers in the Z-80?
9. The Z-80 has a 16-bit address bus. How many memory locations can be addressed?
10. What register is always associated with the ALU?
11. What is the purpose of the F register?
12. What does the use of parentheses indicate, for example, (HL)?
13. What addressing mode is indicated by the parentheses?
14. A zero (Z) flag that is set has what value?
15. What are the flags used for?
16. In the instruction LD B,C, which is the source and which is the destination register?
17. How is the two-byte data value, 1A19H, actually stored in memory?
18. How are indexed and relative addressing modes related?
19. What is the op-code for a 16-bit exclusive-OR instruction?
20. With reference to the PC register, what is the difference between a jump and a call instruction?

CHAPTER 3

Getting Acquainted With T-Bug

In this chapter we will discuss the Radio Shack T-BUG monitor and how it is used to create object code programs in memory. You will be introduced to T-BUG's commands and their use and will learn how to examine and change the contents of the Z-80's registers. You will also become familiar with assembly-language programming using the Z-80 instruction set discussed in Chapter 2.

T-BUG VERSUS AN EDITOR/ASSEMBLER

From the previous discussions, you saw that assembly language and machine language are very closely related. In fact, assembly language may be thought of as machine language made easy, with mnemonics and labels replacing op-codes and operands (see Table 3-1). However, the programmer still must possess a knowledge of the microprocessor's internal organization, the registers, status flags, and interrupts. In addition to learning the mnemonics representing each of the microprocessor's instructions, the programmer also needs to know the actual op-codes. This is because programs are typically *written* in assembly language using menmonics, but are *debugged* or "checked" using a monitor, such as T-BUG, which only works with machine language or op-codes.

So, why use T-BUG instead of an editor/assembler? The answer is simply that it is less costly, simpler, faster, and more effective to use a monitor, especially when writing short (under 100 lines) programs. About the only operation that cannot be done using T-BUG is the generation of a source code program. To do this, you would need an editor/assembler.

The Cost of Programs

From an economic viewpoint, using a monitor such as T-BUG to implement assembly-language programs makes good sense for several reasons. First, a monitor is needed in most cases to "debug" the final object code. Second, having a monitor eliminates the need to have *both* an editor/assembler and a monitor. The editor/assembler costs twice as much as the T-BUG monitor, so you save money. Finally, a monitor is usually faster when writing short programs, and time costs money, too.

Table 3-1. Machine Language Versus Assembly Language

Machine Language (Object Code)	Assembly Language (Source Code)
6000 CD 49 00	GETNUM CALL GETCHR ;GET 1ST DIGIT
6003 CA 00 60	JZ GETNUM ;LOOP TIL DIGIT
6006 FE 0D	CP ODH ;IS IT CR?
6008 CA 14 60	JZ POP ;IF CR GO POP
600B 77	LD (HL),A ;MOVE IT TO CRT
600C 23	INC HL ;NEXT CRT POS.
600D D6 30	SUB 30H ;ASCII TO HEX
.	.
.	.
.	.

With few exceptions, notably Microsoft's *Editor-Assembler+Plus*, most editor/assemblers do not include "debugging" capabilities. These tasks are performed by monitors, such as T-BUG. The principal function of a monitor is to provide access to, and control over, the computer's microprocessor and memory. The purpose of an editor/assembler, however, is to create source- and object-code programs. So, unless the editor/assembler that is used has built-in "debug" capabilities, you will also need a monitor to help you locate and correct the inevitable "bugs" that occur in programs.

Since an editor/assembler will not be used, programs will be written out and will then be assembled by hand, using tables of Z-80 op-codes. The T-BUG program will then be used to enter the op-codes into memory, and then debug it. Thus, through the use of a technique called *hand assembly*, we are able to use mnemonics and labels as well as op-codes and operands. This technique, when used in conjunction with the Level II BASIC ROM subroutines, forms the basis of the "shortcut" assembly-language programming described in this book.

Hand Assembly

Hand assembly consists of little more than the addition of two steps to the "normal" assembly-language programming procedures: (1) the programmer translates mnemonics and labels to op-codes and hexadecimal addresses, and (2) the programmer manually determines the addresses used by the program. These tasks are handled quite easily using mnemonic-to-op-code and decimal-to-hexadecimal conversion tables, such as those provided in Appendices B and E, respectively.

Programs are written in the same format used by an editor/assembler, *except* addresses are not entered at this time, and a new column is added, as shown in Fig. 3-1. After the program has been written, the programmer goes back over it and translates each mnemonic and label or operand into its corresponding hexadecimal equivalent. This value is entered into the OP-CODE column. When a reference is made to a particular line in the program, it is assigned an appropriate label. Starting at the first address used by the program, the programmer counts the number of bytes per op-code and operand(s) and assigns addresses accordingly. As each label is encountered, the hexadecimal equivalent of its address is entered in the appropriate OP-CODE column position. The program is now ready to be stored in memory, using T-BUG. At this point, only the addresses and op-codes are needed to enter the object code version of the program into memory. The program with mnemonics, labels, and added REMARKS becomes your *documentation*. The REMARKS provide information about what each instruction does.

Programs written using an editor/assembler must generally be *re*-assembled *each* time a change or correction is made. Suppose, that once the object version of a program is loaded into memory, it is executed and a "bug" is found in the program. What operations have to be performed, in order to correct this bug? If an editor/assembler is being used, the editor/assembler would have to be reloaded into

	Assembly Source Code			
(Hex) New	**Label**	**Mnemonic/Operand**		**Remarks**
CD 00 70	BEGIN	CALL	DELAY	;KEYBD DEBOUNCE
21 00 3C		LD	HL,3C00	;CRT ADDRESS
CD 00 60	1ST N	CALL	GETNUM	;GET 1ST NUMBER
08		EX	AF,AF'	;SWAP AF
3E 2B		LD	A,"+"	;ASCII "+"
77		LD	(HL),A	;DISPLAY IT
		.		
		.		
		.		

Fig. 3-1. New column (HEX) used in hand-assembly.

memory, the source program would have to be reloaded into memory, and then the program would have to be edited. Once the program is edited, the new source program is saved on tape and then it is assembled. Once the program is assembled, the monitor can be used to execute and locate any additional bugs. As you can see, a lot of time is used up loading and storing information from/to tapes.

Using the hand assembly technique, instructions can be added, deleted or changed, using a pencil and eraser. Once this is done, the program is reassembled, *by hand*, and the op-codes for the new instructions are added. *Many of the memory addresses contained in the program may have to be changed.*

As you can see, for *short* programs, it takes less time to change the program by hand than it does to load a number of cassette tapes into the microcomputer. On the other hand, for *large* programs, it makes more sense to use an editor/assembler, since it is less prone to make errors, and it is easier for the computer to translate hundreds or thousands of mnemonics to op-codes, than for us to do it.

Ease of Use

Monitors typically have fewer commands than do the editor/assemblers, and T-BUG is no exception, with only seven commands to remember. Although not as flexible or versatile as the Radio Shack *Editor/Assembler,* T-BUG is nevertheless a very powerful programming tool. With these seven commands and only 1535 bytes of memory used to store them, T-BUG provides the programmer with the ability to:

- Create and modify object-code programs directly in memory.
- Debug object-code programs.
- Inspect and change the contents of memory and CPU registers.
- Save and load object-code (SYSTEM) programs to and from cassette.
- Execute object-code programs created by T-BUG or an editor/assembler.

NOTE: In Radio Shack terminology, a machine-language program is called a SYSTEM program. Both names refer to an object-code program.

These seven commands enable the programmer to examine the contents of *any* memory location, including those in ROM, and to change the contents of read/write (RAM) memory or the Z-80's registers. They also permit the setting of "breakpoints" for debugging programs as they are executed and the saving of object-code programs on cassette as SYSTEM programs. T-BUG is also easy to load, simple to understand, and simple to use.

T-BUG—An Effective Programming Tool

But, is T-BUG effective? Can it really be used to implement assembly-language programs without using an editor/assembler? The answer is a positive, but qualified, YES.

T-BUG can be used to create an object program directly in memory, debug the program, and execute or save the final results. But, it cannot convert mnemonics and labels into op-codes and operands. These tasks are performed by the programmer, using the "hand assembly" technique. With the exception of creating and assembling source code, a monitor such as T-BUG *can* be used to do assembly-language programming; it is just a little more work for the programmer, that's all.

Thus, the basic tradeoff is saving some money by not buying the editor-assembler versus letting the TRS-80 assemble the programs, and make fewer errors.

T-BUG

T-BUG is a machine-language monitor and debug program that provides the programmer with the ability to directly inspect and change the contents of the Z-80's registers and read/write (RAM) memory. T-BUG is loaded into *low* memory using the SYSTEM command and occupies only 1535 bytes of memory (memory locations 4380H through 497FH), stack included. Unlike Level II BASIC, which was written in 8080 assembly language, T-BUG was written in Z-80 assembly language. The significance of this will be explained later.

LOADING T-BUG

T-BUG loads into the TRS-80 from cassette just like any other SYSTEM program. The steps that are required to load T-BUG are summarized in Table 3-2. T-BUG occupies memory locations 4380H through 497FH. The stack pointer (SP) is preset to 4980H, but can be relocated if necessary. With T-BUG loaded in memory, there are 13,949 bytes of memory available for the user (locations 4982H through 7FFFH (16K)).

Why is T-BUG loaded into low memory instead of high memory as most other utility programs are? Because, by residing in low memory, T-BUG "frees" the remaining memory locations for user programs and permits programs to be written *where* they will be used. This is a very definite "plus" when a *relocator* routine or program is not available. One of the disadvantages of having T-BUG in low memory is that you normally cannot have both T-BUG and a BASIC

Table 3-2. Loading T-BUG Into Memory

Step 1.	Insert T-BUG cassette (Level II side up) in recorder; rewind if necessary.
Step 2.	Adjust volume control as necessary and depress PLAY.
Step 3.	Enter SYSTEM.
Step 4.	Enter T-BUG . . . the cassette will begin loading into the computer. Two asterisks (**) will appear in the upper-right-hand corner of the display; the right asterisk should blink on and off. The appearance of a "C" indicates a **checksum** error, so try loading again with a slightly different volume setting. A "good" load is indicated by the simultaneous stopping of the cassette recorder and the appearance of the TRS-80's SYSTEM prompt *? (loading time about 15 seconds).
Step 5.	Press the slash (/) key and then ENTER key . . . T-BUG will respond by clearing the first 16 columns of the display and displaying its prompt (#) in the upper-left-hand corner of the video display.

program in memory at the same time. Later, we will see how this *can* be done.

T-BUG COMMANDS

T-BUG has seven commands. These seven commands with their format and function are listed in Table 3-3.

In addition to the seven commands, T-BUG has two operators, the ENTER key, which is used after the memory command is entered, and the X key, which is used after the memory, jump, breakpoint, or punch commands. The ENTER key causes the currently displayed memory address to be incremented by one (nnnn + 1) and the content of memory at this new address is displayed below the first address.

Table 3-3. A Command Summary of T-BUG

Command	Format	Function
M, MEMORY	# M **nnnn**	Display/change contents of memory location **nnnn.**
J, JUMP	# J **nnnn**	Jump to memory location **nnnn** and execute.
B, BREAKPOINT	# B **nnnn**	Set breakpoint at address **nnnn.**
F, FIX	# F	Restore instruction displaced by breakpoint.
G, GO	# G	Continue execution after breakpoint and fix.
R, REGISTER	# R	Display contents of CPU registers.
P, PUNCH	# P **aaaa bbbb cccc XXXXXX**	Write to cassette contents of memory locations from **aaaa** to **bbbb** with a starting address of **cccc** and file name **XXXXXX.**

Pressing the X key (EXIT) while executing the instructions for the M, J, B, or P commands causes an immediate termination of that command and an "exit" back to T-BUG's command mode, indicated by the reappearance of the # prompt. This prompt (#) is only displayed when in the command mode.

Now let's examine each individual command and its function.

The MEMORY Command

The MEMORY command (#M nnnn) is executed by pressing the M key followed by the four-digit hexadecimal address (nnnn) of the memory location to be inspected or changed. For example, entering M 5000 produces the following:

```
# M 5000 FF
```

What happened as you pressed the last zero of the memory address? T-BUG immediately responded with the contents (in hexadecimal) of that address, which in this case was FF. Pressing the ENTER key causes the display to increment to the next memory address (NOTE: (ENTER) means press the ENTER key):

```
# M 5000 FF (ENTER)
5001 FF
```

To change the contents of memory location 5001 from FFH to 00H, simply type the new characters, 00, instead of pressing the ENTER key:

```
# M 5000 FF (ENTER)
5001 FF 00
5002 FF
```

T-BUG automatically increments and displays the next higher memory address after the second character is typed. This feature becomes quite handy when entering lengthy programs and is similar to the AUTO (line-numbering) statement in Level II BASIC.

But, what happened to the T-BUG prompt # after the address 5000 was entered? The T-BUG prompt appears only when in the command mode, and typing M causes T-BUG to execute the instructions for the MEMORY command. Thus, the prompt is not displayed. How do we get back into the command mode? Simple, press the X key (EXIT):

```
# M 5000 FF (ENTER)
5001 FF 00
5002 FF (X)
#
```

You do not have to press the ENTER key after pressing the X key. Did you notice that the character X did not appear on the display? Only the T-BUG prompt # appeared, signalling our return to the command mode.

The REGISTER Command

The REGISTER command (#R) is executed by pressing the R key while in the command mode. T-BUG responds by displaying the *current* content of the Z-80's 20 internal registers as follows:

```
A'F'            B'C'
D'E'            H'L'

AF              BC
DE              HL

IX(MSB,LSB)     IY(MSB,LSB)
SP(MSB,LSB)     PC(MSB,LSB)
```

What T-BUG displays is the hexadecimal representation of the content of each register at the instant the R key was pressed. The display does not indicate which register is which, so you should either commit the above format to memory, or copy it on a 3×5 card.

Press the R key. Your display should look something like this:

```
#  FFFF        FFFF
   FFFF        FFFF

   0042        00FD
   41E9        43A0

   FFFF        FFFF
   4980        FFFF
```

A display of other than all Fs in any of the complement registers indicates "garbage" and is not important at this time. Typing NEW prior to loading T-BUG generally eliminates this occurrence.

Let's examine what T-BUG has displayed. The A register is the accumulator and contains all zeros (00). The F register is the status or "flag" register and contains 42. Unfortunately, 42 by itself doesn't mean much. To be useful, it must be expressed in *binary* so that the status of each bit can be determined. This can be easily accomplished by breaking the hexadecimal byte into two parts; a high *nibble* (4 bits), which in this case is 4, and a low nibble of 2. Now, simply express these as binary numbers:

42H = 4 2 = 0100 0010

This can be done, because each character in a hexadecimal number represents four bits. Now, going back to Chapter 2, these binary bits

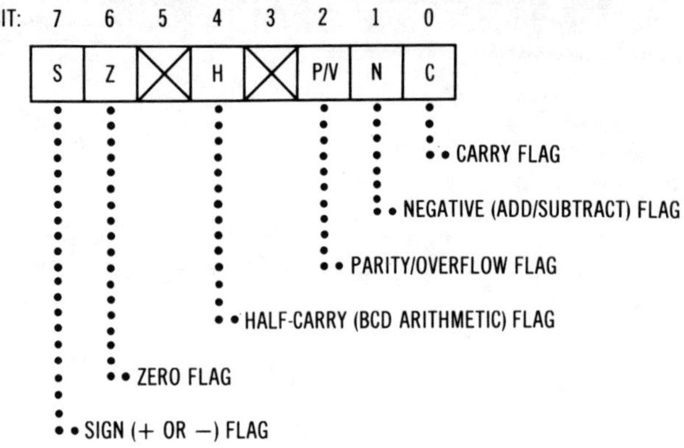

Fig. 3-2. Z-80 flag register format.

can be compared to the Z-80's Flag Register (Fig. 3-2). Thus, the ZERO and NEGATIVE flags are set. The structure of the flag word should also be written on the 3×5 "register" card.

Getting back to the other registers, the B register contains zeros (00), and the C register contains FD. The DE register pair contains 41E9H, which is the address of the TRS-80's *Keyboard Input Buffer Area* in RAM memory (a "reserved" area in the Radio Shack Memory Map). The HL register pair contains 43A0H, the *starting address* (also called auto-start address) of T-BUG. This is the hexadecimal equivalent of the decimal number, 17312, which is entered after the slash (/) when executing T-BUG from BASIC using the SYSTEM command. The SP register contains 4980H, the address noted earlier as the user stack, which is established by T-BUG.

Once we know what is *in* each register, how do we *change* the contents of each one? To do this, T-BUG's *Register Save Area* (memory locations 4825H through 483CH) must be discussed. T-BUG uses this area to "save" the contents of the CPU registers while it is performing one of its operations or commands. The Z-80's internal registers are loaded with this information *prior to* executing a user program when either a JUMP or GO command is executed. The individual addresses for each register are summarized in Table 3-4. Where two addresses are given, as with the index registers (IX and IY), stack pointer (SP), and program counter (PC), the first address is for the most-significant byte (MSB) and the second address is for the least-significant byte (LSB). T-BUG always displays the MSB on the left and LSB on the right for these 4 registers, making it easier for us to read.

Now, press the M key to execute the MEMORY command and then enter the address of the A register, 482E:

Table 3-4. Register Save Area/Memory Assignments

A'(4826H)	F'(4825H)	B'(4828H)	C'(4817H)
D'(482AH)	E'(4829H)	H'(482CH)	L'(482BH)
A(482EH)	F(482DH)	B(4830H)	C(482FH)
D(4832H)	E(4831H)	H(4834H)	L(4833H)
IX(4836H,4835H)		IY(4838H,4837H)	
SP(483AH,4839H)		PC(483CH,483BH)	

```
# M 482E 00
```

Typing FF changes the content of memory location 482E from 00 to FF:

```
# M 482E 00 FF
482F FD
```

Note that T-BUG automatically incremented the memory address to the next higher memory address, 482FH, which in this case is the memory location used to store the content of the C register. Pressing the X key returns control to T-BUG's command mode, and pressing the R key lets us see what we've done:

```
#  FFFF  FFFF
   FFFF  FFFF

   FF42  00FD
   41E9  43A0

   FFFF  FFFF
   4980  FFFF
```

As you can see, the value for AF has been changed from 0042 to FF42. Remember, however, that the value FF is *not* actually transferred into the Z-80's accumulator *until* either a JUMP or GO command is executed. For now, change the A register back to zeros:

```
# M 482E 00
482F FD
```

The JUMP Command

The JUMP command (#J nnnn) is executed by pressing the J key and then typing the four digit hexadecimal destination address (nnnn). For example, typing a destination address of 1A19H produces an interesting result:

```
# J 1A19
READY
>9_
```

This is the re-entry point for Level II BASIC! Remember, BASIC's prompt is a right arrow followed by an underline (>__). Typically, unless a "debounce" routine is in use, the 9 from the destination address also appears on the display. Simply erase it by pressing the back arrow (<) key.

How do we get back to T-BUG? Type SYSTEM and press ENTER, then type /17312 and press ENTER. The slash tells the computer to execute the program at the decimal address following the slash. The decimal number 17312 is the starting address of T-BUG (43A0H). If no address is entered, and ENTER is pressed instead, the computer defaults to the address stored in the HL register pair:

```
SYSTEM (ENTER)
*? /17312 (ENTER)
#
```

If the jump had been made to address 0000H instead of 1A19H, a *complete restart* would have occurred, resulting in the MEMORY SIZE? message appearing. When that occurs, it is fairly certain that what was in memory has been "lost."

The BREAKPOINT Command

The BREAKPOINT command (# B nnnn) is executed by pressing the B key followed by the four digit hexadecimal address of a program *instruction!* It is used in conjunction with the FIX and GO commands to perform "debugging" of machine-language programs.

Failure to set a breakpoint at the address of a *program instruction* produces erratic results! So, *always* set the BREAKPOINT at the *beginning* of an instruction.

When the BREAKPOINT command is executed, T-BUG replaces three program bytes (starting at nnnn) with a *call* instruction. Since a *call* instruction is three bytes long, these bytes are moved from memory, starting at address nnnn, to the stack. The *call* instruction op-code is followed by the low- and high-address bytes, 80 and 43. The address nnnn is then stored in the Register Save Area, in the two memory locations used to store the PC.

NOTE: Only *ONE* BREAKPOINT may be implemented at any one time, because the FIX command will work only upon the *last* BREAKPOINT entered.

The FIX Command

The FIX command (#F) is used *only after a BREAKPOINT has been executed,* otherwise a portion of your program will be destroyed. It "restores" the original three bytes of the program that are stored in the stack to the program, beginning at the address held in the PC register. This is the reason a FIX must be used only after a BREAKPOINT has been set. If the FIX command is entered without there first being a BREAKPOINT, whatever is currently on the stack will be written into your program at the address pointed to by the PC register, destroying three bytes in your program.

The GO Command

The GO command (#G) is executed by pressing the G key and should only be used after a BREAKPOINT has been set in your program. It instructs T-BUG to begin program execution at the address stored in the PC register—the BREAKPOINT address—*after* a FIX has restored the program's original program instructions. Like the FIX command, GO must be used only after a BREAKPOINT.

Now, let's see what actually happens when the BREAKPOINT, FIX, and GO commands are used. Enter the short program listed in Example 3-1 using the MEMORY command.

Example 3-1. A short demonstration program.

ADDR	OP-CODE			LABEL	MNEMONIC/ OPERAND		REMARKS
5000	11	FF	FF		LD	DE,FFFF	;LOAD DE WITH FFFF
5003	1D			LOOP1	DEC	E	;ONE LESS E
5004	C2	03	50		JP	NZ,LOOP1	;DONE?
5007	15				DEC	D	;ONE LESS D
5008	C2	03	50		JP	NZ,LOOP1	;DONE?
500B	CD	C9	01	CLS	CALL	CLS	;CLEAR SCREEN
500E	C3	A0	43	END	JP	43A0	;RTN TO T-BUG

Once the program is loaded, exit the MEMORY command by pressing the X key and enter the BREAKPOINT command by pressing the B key. Because of the restriction of setting a breakpoint only on an instruction (op-code), the first address that can be used is 5003H, where the DEC E instruction is stored. So, enter that address:

```
# B 5003
#
```

Notice that nothing visible happens; however, if we use the MEMORY command and inspect the program, we will find that T-BUG has replaced three program bytes:

```
# M 5003 CD (ENTER)
5004 80 (ENTER)
5005 43 (ENTER)
5006 50 (X)
#
```

T-BUG has replaced the 1D C2 03 values with CD 80 43, the address of the stack pointer (remember LSB first, MSB second). Where did the original instructions go? Let's look at the content of memory locations 484FH-4851H in the stack area:

```
#  M  484F  1D  (ENTER)
4850  C2  (ENTER)
4851  03  (ENTER)
4852  FD  (X)
#
```

So, when T-BUG executes a BREAKPOINT command, it automatically places the program instruction (nnnn) and the next two bytes (nnnn + 1 and nnnn + 2) on the stack for temporary storage, and replaces them with a *call* instruction (CD) and a two byte address (80 43) pointing to the stack area.

If a FIX command is executed at this time to remove the "breakpoint," problems will occur, because the PC register no longer holds the address of the breakpoint! What should be done? The answer is: put the BREAKPOINT address back into the PC register. This is accomplished by referring back to the Register Save Area memory addresses and by determining which contain the PC register bytes. There, we find: PC(483C,483B) . . . where address 483BH is the least-significant byte and 483CH is the most-significant byte. Using the MEMORY command, load the PC register with the address of the BREAKPOINT, 5003:

```
#  M  483B  00  03
483C  50  (X)
#
```

Where was the PC register pointing before we changed its contents? That's right! It pointed to 5000H, the starting address of our program, and *not* to the BREAKPOINT address, 5003H. Since the MSB is 50 in both addresses, it does not have to be changed.

Now, press the F key to execute a FIX to remove the breakpoint, and then jump to the beginning of the program:

```
#  F
#  J  5000
#
```

Did the display "erase" after a moment's hesitation? Good, that's what it is supposed to do. If we inspect the program now we will find it exactly as we wrote it:

```
#  M  5000  11  (ENTER)
5001  FF  (ENTER)
5002  FF  (ENTER)
```

```
5003  1D  (ENTER)
5004  C2  (ENTER)
5005  03  (ENTER)
  .    .    .
  .    .    .
  .    .    .
5010  43  (X)
#
```

The PC register must be reset only if its contents have been changed. When in doubt, check the contents of memory locations 483B-483C—the PC register—using the REGISTER command. Normally, this procedure is only necessary when either MEMORY or JUMP commands have been executed prior to using the FIX command. These commands cause the PC register contents to be altered, so the BREAKPOINT address is lost.

When the 0 key is pressed the last time in the command J 5000, why does the computer seem to wait for a second, before clearing the screen? Well, let's examine the program and determine what it does. The first 11 bytes are a "delay" loop, which causes the slight delay before the display is erased. The next three bytes are a *call* to the Level II BASIC's CLEAR SCREEN (CLS) subroutine, and the last three bytes are an unconditional JUMP back to the starting address of T-BUG.

We now have a machine language version of the BASIC CLS command, CALL 01C9H. Instead of having to jump back into BASIC and press the CLEAR key, we simply place the following six byte program in memory and JUMP to it when we wish to "clear" the video display:

```
#  M  7FFA  CD
7FFB  C9
7FFC  01
7FFD  C3
7FFE  A0
7FFF  43
```

Once the screen is cleared, the Z-80 jumps back to the beginning of T-BUG.

The PUNCH Command

The PUNCH command (#P *aaaa bbbb cccc xxxxxx*) is T-BUG's answer to Level II BASIC's CSAVE statement. It permits object code programs to be "saved" on cassette for later use. Unlike BASIC, however, the PUNCH command allows file names of up to *six* characters (BASIC uses only the *first* character).

With the PUNCH command, programs DO NOT have to be complete or functional to be saved. T-BUG simply "copies" the contents of all memory locations between the beginning address, *aaaa*, and the ending address, *bbbb*, out to the cassette, similar to core image- or memory-dump. Both programs and data can be "saved" using this command; T-BUG doesn't know the difference.

The autostart address, *cccc*, is used to specify the address of the first instruction in the program to be executed. If the first instruction is actually the first byte in the program, then *aaaa* and *cccc* will be the same. Why have a "starting" address different than the beginning of the program? Sometimes, programmers like to put all the temporary storage memory locations and subroutines at the beginning of a program (low memory) and the main program at the end. Other programmers like the lowest memory address used by the program to be the starting address of the program, with subroutine and temporary storage locations in high memory. With T-BUG, the former is the case. The instructions at 4380H are not the instructions for the "main program" but are the instructions that are executed when a breakpoint is "hit" and the Z-80 calls the "subroutine" at 4380H.

To "save" our simple program on cassette, simply collect the necessary information:

- Beginning address, *aaaa:* 5000
- Ending address, *bbbb:* 5010
- Autostart address, *cccc:* 5000
- File name, *xxxxxx:* SAMPLE

and set up the cassette recorder to RECORD. Then execute the PUNCH command as follows:

```
# P 5000 5010 5000 SAMPLE
```

NOTE: If fewer than six characters are used for the file name, the ENTER key must be pressed to initiate the PUNCH command, otherwise execution automatically begins when the sixth character is pressed.

The recorder will start and run until the program is completely "saved" onto the cassette. The PUNCH command may be terminated at anytime using the X key—*except* when entering the file name! Here, the BREAK key must be pressed instead. This occurs because X is a valid file name character and cannot be differentiated from the X in an EXIT command.

One of the first rules of programming is "always make a back-up copy" and this rule is just as valid for assembly-language programming. Hence, we must know *how* to make a "back-up" copy of object code programs. T-BUG is an object code (machine language) program, so let's learn how to make a back-up copy of it. That way we can put the *original* copy away in a safe place and operate with the *copy*. The necessary information about T-BUG is summarized in PUNCH command:

```
# P 4380 497F 43A0 T-BUG (ENTER)
```

The cassette should start and run for about 20 seconds, and then stop. You have just "backed-up" your T-BUG program. Now, put the original away in a safe place and use only the copy from now on. Should something happen to the copy, simply make another "copy" from the original. If you have any other SYSTEM programs where you know this address information, now would be a good time to make back-up copies of them, too.

Table 3-5. Addresses Used to Save T-BUG on Tape

Beginning address, **aaaa**:	4380H
Ending address, **bbbb**:	497FH
Autostart address, **cccc**:	43A0H
File name, **xxxxxx**:	T-BUG

Did you notice that T-BUG automatically placed a "space" between entries in the PUNCH command? If not, that might explain any problems you may be having. Remember, the "space" you enter is ignored in the numeric entries, but *will* be used in the File Name!

Unless T-BUG is modified, there is no provision for verifying or "checking" the information on the cassette against the contents of memory, as there is with BASIC's CLOAD? statement. However, for the adventurous reader, some modifications to T-BUG have been published.[1] When implemented, these modifications to T-BUG provide the ability to: (1) VERIFY (V) a program PUNCHed to cassette, (2) DUMP (D) onto the video display 16 consecutive memory addresses at once, and (3) step both forward (ENTER key) and backward (SPACE bar) through memory. Although these enhancements are neither covered nor used in this book, you might like to add them to T-BUG.

LOADING MULTIPLE PROGRAMS

When more than one program must be loaded into memory, just use the SYSTEM command as often as required. This technique works well as long as none of the programs "overlap" or try to use the same memory areas. It can also be used as often as necessary, not just once or twice.

The trick here is NOT to press the slash (/) and then the ENTER key accidentally! If you do, you'll end up executing the *last* program entered. The correct procedure is to type the slash and decimal address (/.....) of the program you actually want to use, once all the programs and data have been loaded from cassette, forcing T-BUG to jump to that program and begin execution. This lets us load data and programs from cassette into memory.

The following is an example of how to load a second SYSTEM tape (program or data) with T-BUG already in memory and operating:

```
#  J 1A19                    ;JUMP back to BASIC
   SYSTEM (ENTER)            ;enter SYSTEM command mode
   *? FILE NAME (ENTER)      ;Load FILE NAME from cassette
   *? /17312 (ENTER)         ;T-BUG's autostart address
```

T-BUG AND ASCII

We have already discussed the fact that decimal numbers must be converted into binary numbers before the computer can actually operate on them. The same is true for *letters* and *symbols.* The letters of the alphabet (A-Z), numerals (0-9), and symbols (!,$,* etc.) are implemented using the *A*merican *S*tandard *C*ode for *I*nformation *I*nterchange (ASCII), a standardized set of 7-bit binary values that represent 128 different characters or operations. The complete set of ASCII values is listed in Appendix F, and is shown in an abbreviated form, along with the TRS-80 modifications, in Table 3-6. Due to the manner in which graphics and alphanumerics are operated on in the Model I TRS-80, lowercase (a...z) letters cannot be displayed on the Video Display, but are *output* to peripherals, such as the line printer, cassette tape deck, etc. This is indicated by the UPPER-lower (Aa...Zz) case pairs in the 6-H and 7-H columns of Table 3-6. The Model I TRS-80 automatically converts lowercase letters to uppercase for display purposes.

Because Radio Shack has used several different character generator chips (Z29 on the Model I TRS-80 schematic), the actual characters displayed in response to the different hexadecimal codes *may be* different from those shown in Table 3-6. In the Model III, the character generator chip is U36 (MCM68A316E). Four ASCII characters have been modified to accommodate the TRS-80's four ARROW keys (↑,→,↓,←) as shown in Table 3-7. Most TRS-80 compatible peripherals (i.e., Centronics printers, plotters, etc.) recognize these new symbols.

Did you notice that the numerals (0-9) are converted to ASCII by simply *adding 30* to the decimal number?

The program in Example 3-2 causes the Model I TRS-80 to display all the above ASCII characters and symbols, as well as the 64 different graphic symbols.

Table 3-6. TRS-80 ASCII Table

MSB →	2	3	4	5	6	7	LSB↓
	SPACE	0	@	P	↓	Pp	0H
	!	1	A	Q	Aa	Qq	1H
	"	2	B	R	Bb	Rr	2H
	#	3	C	S	Cc	Ss	3H
	$	4	D	T	Dd	Tt	4H
	%	5	E	U	Ee	Uu	5H
	&	6	F	V	Ff	Vv	6H
	'	7	G	W	Gg	Ww	7H
	(	8	H	X	Hh	Xx	8H
	)	9	I	Y	Ii	Yy	9H
	*	:	J	Z	Jj	Zz	AH
	+	;	K	[	Kk	{	BH
	,	<	L	\	Ll	¦	CH
	—	=	M	]	Mn	}	DH
	.	>	N	↑	Nn	→	EH
	/	?	O	←	Oo	DEL	FH

Table 3-7. Nonstandard Characters for Four ASCII Values

Normal ASCII:	Hex Code	TRS-80 Symbol:
^	5E	↑
_	5F	←
`	60	↓
~	7E	→

Example 3-2. Display characters on the CRT screen.

```
                                 Mnemonic/
Addr   Op-Code       Label       Operand          Remarks
5000   CD  C9  01    CLS         CALL  CLS        ;CLEAR SCREEN
5003   21  FF  3B                LD    HL,3BFF    ;3C00H - 1 (CRT)
5006   06  1F                    LD    B,1F       ;20H - 1 (COUNTER)
5008   23            TAB         INC   HL         ;4 SPACES ON CRT
5009   23                        INC   HL         ;
500A   23                        INC   HL         ;
500B   23                        INC   HL         ;
500C   04                        INC   B          ;NEXT ASCII VALUE
500D   70                        LD    (HL),B     ;DISPLAY IT
500E   78                        LD    A,B        ;ASCII INTO ACCUM
500F   FE                        CP    BF         ;IS IT 191 (DECIMAL)?
5011   C2  08  50                JP    NZ,TAB     ;IF≠191 THEN GO TAB
5014   C3  14  50    LOOP        JP    LOOP       ;ENDLESS LOOP
```

Unless your TRS-80 has been modified (Radio Shack or "add-on") for lowercase, a rather peculiar display occurs, *there are no lowercase letters!* The Model III does not have this problem as it features both uppercase and lowercase display.

Luckily, all is not lost for the un-modified Model I TRS-80, because the lowercase to uppercase translation does not occur when data is sent to peripheral (external) devices. For example, the BASIC program in Example 3-3 outputs ASCII characters 20H (SPACE) through the last graphics symbols BFH (⠿) to the line printer.

Example 3-3. Printing uppercase and lowercase characters on a printer.

```
10  FOR X=32 TO 191
20  LPRINT CHR$(X);"    ";REM 4 BLANK SPACES!
30  NEXT X
40  END
```

This program must only be used with a TRS-80 that is connected to a printer, or the computer will "lock up," and it will have to be reset. Also, if you enter this program into memory, you will wipe out T-BUG.

When this BASIC program is run, you should see the same ASCII characters being printed as were displayed. However, there will be a very noticeable difference, the lowercase letters are back! Actually, they were never "lost," just that they are not displayed on the un-modified Model I TRS-80. Also, if the printer has provisions to print the TRS-80 graphics symbols (Okidata Microline 80, Paper Tiger, etc.), you will see them also. Otherwise, the printing becomes somewhat erratic as the characters end and the graphic symbols (80H-BFH) begin. This seemingly contradictory behavior concerning uppercase and lowercase characters must be remembered, or your lowercase *w* will end up a 7 on the display, but will look all right on a printer. Forewarned is forearmed.

REFERENCE

1. Curtis, H. A., "T-BUG for II," *80 Microcomputing*, April, 1980, pp. 84-86.

REVIEW QUESTIONS

1. What is the significance of the two numbers 17312 and 43A0H?

2. What happens when a JUMP command is executed to address 1A19H?

3. What is the purpose of T-BUG's "R" command?

4. When are the F and G commands used?

5. What must be done to change the content of the D register?

6. While operating, what does T-BUG hold in the HL register pair?

7. What is the Level II BASIC prompt symbol?

8. What is the T-BUG prompt symbol?

9. What is the SYSTEM prompt symbol?

10. What is the first address (lowest address) of the Video Display?

11. How are the letters of the alphabet (A-Z) and numerals (0-9) handled within the TRS-80?

12. If 6AH is sent to the Video Display, what will be seen?

13. What ASCII value is used to send a DOWN-ARROW (↓) to a *printer?*

14. How can the Video Display be "cleared" from assembly language?

15. What must be done to display the number "1" on the CRT Video Display?

CHAPTER 4

TRS-80 Memory Map

The purpose of this chapter is to provide you with an introduction to the memory map of the TRS-80 and the Level II BASIC ROMs. We will discuss in general terms what the TRS-80 memory map is, and what the Level II ROMs contain. Detailed discussions and specific examples will be covered in later chapters.

The TRS-80 memory map consists basically of two areas, the Level II BASIC ROMs and the user read/write (RAM) memories. The memory map is nothing more than a memory-location by memory-location accounting of those addresses that are either "dedicated" or "reserved" for use by the CPU and are not generally available to the programmer. Some addresses are actual locations within memory chips, others are *hardwired* locations which *act* like memory, and some areas of the map are *blank*.

Table 4-1 presents the general organization of the TRS-80 memory map addresses in both hexadecimal and decimal notations. The major areas of interest in the map are summarized in Table 4-2. Let's look at each of these areas in closer detail.

Table 4-1. General Organization of the TRS-80 Memory Map

Address	Contents
0000H-2FFFH	(12K ROM) Level II BASIC ROMS.
3000H-37DDH	Model I—Empty (2013 bytes); no memory. Model III—System routines (2K ROM).
3800H-3880H	(HARDWIRED) Keyboard matrix.
3C00H-3FFFH	(1K RAM) CRT video display memory.
4000H-42E8H	(RAM) "Reserved" memory; system work area.

Table 4-2. Major Areas of TRS-80 Memory Map

Hexadecimal Address	Memory Contents	Decimal Address
0000H 2FFFH	(12K) LEVEL II BASIC ROMs	0 12287
3000H 37DDH	(2013 bytes) Model I: Empty, nothing here Model III: Date/Time & cassette Baud routines	12288 14301
37DEH	DOS Communication Status Address	14302
37DFH	DOS Communication Data Address	14303
37E0H	Interrupt Latch Address	14304
37E1H	Disk Drive Select Latch Address	14305
37E4H	Cassette Select Latch Address	14308
37E8H	Line Printer Port Address	14312
37ECH	Floppy Disk Controller Address	14316
3800H 3880H	KEYBOARD MEMORY MATRIX	14336 14464
3C00H 3FFFH	(1K) VIDEO MEMORY	15360 16383
	.... beginning of user read/write (RAM) memory	
4000H 4012H	VECTORS (RSTs 1 through 7)	16384 16402
4016H	KEYBOARD Driver entry point	16406
401EH	VIDEO Driver entry point	16414
4020H	Video memory address of current CURSOR position	16416
4026H	LINE PRINTER Driver entry point	16422
403DH	PRINT SIZE Flag (00 = 64 ch; 08 = 32 ch)	16445
403EH 407FH	Unused by Level II BASIC (used by DOS)	16446 16511
4080H 408DH	Single-precision DIVIDE work area	16512 16525
408EH	USR Routine entry pointer	16526
4090H	RND Function Multiplicative Constant Mantissa	16528
4093H	INP Routine (4093="IN" inst; 4094=port#; 4095=Ret)	16531
4096H	OUT Routine (4096="OUT" inst; 4097=port#; 4098=Ret)	16534
4099H	INKEY$ Buffer (holds last entry from keyboard)	16537
409AH	ERROR CODE Buffer (for RESUME use)	16538
409BH	LINE PRINTER Line position	16539
409CH	Output Device Flag (00=VIDEO; 01=LPRINTER; FF=CASSETTE)	16540
409DH	Max. Line-length of VIDEO (00=64 ch)	16541
409EH	Next Print Zone (reached after comma as: ?X,Y,Z)	16542
409FH	Unused by Level II BASIC	16543
40A0H	Beginning of STRING Space Pointer	16544
40A2H	Current Line-number being processed	16546
40A4H	Beginning of BASIC Program Pointer	16548
40A6H	Current Line CURSOR Position in VIDEO (used by TAB)	16550
40A7H	Input Buffer Pointer	16551
40A9H	Flag Byte for INPUT# −1 Routine	16553
40AAH	RND Function "seed" (also used with RANDOM)	16554

Table 4-2—cont. Major Areas of TRS-80 Memory Map

Hexadecimal Address	Memory Contents	Decimal Address
40ADH	Unused by Level II BASIC	16557
40AEH	DIM and LET Flag	16558
40AFH	NUMBER TYPE FLAG (NTF1) 2=INT; 3=STR; 4=SGL; 8=DBL	16559
4031H	Address of last usable byte in memory (MEM SIZE?)	16561
40B3H	String work area pointer	16563
40B5H	String work area	16565
40D3H	Current string length	16595
40D4H	Address of current string	16596
40D6H	Next free byte in string area	16598
40D8H	PRINT USING format byte (bit 2=*; 3=+; 4=$; 6=comma(,))	16600
40DAH	Last DATA line-number read	16602
40DCH	DIM use (set = 64 to prevent subscripted variable)	16604
40DFH	Entry point storage for SYSTEM tapes	16607
40E1H	AUTO Flag (00 = not AUTO, else AUTO; set 00 after BREAK)	16609
40E2H	AUTO line-number	16610
40E4H	AUTO increment size	16612
40E6H	Pointer to end of previous/current line	16614
40E8H	STACK POINTER save area	16616
40EAH	Used by RESUME (holds "error" line-number)	16618
40ECH	EDIT current line-number	16620
40EEH	Used by RESUME (points to end previous/current line)	16622
40F0H	Address of ON ERROR	16624
40F2H	ON ERROR Flag (FF after error, 00 if no error)	16626
40F5H	Last line-number executed	16629
40F7H	Pointer to next byte used after CONT	16631
40F9H	Pointer to Simple (scalar) Variables	16633
40FBH	Pointer to Array Variables	16635
40FDH	Last Array Variables memory location	16637
40FFH	Used by RESTORE (holds current line-number for READ)	16639
4101H 411AH	VARIABLE TYPE TABLE (A-Z) (2=INT; 3=STR; 3=SGL; 8=DBL)	16641 16666
411BH	TRON Flag (00 = TROFF; AF = TRON)	16667
411DH 4124H	Floating-point Accumulator (FPA1)	16669 16676
4127H 412EH	Floating-point Accumulator (FPA2)	16679 16686
4130H 4151H	Numeric work area / PRINT USING buffer	16688 16721
41E8H 42E8H	Input (and output) Buffer area	16870 17127
42E9H	Beginning of user-available memory	17129
. . .		. . .
4288H	STACK POINTER for SYSTEM	17032
.		.

Table 4-2—cont. Major Areas of TRS-80 Memory Map

Hexadecimal Address	Memory Contents	Decimal Address
.		.
.		.
4FFFH	End of 4K memory	20479
.		.
.		.
.		.
7FFFH	End of 16K memory	32767
.		.
.		.
.		.
BFFFH	End of 32K memory	49151
.		.
.		.
.		.
FFFFH	End of 48K memory	65535

THE BASIC ROMs (0000H–2FFFH)

This is the 12K ROM area of the memory map that contains Level II BASIC. The general organization of the BASIC ROMs is given in Table 4-3. There have been at least four different ROM versions of Level II: 1.0, 1.1, 1.2, and 1.3. ROM 1.3 is currently used in both Model I and Model III computers and is easily recognized by its abbreviated "MEM SIZE?" and "R/S L2 BASIC" sign-on messages. This area of the memory map is read-only memory (ROM) and can be "read" but not "written" to, that is, you can *inspect* but not *change* the contents of these memory locations. You can attempt to change

Table 4-3. General Organization of BASIC ROMs

Address	Contents
0000H-01D8H	System power-up initialization and I/O.
01D9H-03E2H	Cassette subroutines.
03E3H-0457H	Keyboard driver.
0458H-058CH	Video display driver.
0674H-070AH	Initialization code.
070BH-1607H	Floating-point arithmetic/mathematic.
1608H-164FH	Table of entry points for functions.
1650H-1820H	Table of Level II BASIC reserved words.
1821H-1899H	Table of entry points for Level II commands.
189AH-18C8H	Table of precedent operators.
18C9H-18F6H	Non-DOS error messages.
18F7H-191CH	Non-DOS power-up initialization.
191DH-1953H	Message table.
1936H-2FFFH	Level II BASIC interpreter subroutines.

the content of one of these memory locations using the M command in T-BUG, but the information in the ROMs will not be altered.

To determine which version you have use the following BASIC program:

```
10  FOR  I=11264  TO  12287:V=PEEK(I):S=S+V:NEXT  I:X=S/16
20  A=(X—FIX(X))*16:Y=FIX(X)/16:B=(Y—FIX(Y))*256
30  PRINT  (A+B)
```

If the result is 176, it is ROM 1.0; 142 = ROM 1.1; 10 = ROM 1.2 and 162 = ROM 1.3.

EMPTY, NO MEMORY, OR SYSTEM ROUTINES (3000H–37DDH)

In the Model I TRS-80 computers, this area of the memory map is empty—there is *nothing* there—and is simply wasted memory space. Some peripherals use this area to insert their own ROM software, such as Exatron's *Stringy Floppy*, and are easily recognized by their decimal addresses between 12288 and 14301. For example, Exatron uses the extremely easy-to-remember address, 12345.

In Model III TRS-80s, this area contains a 2K ROM that holds the Date, Time, and Cassette (500/1500 baud) subroutines.

KEYBOARD MATRIX (3800H–3880H)

This is the *hardwired keyboard matrix* area of the memory map which "pretends to be" memory. As a key is pressed, *one bit* of one memory address is connected to +5 V dc, assigning a decimal value of 1, 2, 4, 8, 16, 32, 64, or 128 to that "memory location." A special subroutine then translates the address and value into the appropriate keyboard (ASCII) character value. The keyboard matrix is depicted in Fig. 4-1.

More than one key may be pressed at the same time, resulting in a value equal to the *SUM* of the values of the keys pressed. For example, simultaneously pressing the "J," "K," and "L" keys assigns a value of 28 to memory location 3802H (J + K + L = 4 + 8 + 16 = 28). More on this later!

The keyboard matrix area of the memory map is essentially an *input only* set of contacts connected across specific memory address lines (see p. 44, *TRS-80 Microcomputer Technical Reference Handbook*). Data (the key(s) that is (are) pressed) can be read *from,* but not written *to,* the keyboard.

VIDEO DISPLAY (3C00H–3FFFH)

This 1k RAM area is the CRT Video Display memory and consists of *seven* (unmodified Model I's) 2102-type static memory chips. Six

Addr.		Keyboard								
3801H	=	@	A	B	C	D	E	F	G	
3802H	=	H	I	J	K	L	M	N	O	
3804H	=	P	Q	R	S	T	U	V	W	
3808H	=	X	Y	Z						
3810H	=	 0	! 1	" 2	# 3	$ 4	% 5	& 6	' 7	(shifted)
3820H	=	(8	) 9	* :	+ ;	< ,	= -	> .	? /	(shifted)
3840H	=	ENTER	CLEAR	BREAK	↑	↓	←	→	SPACE	
3880H	=	SHIFT								
VALUE	=	1	2	4	8	16	32	64	128	

Fig. 4-1. TRS-80 Keyboard Matrix.

chips are used to store ASCII characters while the seventh chip determines whether the display is "characters" or "graphics symbols." The TRS-80 *assumes* that any data stored here is either ASCII characters or graphics symbols. Because the video display is normally 64 characters per line, the 1024 video memory locations can display up to 16 lines of data (1024/64 = 16). The memory addresses for each of the 16 rows in the video memory area are summarized in Table 4-4. This area of the memory map *can* be used for temporary data storage and simultaneous display *only if* the eighth 2102 has been installed. Without the eighth memory chip, a value of 10H stored at 3C00H will be converted to 61H, because an offset is "added" to values less than 20H in unmodified Model I TRS-80s. Also, the display is subject to erasure when errors occur that cause the display to be "cleared." For these reasons, this area of the memory map should be used with caution.

Table 4-4. CRT Video Display Memory Locations

Address	Row	Position (0-1023) decimal
3C00H-3C3FH	1	0-63
3C40H-3C7FH	2	64-127
3C80H-3CBFH	3	128-191
3CC0H-3CFFH	4	192-255
3D00H-3D3FH	5	256-319
3D40H-3D7FH	6	320-383
3D80H-3DBFH	7	384-447
3DC0H-3DFFH	8	448-511
3E00H-3E3FH	9	512-575
3E40H-3E7FH	10	576-639
3E80H-3EBFH	11	640-703
3EC0H-3EFFH	12	704-767
3F00H-3F3FH	13	768-831
3F40H-3F7FH	14	832-895
3F80H-3FBFH	15	896-959
3FC0H-3FFFH	16	960-1023

COMMUNICATION AREA (4000H–42E8H)

This 744 byte section of user read/write (RAM) memory is used by Level II BASIC as a temporary storage area, and contains *buffer* and *control block* areas used by both BASIC and DOS. The use of this section of memory is summarized in Table 4-5. This area is called the *communication area* of the TRS-80 memory map.

This area should be used with caution, especially when operating in BASIC, as accidental changes can have drastic results, i.e., complete loss of programs! Specific portions of this "reserved" area of the memory map will be discussed further in later chapters. For now,

Table 4-5. The Communications Region of RAM

Address	Contents
4000H-4012H	VECTORS (RSTs 1 through 7).
4015H-401CH	KEYBOARD Device Control Block.
401DH-4024H	VIDEO DISPLAY Device Control Block.
4025H-402CH	LINE PRINTER Device Control Block.
4036H-403CH	KEYBOARD work area.
403DH	PRINT SIZE Flag (00=64 ch; 08=32 ch).
403EH-407FH	Used by DOS.
4080H-408DH	Single precision DIVISION work area.
408EH-411CH	"Reserved" area used by Level II BASIC.
411DH-412EH	Floating-point Accumulators (FPA1 & FPA2).
4130H-4151H	Numeric work area (binary to ASCII & FPA3).
4152H-41E7H	DOS Entry and Link addresses.
41E8H-42E8H	Input Buffer area.

it is sufficient to know that the first 744 bytes of the user read/write memory is from 4980H through the end of memory. With a 16K-RAM Model I TRS-80, this means about 13,950 bytes of memory available.

USER RAM (42E9H–7FFFH/BFFFH/FFFFH)

This portion of the memory map is where your programs and data reside. It is the memory available to you when you enter the BASIC "?MEM" statement. The last addresses and amount of usable memory for the three RAM configurations are listed in Table 4-6. With T-BUG loaded into memory locations 4380H-497FH, free (usable) memory is from 4980H through the end of memory. With a 16K-RAM Model I TRS-80, this means about 13,950 bytes of memory available.

Table 4-6. TRS-80 Memory Size and Usable Memory

Hex Address	Memory	Usable Memory*
4000H-4FFFH	4K	3,284 bytes
4000H-7FFFH	16K	15,572 bytes
4000H-BFFFH	32K	31,956 bytes
4000H-FFFFH	48K	48,340 bytes

Note: *Subtract 2 bytes for computers with ROM 1.3.

THE ROMs

The ROMs contain the TRS-80's Level II BASIC, which was written by Paul Allen and Bill Gates of Microsoft. The BASIC interpreter was written in 8080- and not Z-80-assembly language as you might expect, which explains its less than spectacular speed. Although the

Table 4-7. TRS-80 Level II BASIC ROM Entry Addresses

Command	Address	Command	Address
ABS	0977H	MID$	2A9AH
ASC	2A0FH	MEM	27C9H
ATN	15BDH		
AUTO	2008H	NEW	1B49H
		NEXT	22B6H
CDBL	0ADBH	NOT	25C4H
CHR$	2A1FH		
CINT	0A7FH	ON	1F6CH
CLEAR	1E7AH	OUT	2AFBH
CLOAD	2C1FH		
CLS	01C9H	PEEK	2CAAH
CONT	1DE4H	POINT	0132H
COS	1541H	POKE	2CB1H
CSAVE	2BF5H	POS	27F5H
CSNG	0AB1H	PRINT	206FH
DATA	1F05H	RANDOM	01D3H
DEFDBL	1E09H	READ	21EFH
DEFINT	1E03H	REM	1F07H
DEFSNG	1E06H	RESET	0138H
DEFSTR	1E00H	RESTORE	1D91H
DELETE	2BC6H	RESUME	1FAFH
DIM	2608H	RETURN	1EDEH
		RIGHT$	2A91H
EDIT	2E60H	RND	14C9H
ELSE	1F07H	RUN	1EA3H
END	1DAEH		
ERL	24DDH	SET	0135H
ERR	24CFH	SGN	098AH
ERROR	1FF4H	SIN	1547H
EXP	1439H	SQR	13E7H
		STOP	1DA9H
FIX	0B26H	STR$	2836H
FOR	1CA1H	STRING$	2A2FH
FRE	27D4H	SYSTEM	02B2H
GOSUB	1EB1H	TAN	15A8H
GOTO	1EC2H	TROFF	1DF8H
		TRON	1DF7H
IF	2039H		
INKEY$	019DH	USR	27FEH
INP	2AEFH		
INPUT	219AH		
INT	0B37H	VAL	2AC5H
		VARPTR	24EBH
LEFT$	2A61H		
LEN	2A03H		
LET	1F21H		
LIST	2B2EH		
LLIST	2B29H		
LOG	0809H		
LPRINT	2067H		

alternate (complementary) registers are occasionally used for temporary storage (look at the content of memory at 005AH, 1479H, 1619H, etc., using T-BUG), the bulk of the interpreter was written in 8080 assembly language.

What does this mean to the programmer? Simply, the alternate registers are not used, unless BASIC has executed an 08H or D9H register exchange instruction within the subroutine accessed. This means that the programmer may "swap" the registers to preserve their contents when interrupting normal computer operation to insert special-purpose routines! This technique is demonstrated in the Mumford and Richardson "JKL" LPRINT subroutine that will be discussed later.

Table 4-7 lists the *entry* or starting addresses of some of the Level II BASIC's ROM subroutines. Some of these "routines" may be accessed only through a Call (CDH) instruction, others may be simply Jump'ed to. Also, some routines require one or two variables for operation, and these must be stored in the proper memory locations and buffers by the programmer or errors occur. Exactly which register(s) and buffers are required by each "routine" will be covered in following chapters. However, some routines use neither variables nor buffers and can be used "as is." The CLEAR SCREEN (CLS) routine (01C9H) and BASIC re-entry point (1A19H) are examples of routines that require no additional information. Another no-argument routine is the BASIC "SYSTEM" routine (02B2H) which jumps directly to the SYSTEM prompt. Its use allows you to branch directly to the SYSTEM command from T-BUG when loading-in additional cassette tapes:

```
# J 02B2
*? _
```

Why type and enter something that can be jumped directly to? In a later chapter we will learn how to input data from cassettes directly from T-BUG and assembly-language programs without having to use this routine.

In closing this chapter, try the following exercise and see what happens:

```
# M 403D 00 08
403E 00 X
# J 1A19
```

What happened? Can you explain what occurred? How can the display be restored to the original state? HINT: check the TRS-80 memory map for the significance of address 403DH.

CHAPTER 5

Formatting, Moving, and Converting Data

In this chapter we will begin to explore and use the Level II BASIC ROM subroutines that format, move, and convert data within the TRS-80. We will discuss numerical and string data and their formats, the operation and use of the keyboard and CRT video display subroutines, and the operation and use of the ROM subroutines that can move and convert data.

Throughout this and following chapters, you will be introduced to many special-purpose terms and labels and memory addresses associated with the Level II BASIC ROM subroutines. Their purpose is strictly to give you a "handle" with which to grasp the whats and wherefores of using the ROM subroutines. The terms and labels provide mnemonic-like descriptions of a function or operation, and the addresses tell you where the desired subroutine or buffer resides. The addresses are important, but you DO NOT have to memorize them! Instead, you should concentrate on understanding what each subroutine *does* and what it can do *for you.* It is much easier to look up an address than to re-read a complete explanation of each ROM subroutine's purpose and use.

The TRS-80 Level II BASIC handles *numeric* (numbers) and *string* (characters and symbols) data differently. Numeric data is represented in one of four formats depending upon their use. These four formats are: integer, single precision, double precision, and 16-bit unsigned integer. String data, however, is always represented as ASCII values. With the exception of the 16-bit unsigned integer format, it is the programmer who determines which format is used.

In BASIC, this is accomplished by using the variable specifiers: % for integer, ! for single precision, # for double precision, and $ for string. In assembly language, you do not use these specifiers. However, you *can* use the ROM subroutines that implement them.

NUMERIC FORMATS

All numeric data within the TRS-80 are represented in either integer, single-precision, or double-precision formats; plus a specialized-use format–16-bit unsigned integer. Integers are numbers without a decimal point, while single-precision and double-precision numbers (also called *floating-point numbers*) have a decimal point and, respectively, up to six or sixteen significant digits. The TRS-80 handles each format differently. Let's examine each format.

Integer (INT)

Integer numbers are stored in two consecutive bytes in memory, or in the register pairs BC, DE, or HL, and may be either positive or negative. Positive integers are those numbers from 0 to +32767; negative integers are from −1 to −32768.

The most-significant *bit* of the most-significant *byte* of the two bytes that comprise an integer is the *sign bit.* If this bit is set (logic 1) the number is *negative;* if it is reset (logic 0) the number is *positive.* Fig. 5-1 illustrates the use of the sign bit within the integer format. Positive integers are stored as simple, 15-bit binary (plus sign bit) numbers, but negative integers are stored in *two's complement* form.

```
(+) = 0XXXXXXX  XXXXXXXX = "positive" integer.
(−) = 1XXXXXXX  XXXXXXXX = "negative" integer.
```

Fig. 5-1. Sign bit representation in integer format.

To convert a decimal number into its two's complement equivalent, you simply subtract the absolute value of the decimal integer from 65,536, and then convert the integer difference into hexadecimal using the conversion table provided in Appendix E. This technique is shown in Example 5-1.

Example 5-1. Decimal Two's-Complement Conversion.

```
Example: Convert −12345 into its proper 2's-complement.
       (1)   65536 − (12345) = 53191
       (2)   53191 = 52992 → (CF—H)
                     +199 → (—C7H)
                     ---------------
            −12345 = 53191 = CFC7H
```

The same technique may also be used with hexadecimal numbers, but you must *add 1* to the result (FFFFH = 65535 as compared to the 65536 used previously), as shown in Example 5-2.

Example 5-2. Hexadecimal Two's-Complement Conversion.

Example: Convert −(3039H) into its proper 2's-complement.
(1) FFFFH − (3039H) = CFC6H
(2) Add 1: CFC6H + 1 = CFC7H

Integer numbers are stored in memory least-significant byte first, and most-significant byte second, in normal 8080/Z-80 fashion. For example, the number CFC7H would be stored in memory as C7 (LSB), then CF (MSB).

Single Precision (SGL)

Single-precision numbers are stored in four consecutive bytes in memory, or in two register pairs, and are represented in *normalized, excess-128, base-2 exponential* format. The most significant of the four bytes that comprise a single precision number is the *exponent* byte (EXP) and contains the *base-2 exponent* of the "floating-point" number. Its purpose is to specify *where* the decimal point goes. The exponent is stored in *excess-128* format, where the "true" exponent is actually *128 less* than the number represented. For example, if the exponent byte is 84H, the "true" exponent is 4 (84H = 132-128 = 4). This format allows both positive and negative exponents to be represented using only a single byte. The remaining three bytes form the *mantissa,* or numerical value, of the number represented, and are in *normalized* floating-point format. The most significant bit in the mantissa (in the most significant byte) is used to indicate the *sign* of the mantissa. Thus, a 1 indicates that the mantissa is negative, a 0 indicates that the mantissa is positive. The remaining 23 bits in the mantissa actually represent the numerical value. If the most significant bit of these 23 bits (the second to the most significant bit) in the most significant byte of the mantissa is a 1, then the mantissa is normalized. Thus, a mantissa of 1*1*001010 11101011 00101100 is normalized, and a mantissa of 1*0*000100 10111101 00010111 is not normalized. As an example of positive and negative mantissas, the single-precision number +12.345 is represented as 84H 45H 85H 1EH, but −12.345 is represented as 84H *C*5H 85H 1EH. If you break down the hexadecimal numbers 45H and C5H to their respective binary equivalents (45H = 0100 0101; C5H = 1100 0101) you see that the only difference is that the most-significant bit (sign bit) has been set, indicating a negative number. Only this sign bit is used to designate whether a single-precision number is positive or negative, because two's complement is NOT used with floating-point numbers. Example 5-3 illustrates how a single-precision number is represented in the TRS-80.

Example 5-3. Single-Precision Representation.

```
Example: 12.345 = 1.2345E+1 = 84H   45H   85H   1EH
                              ---   ---------------
                     EXPONENT ↙                  ↘ MANTISSA

  Exponent: 84H = 132−128 = +4 decimal places
  Mantissa:          45H            85H            1EH
                    (MSB)          (. . .)         (LSB)
                  4H     5H      8H     5H      1H     EH
              -------------- -------------- --------------
                0100   0101    1000   0101    0001   1110
  Normalize:   +1
              -------------- -------------- --------------
                1100   0101    1000   0101    0001   1110
  Move decimal point 4 positive places:
                  1100.0101    1000   0101    0001   1110
```

The one-byte exponent (EXP) and the three-byte mantissa (MSB ... LSB) are stored in memory in normal 8080/Z-80 fashion: LSB ... MSB EXP. Single precision in the TRS-80 yields six significant decimal digits.

Double Precision (DBL)

Double-precision numbers are stored in eight consecutive bytes of memory, and use the *same single-precision representation except with four additional mantissa bytes*. Thus, double-precision format looks like: EXP MSB . . . . LSB. However, like both integer and single-precision numbers, double-precision numbers are also stored in memory in reverse order, so the arrangement *in memory* would appear as: LSB ... ... MSB EXP. Again, the only difference between double-precision and single-precision formats is the number of mantissa bytes, 7 *vs* 3, all else is identical. Double precision in the TRS-80 yields 16 significant decimal digits.

16-Bit Unsigned Integer

This special format is used by the TRS-80 for *line numbers* and *memory addresses* only, and because there is no sign bit, only positive integers may be represented. Without a sign bit, all 16 bits of the two bytes are used to represent integers up to 65,535.

The four numerical representations used within the TRS-80 are summarized in Table 5-1. Luckily, the Level II BASIC ROMs contain subroutines that will automatically format data to integer, single precision, or double precision for us. They will be discussed later in this chapter.

Table 5-1. Summary of TRS-80 Numeric Formats

	Sign	Range/Precision	Bytes as Stored in Memory
INTEGER	+/−	−32768 to +32767	LSB MSB (− in 2's complement)
SINGLE PRECISION	+/−	SIX significant decimal digits	LSB ... MSB EXP (EXP = XXH−128)
DOUBLE PRECISION	+/−	16 significant decimal digits	LSB ... ... MSB EXP
16-BIT UNSIGNED INTEGER	+	0-thru-65535	LSB MSB (no sign bit)

STRING DATA FORMAT

String data (anything not numeric) is handled as ASCII values. Examples of string data are the letters of the alphabet (A,a-Z,z), the symbols ($, ?, *, etc.), and the numerals (0-9). String data is stored as consecutive, single-byte hexadecimal ASCII values. For example, the uppercase letter A is stored as a 41H value, and the character string ABC would be stored as 41H 42H 43H.

REGISTERS, BUFFERS, AND FPAs

With the exception of the "service" ROM subroutines, which require no variables or arguments, most of the Level II BASIC ROM subroutines expect to use either one or two input values, called *operands,* and return a single output value, called the *result,* to the user. Depending upon the subroutine, these operands and result are stored in either specific memory locations, called *buffers,* or in certain register pairs. The subroutine always looks for its operands in these assigned locations or registers, and always stores its result in a specific place. With this in mind, we must first discuss *which* buffers and registers are used by which subroutines before we can begin to use the Level II ROM subroutines in our assembly-language programs. In doing so, we will learn where to place the operands for the subroutines, and where to expect the result.

Integer

In general, integer operands are *passed,* or transferred, to the using ROM subroutine via the HL (single operand), or HL and DE (two operand) register pairs, and the result from the subroutine is stored in the *integer buffer area* (4121H-4122H) located in the Communication Area of user read/write memory (RAM). Register pair HL is used by the integer subroutine to address this section of RAM.

Single Precision

Single-precision operands are passed to subroutines via the single-precision buffer areas, 4121H-4124H and 4127H-412AH, and/or the BC and DE register pairs. Subroutines that require only a single operand use only the buffer area 4121H-4124H for both input and output. When two operands are required, *both* of the buffer areas *and* the BC and DE register pairs are used. One operand is stored in buffer area 4121H-4124H and the other is stored in the second buffer area 4127H-412AH. Although the actual operand is stored in the second buffer area, the BC and DE register pairs are used

Table 5-2. Single Precision Use of BC and DE Register Pairs

Register	Content
B	(EXP) Exponent
C	(MSB) Most-significant Mantissa
D	(. . .) Next-significant Mantissa
E	(LSB) Least-significant Mantissa

to pass the operands to and receive the result from the subroutine. When this occurs, the second operand is handled in the manner shown in Table 5-2. The result returned from both single-precision and double-precision subroutines is stored in the buffer area 4121H-4124H, destroying the original contents.

Double Precision

Double-precision operands are passed to subroutines via the buffer areas, 411DH-4124H and 4127H-412EH. Single operand subroutines use the buffer area 411DH-4124H for both input and output. Two operand subroutines use the buffer area 411DH-4124H for the first operand, and the buffer area 4127H-412EH for the second operand. The result is returned in the buffer area 411DH-4124H, destroying the original contents.

These buffer areas are referred to as *F*loating-*P*oint *A*ccumulators (FPAs) in reference to their accumulator-like handling of data. Level II BASIC ROM subroutines utilize three different FPAs. The first floating-point accumulator (FPA1) consists of memory locations 411DH-4124H and is the most frequently used FPA. The second floating-point accumulator (FPA2) consists of memory locations 4127H-412EH and is used only with two operand subroutines. The third floating-point accumulator (FPA3) consists of memory locations 414AH-4151H and is the least used, because it is only used with single-precision MULTIPLICATION and double-precision subroutines. Thus, we will limit our discussion to FPA1 and

Table 5-3. Floating-Point Accumulators (FPAs)

FPA1 = Buffer Area 411DH—4124H. FPA2 = Buffer Area 4127H—412EH. FPA3 = Buffer Area 414AH—4151H.

FPA2. The use and addresses of the FPAs are summarized in Table 5-3.

NUMBER TYPE FLAGS

Associated with these two FPAs are the two *N*umber *T*ype *F*lags (NTFs) which indicate the *type* (integer, single precision, double precision, or string) of the operand stored in the respective FPAs. The first buffer area (FPA1) is represented by NTF1 which resides at memory location 40AFH. The second buffer area (FPA2) is represented by NTF2 which resides at memory location 40B0H and is the least used of the two NTFs.

The "type" of operand stored in the respective FPAs is *flagged*, or indicated, as shown in Table 5-4. The NTF flag value is actually the number of bytes used by the operand stored in the FPAs. If the NTF and the actual operand do not match, too few or too many bytes will be passed to the using subroutine, producing erroneous and unpredictable results. Thus, it is up to the programmer to ensure that the NTF and the operand agree. For example, the NTF must be 02H for an integer, but 04H for a single precision number, etc.

Table 5-4. Number-Type Flags (NTFs)

NTF1	FPA1 Contents
02H	INTEGER
03H	STRING
04H	SINGLE PRECISION
08H	DOUBLE PRECISION

There are two ways to assign the NTF values. The first way is to manually "load" the proper value into the appropriate NTF memory location. The second, and easiest, way is to use certain ROM subroutines that automatically load the NTF for us. These subroutines are:

CALL 0A9DH SETINT: sets NTF1 = 2 by loading 02H into memory location 40AFH; uses only the A register.

CALL 0AEFH SETSGL: sets NTF1 = 4 by loading 04H into memory location 40AFH; uses only the A register.

CALL 0AECH SETDBL: sets NTF1 = 8 by loading 08H into memory location 40AFH; uses A register and BC register pair.

Now that you know how to *load* the FPAs, is there a way that you can determine their contents? Is the variable currently stored in the FPA an integer, single-precision, or double-precision number? This can be done by using the ROM subroutine RST32 which is located at address 25D9H:

CALL 25D9H RST32: tests the content of FPA1 and returns the result in the F register by setting the ZERO, NEGATIVE, PARITY ODD, or NO CARRY flags as follows:
Set ZERO (Z = 1) = STRING variable.
Set NEGATIVE (S = 1) = INTEGER variable.
Set PARITY ODD (P/V = 1) = SINGLE-PRECISION variable.
Set NO CARRY (C = 0) = DOUBLE-PRECISION variable.

Using this subroutine and the short program shown in Example 5-4, a simple four-way branch to other processing routines can be made.

Example 5-4. Four-way Branch Using RST32 (25D9H).

Addr	Op-Code (Hex)	Label	Mnemonic/ Operand	Remarks
5000	CD D9 25	RST32	CALL 25D9H	;TEST NTF1
5003	CA XX XX		JP Z,STR	;go STRING if ZERO set
5006	FA XX XX		JP M,INT	;go INTEGER if MINUS set
5009	E2 XX XX		JP PO,SGL	;go SINGLE if PARITY-ODD set
500C	D2 XX XX		JP NC,DBL	;go DOUBLE if CARRY reset

STRINGS

String variables are stored as consecutive ASCII values in memory, beginning at the address pointed to by the *input buffer pointer* (40A7H), and are terminated with either a *zero byte* (ASCII control code: NULL, 00H) or a BREAK (01H).

String variables may be input from the keyboard using the multipurpose ROM subroutine called QINPUT which is located at 1BB3H. This subroutine not only sets the NTF1 to the proper code (03H = string) for us, but it also directs the string to memory and loads the beginning address of the string into the input buffer pointer (40A7H). We will discuss QINPUT in greater detail later in this chapter.

Table 5-5 summarizes the TRS-80's use of registers, buffers, FPAs, variable types, and NTFs. Notice that integer and single-precision numbers use *both* FPAs *and* registers to store data, depending upon the ROM subroutine used.

Table 5-5. Summary of Registers, Buffers, FPAs, and NTFs

NTFs	Operand	FPA1	Inputs INT	Inputs SGL	Inputs DBL	Outputs INT	Outputs SGL	Outputs DBL	Registers
		411DH			LSB			LSB	
		411EH			...			...	
		411FH			...			...	
NTF1	SINGLE FIRST	4120H			...			...	
40AFH		4121H	LSB	LSB	...	LSB	LSB	...	H = MSB INT
		4122H	MSB	...	...	MSB	...	...	L = LSB
		4123H		MSB	MSB		MSB	MSB	
		4124H		EXP	EXP		EXP	EXP	
		FPA2							
		4127H	LSB	LSB	LSB				D = MSB INT
		4128H	MSB	...	...				E = LSB
		4129H		MSB	...				
NTF2	SECOND	412AH		EXP	...				B = EXP
40B0H		412BH			...				C = MSB SGL
		412CH			...				D = ...
		412DH			MSB				E = LSB
		412EH			EXP				

MOVING VARIABLES

Now that you know where the operands and results belong, how do you actually get them there? One way is to manually load them directly into the appropriate memory locations using T-BUG's M command. Another way is to let some ROM subroutines move them for us. Some of these subroutines use the stack, while others use memory locations.

Single Precision Variables

The following ROM subroutines can be used to move single-precision variables between memory locations, buffer areas, register pairs BC and DE, and the stack:

CALL 09B1H HLFPA1: Memory-to-FPA1 ((HL)-to-FPA1), moves a single-precision variable from any memory location pointed to by the HL register pair into FPA1 (4121H-4124H); uses the HL, BC and DE register pairs, all saved.

CALL 09CBH FPA1HL: FPA1-to-memory (FPA1-to-(HL)), moves a single-precision variable from FPA1 into any memory location pointed to by the HL register pair; uses HL, DE, and B registers, none saved.

CALL 09B4H REGFPA: Register-to-FPA1 (BCDE-to-FPA1), moves a single-precision variable from the BC and DE register pairs into FPA1; uses HL, BC and DE registers, all saved. NTF not updated.

CALL 09BFH FPAREG: FPA1-to-register (FPA1-to-BCDE), moves a single-precision variable from FPA1 into the BC and DE register pairs; uses HL, BC and DE register pairs, none saved.

CALL 09C2H HLBCDE: Memory-to-register ((HL)-to BCDE), moves a single-precision variable from any memory location pointed to by the HL register pair into the BC and DE register pairs.

CALL 09A4H FPASTK: FPA1-to-stack, moves a single-precision variable from FPA1 onto the stack; uses HL and DE register pairs; HL is saved, DE is not saved.

POP BC
POP DE Stack-to-register (stack-to-BCDE): retrieves a single-precision variable from the stack and places it in the BC and DE register pairs in proper order.

Single-Precision and Double-Precision Variables

The following two ROM subroutines move either single-precision or double-precision variables between any two sections of memory:

CALL 09D2H HLTODE: Memory-to-memory ((HL)-to-(DE)), transfers the contents of the memory locations pointed to by the HL register pair into the memory locations pointed to by the DE register pair. The content of NTF1 (40AFH) specifies the number of bytes to be moved.

CALL 09D3H DETOHL: Memory-to-memory ((DE)-to-(HL)), performs the inverse of 09D2H by transferring the contents of the memory locations pointed to by the DE register pair into the memory locations pointed to by the HL register pair. The content of NTF1(40AFH) specifies the number of bytes to be moved.

Table 5-6. Summary of Data Movement Subroutines and Op-Codes

Movement	Label	Call	NTF1 (40AFH)				Notes
			INT	SGL	DBL	STR	
FPA1-to-Stack	FPASTK	09A4H	2	4			
(HL)-to-FPA1	HLFPA1	09B1H		4			
BCDE-to-FPA1	REGFPA	09B4H		4			
FPA1-to-BCDE	FPAREG	09BFH		4			
(HL)-to-BCDE	HLBCDE	09C2H		4			
FPA1-to-(HL)	FPA1HL	09CBH		4			
(HL)-to-(DE)	HLTODE	09D2H	2	4	8	3	General purpose
(DE)-to-(HL)	DETOHL	09D3H	2	4	8	3	Inverse of above
(DE)-to-(HL)	DEHLA	09D6H	2	4	8	3	A=number bytes moved (up to 255).
(DE)-to-(HL)	DEHLB	09D7H	2	4	8	3	B=number bytes moved (up to 255)
FPA2-to-FPA1	DBLSGL	09F4H	2	4	8		
FPA1-to-FPA2	SGLDBL	09FCH	2	4	8		
HL-to-FPA1		0A9AH	2				
DE-to-HL		EX DE,HL	2				Z-80 Op-Code
HL-to-DE		EX DE,HL	2				"
BC-to-stack		PUSH BC	2	4			"
DE-to-stack		PUSH DE	2	4			"
HL-to-stack		PUSH HL	2				"
Stack-to-HL		POP HL	2	4			"
Stack-to-BC		POP BC	2	4			"
Stack-to-DE		POP DE	2	4			"

The following ROM subroutine moves either single-precision or double-precision variables from the first floating-point accumulator (FPA1) into the second floating-point accumulator (FPA2):

CALL 09FCH SGLDBL: FPA1-to-FPA2, works only with NTF1 equal to 04H or 08H. If NTF1 = 4, then the four bytes comprising a single-precision variable beginning at FPA1 address 4121H are moved into FPA2 beginning at address 4127H. If NTF1 = 8, then the eight bytes comprising a double-precision variable beginning at FPA1 address 411DH are moved into FPA2 beginning at address 4127H (see Table 5-5).

Table 5-6 lists the most useful ROM subroutines and Z-80 op-codes for moving variables. Two of the subroutines listed, CALL 09D6H and CALL 09D7H, deserve special attention. Both move variables of up to 255 bytes between memory addressed by the DE and HL register pairs as the "source" and "destination" pointers, respectively. Their only difference lies in *where* the number of bytes to be moved is held. Subroutine 09D6H requires the number of bytes to be moved be held in the A register, while subroutine 09D7H requires the number of bytes to be moved be held in the B register. Also, notice that the last eight entries in Table 5-6 are just Z-80 op-codes. Since these instructions are used to move information around in memory, they deserve to be included in this table.

KEYBOARD INPUT

Now that you know where the variables go and how to get them there, it is time to investigate how to get them into the TRS-80 in the first place. The Level II BASIC ROMs provide at least four different subroutines for inputting data. One subroutine is rather primitive and is seldom used. Two other subroutines are essentially the same, differing only in that one saves the contents of the DE register pair before being executed and the other does not. The fourth, and most powerful, subroutine accepts a string of up to 240 characters from the keyboard and displays them on the CRT. Let's look at each of these subroutines in closer detail:

CALL 002BH KBSCAN: performs a primitive keyboard scan and returns an ASCII value in the A register if a key is pressed; if no key is pressed, a zero is returned. It uses the DE register to store the address of the *keyboard control block* (4015H) and so destroys the original contents of the DE register pair. It requires the programmer to supply a "loop" consisting of a compare and jump-zero instructions such as shown in Example 5-5. This subroutine is *similar* to the BASIC INKEY$ function and does not display the character on the CRT.

CALL 035BH KBDSCN: identical to 002BH except the contents of the DE register pair are saved.

CALL 0049H GETCHR: essentially the BASIC INKEY$ function and consists of ROM subroutine 002BH *plus* the necessary loop instructions. It automatically

Example 5-5. Keyboard Scan Using KBSCAN (002BH).

Addr	Op-Code (Hex)	Label	Mnemonic/ Operand	Remarks
5000	D5		PUSH DE	;save DE
5001	CD 2B 00	KBSCAN	CALL 002BH	;scan keyboard
5004	FE 00		CP A,00H	;key pressed?
5006	CA 01 50		JP Z,KBSCAN	;loop back if NO
5009	D1		POP DE	;retrieve DE

scans the keyboard until a key is depressed and returns the ASCII value in the A register, and then returns to the calling program. Again, no CRT display; DE not saved.

CALL 1BB3H QINPUT: displays the SYSTEM prompt "?" (without the asterisk) and accepts numeric and string inputs of up to 240 characters. The input is *assumed* to be *numeric* regardless of what it really is, so whatever is entered is converted to a number, including strings and symbols. This subroutine is typically followed by a Z-80 op-code which sets the C flag, such as RST 10 (D7H). Upon exit, the HL register pair contains a value *one less* than the beginning address in memory where the input string is stored. When followed by the ROM subroutine ASCBIN (0E6CH), the output is automatically converted to the lowest possible representation (integer, single- or double-precision) and directed to the appropriate FPA with the NTF set as shown in Table 5-7.

Now, let's see how numeric data is handled and represented within the TRS-80 using the subroutine QINPUT (1BB3H) and ASCBIN (0E6CH).

Using T-BUG's M command, enter the program shown in Example 5-6 and then "clear" the contents of FPA1 (411DH-4124H) by entering zeros in each memory location.

Example 5-6. Keyboard Input and Conversion Using QINPUT (1BB3H) and ASCBIN (0E6CH).

Addr	Op-Code (Hex)	Label	Mnemonic/ Operand	Remarks
5000	CD B3 1B	QINPUT	CALL 1BB3H	;kybd scan and display
5003	23		INC HL	;next cursor position
5004	CD 6C 0E	ASCBIN	CALL 0E6CH	;convert INT,SGL,DBL
5007	C3 A0 43		JP 43A0H	;return to T-BUG

Table 5-7. QINPUT (1BB3H) vs. FPA1 and NTF1

Result	(FPA1) Stored In	NTF1
INTEGER	4121H-4122H	02H
SINGLE PRECISION	4121H-4124H	04H
DOUBLE PRECISION	411DH-4124H	08H

Now execute the program by jumping to its starting address (5000H) by using the J command. The screen will clear and display the SYSTEM prompt "?" (if an extraneous 0 ends up on the screen too, simply erase it using the BACKSPACE key). Notice that QINPUT recognizes all of the Level II BASIC control functions, such as BACKSPACE, TAB, etc. Type and enter the integer number, 12345. The screen will again clear, and display only the T-BUG prompt "#."

Since we entered an integer, the NTF should be 2. Let's check the content of NTF1 (40AFH) and see for ourselves:

```
# M 40AF 02
```

which is correct for an integer number. Next, let's see what the integer number looks like when stored in FPA1 (411DH-4124H):

```
# M 411D 00
    411E 00
    411F 00
    4120 00
    4121 39
    4122 30
    4123 00
    4124 00
```

Referring back to the earlier example of integer format and storage, you will recall that the decimal integer 12345 is the same as 3039H, used FPA1 memory locations 4121H-4122H, and was stored LSB preceding the MSB, which is exactly what is seen on the display.

Next, let's see how a single-precision number, such as 12.345, is handled. Again, clear the FPA1 buffer area, and execute the program by using the J command to jump to address 5000H. Then type and enter the number 12.345. Using T-BUG's M command, check the content of NTF1 at address 40AFH:

```
# M 40AF 04
```

which is correct for a single-precision number. Next, check the contents of FPA1 buffer area:

```
# M 411D 00
    411E 00
    411F 00
    4120 00
    4121 1E
    4122 85
    4123 45
    4124 84
```

Again, referring to the earlier example given for single-precision format and storage, you will recall that the single-precision number 12.345, is indeed 84H 45H 85H 1EH.

What happens when a number exceeding single precision capacity is entered? Well, let's try one and see. To do this, you can simply carry the single-precision number 12.345 out three additional decimal places with zeros which does not change the arithmetic value of the number to 12.345000. Again, clear FPA1 and execute the program, and then enter the double-precision number 12.345000. A check of NTF1 indicates 08H, which is the correct flag for a double-precision number, and a look at the contents of FPA1 yields:

```
# M 411D  85
    411E  EB
    411F  51
    4120  B8
    4121  1E
    4122  85
    4123  45
    4124  84
```

which, when rearranged, indicates that the decimal number, 12.345000, is represented within the TRS-80 as:

```
84H    45H    85H    1EH    B8H    51H    EBH    85H
(EXP)  (MSB)  (...)  (...)  (...)  (...)  (...)  (LSB)
```

Adding Level II BASIC's CINT ROM subroutine (0A7FH) to the example program produces an integer output regardless of the size of the number input. Note, however, that a fatal error (crash back to "MEMORY size?") will occur when using this subroutine and a number greater than 32767 is either (1) entered from the keyboard, or (2) generated by the conversion routine (see Example 5-7).

The subroutine QINPUT (1BB3H) can also be used to simultaneously input and display string data as well as numeric data. Strings of up to 240 characters in length may be entered from the

Example 5-7. Keyboard Input and Integer Conversion Using QINPUT (1BB3H) and CINT (0A7FH).

Addr	Op-Code (Hex)	Label	Mnemonic/ Operand	Remarks
5000	CD C9 01	CLS	CALL 01C9H	;clear screen
5003	CD B3 1B	QINPUT	CALL 1BB3H	;kybd scan and display
5004	23		INC HL	;next cursor position
5005	CD 6C 0E	ASCBIN	CALL 0E6CH	;convert INT,SGL,DBL
5008	CD 7F 0A	CINT	CALL 0A7FH	;convert INTEGER only
500B	C3 A0 43		JP 43A0H	;return to T-BUG

keyboard and displayed, starting at the current cursor position. The input string will be stored as ASCII values in consecutive memory locations beginning at the address pointed to by the *input buffer pointer* (40A7H-40A8H) and will be terminated with a NULL (00H) character. The input buffer pointer is initialized to 41E8H, the beginning address of the *input buffer area* (41E8H-42E8H), during the power-up sequence. However, by changing the content of the input buffer pointer, you can direct the input string to any memory area that you wish. Using the short, nine-byte program shown in Example 5-8, you can see what happens when string data are used with QINPUT (1BB3H).

Example 5-8. Keyboard Input of String Data Using QINPUT (1BB3H).

Addr	Op-Code (Hex)	Label	Mnemonic/ Operand	Remarks
5000	CD C9 01	CLS	CALL 01C9H	;clear screen
5003	CD B3 1B	QINPUT	CALL 1BB3H	;kybd scan and display
5006	C3 A0 43		JP 43A0H	;return to T-BUG

Enter the example program and execute it. You should see the SYSTEM prompt "?" on the display. Now type and enter the string, ABCD. The T-BUG prompt "#" will reappear, signalling return to the T-BUG command mode. If you examine the contents of the input buffer area (41E8H-41ECH), you will find the following bytes: 41 42 43 44 00, which are, respectively, the ASCII values for: A, B, C, D, and NULL.

How do you direct the input to some other area in memory? Simple, just change the address held in the input buffer pointer (40A7H-40A8H) to the address in memory where you want the string to begin, and you can send the input string *anywhere* in memory (except ROM, of course). Let's try it and see what happens.

Use T-BUG's M command and change the content of the input buffer pointer (40A7H-40A8H) to the address of some area in high memory, such as 6000H (remember, LSB first, then MSB). Then execute the program and enter the string, DCBA. Now examine the contents of memory locations 6000H-6004H, where you will find the ASCII values: 44 43 42 41 00, which represent the characters D, C, B, A, and NULL. Both numeric and string data can be handled in this manner.

CRT VIDEO DISPLAY

In addition to the subroutine QINPUT (1BB3H), there are four other ROM subroutines that can be used to display data on the CRT. Three of these subroutines display the content of the A register. The fourth, and most powerful, subroutine actually consists of two subroutines. Let's examine each subroutine separately:

CALL 0033H CRTBYT: displays the ASCII character represented by the value in the A register at the CRT position specified in the *cursor position block* (4020H-4021H); uses A, DE, and IY registers, content of DE not saved. Because this subroutine accesses the video driver, all of the ASCII control codes (00H-1FH) supported by Level II BASIC are recognized.

CALL 032AH DSPCHR: displays the ASCII character represented by the value in the A register, *if* the *device type flag* (DTF, 409CH) is zero, and stores the current cursor position at 40A6H.

CALL 033AH CRTOUT: same as CRTBYT (0033H) except the content of the DE register pair is saved. This is probably the most used ROM display subroutine by the BASIC interpreter.

The fourth, and most powerful of the display subroutines, actually consists of the two subroutines, BINASC (0FBDH) and OUTLIN (28A7H):

CALL 0FBDH BINASC: converts an integer, single-precision, or double-precision representation into a corresponding *numeric character string* (binary-to-ASCII); uses the NTF1 (40AFH) and the appropriate FPA buffer contents to determine input. The resulting numeric character string is stored in memory beginning at location 4130H and is terminated with a zero byte (00H). The HL register pair contains 4130H upon exit.

CALL 28A7H OUTLIN: automatically displays and updates the cursor position until a zero byte is encountered. The HL register pair must point to the starting address of the character string to be displayed (already done by BINASC). NTF1 automatically set to 3 (string).

Device Type Flag (DTF)

Associated with the keyboard input subroutine QINPUT (1BB3H) and the CRT video display subroutine DSPCHR (032AH)

Table 5-8. Device-Type Flags (DTFs) at 409CH

DTF (409CH)	Output to
01H	(+1) LINE PRINTER
00H	(0) CRT Video Display
FFH	(−1) CASSETTE

is the *device type flag* (DTF) located at memory location 409CH, which determines *where* the output of these (and other) subroutines go. This DTF is shown in Table 5-8. Upon power-up, Level II BASIC initializes this memory location to zero (00H = CRT).

Some Examples

To display a number contained in FPA1, simply ensure that the contents of NTF1 (40AFH) corresponds to the type of number in FPA1, and then call the two subroutines BINASC (0FBDH) and OUTLIN (28A7H) as shown in Example 5-9.

Example 5-9. Data Display Using BINASC (0FBDH) and OUTLIN (28A7H).

Step 1. Load A0H into 4121H and 43H into 4122H.
Step 2. Load 02H into NTF1 (40AFH).
Step 3. Execute program below.

Addr	Op-Code (Hex)	Label	Mnemonic/ Operand	Remarks
5000	CD BD 0F	BINASC	CALL 0FBDH	;binary-to-string
5003	CD A7 28	OUTLIN	CALL 28A7H	;display til zero byte
5006	C3 A0 43		JP 43A0H	;return to T-BUG

Use T-BUG's M command and place the value A0H in memory location 4121H, and the value 43H in the next location, 4122H. These two locations are the integer (INT) area of FPA1. Accordingly, you must also set the NTF1 (40AFH) to 02H to match the integer number 43A0H. After this has been done, execute the program. What do you see? That's right, you will see "17312," which is the *decimal* equivalent of the *hexadecimal* number 43A0H (T-BUG's entry address). With careful attention paid to matching the NTF1 with the content of the FPA1 buffer, these subroutines can be used to perform hexadecimal-to-decimal number conversion and display.

The subroutine OUTLIN (28A7H) can also be used to display string data. The two programs shown in Example 5-10 illustrate how this can be accomplished using a string of data that was previously entered.

Example 5-10. A) Keyboard Input Using QINPUT (1BB3H); B) Display a String Using OUTLIN (28A7H).

A)	Addr	Op-Code (Hex)	Label	Mnemonic/ Operand	Remarks
	5000	CD C9 01	CLS	CALL 01C9H	;clear screen
	5003	CD B3 1B	QINPUT	CALL 1BB3H	;kybd scan and display
	5006	C3 A0 43		JP 43A0H	;return to T-BUG

B)	Addr	Op-Code (Hex)	Label	Mnemonic/ Operand	Remarks
	6000	CD C9 01	CLS	CALL 01C9H	;clear screen
	6003	23		INC HL	;HL = 41E8H
	6004	CD A7 28	OUTLIN	CALL 28A7H	;display til zero byte
	6007	C3 07 60	LOOP	JP 6007H	;endless loop

Note: You must press the RESET button to exit this program due to endless loop at 6007H-6009H.

Load both programs, and then execute Example 5-10A. Type and enter the string, HELLO. Then execute Example 5-10B. You will see the original string input displayed again. Can you explain the purpose of the INC HL instruction (23H) in Example 5-10B? The answer is found by recalling that when string data is input using the input buffer pointer (40A7H-40A8H), the HL register pair contain a value *one less* than the address. For example, if the input buffer pointer contains 41E8H, then the HL register pair contains 41E7H. Thus, by simply adding 1 (incrementing) to the HL register pair, the address held in the input buffer can be obtained! However, when displaying string data that is *not* stored in the input buffer area, you must load the starting address of the string into the HL register pair before calling the OUTLIN subroutine.

Is it possible to "limit" the number of characters input from the keyboard? The answer is yes, if you make use of the *buffer input* subroutine, BUFFIN (05D9H), which accepts up to n-characters and then ignores the rest. The number of characters (n) that will be accepted by BUFFIN is determined by the content of the B register. The HL register pair must point to the memory area where the string of characters is to be stored. Upon completion, the A register contains the ASCII value of the last character entered, either a *carriage return* (CR on the TRS-80 is the ENTER key) or a BREAK character. Since this subroutine also accesses the video display driver, the ASCII control codes supported by Level II BASIC are recognized. The input string characters will be stored as ASCII values in consecutive memory locations beginning at the address pointed to by the HL register pair, and will be terminated with either a CR (0DH) or BREAK (01H) character. Example 5-11 provides a short program that accepts up to six characters (excluding the CR or BREAK) and places them in the input buffer area (41E8H-42E8H).

Example 5-11. Limiting Keyboard Input to N-Characters Using BUFFIN (05D9H) and B Register.

Addr	Op-Code (Hex)	Label	Mnemonic/ Operand	Remarks
5000	CD C9 01	CLS	CALL 01C9H	;clear screen
5003	2A A7 40		LD HL,(40A7H)	;get address of input buffer
5006	06 06		LD B,06H	;number of characters (n)
5008	CD D9 05	BUFFIN	CALL 05D9H	;input to n-characters
5003	C3 A0 43		JP 43A0H	;return to T-BUG

As you can see, the "?" prompt is not displayed by BUFFIN. If this feature is desired, the example program must be modified as shown in Example 5-12.

DATA CONVERSIONS

Now that you know where the variables belong and how to get them there, it's time to investigate getting them converted from one format to another. The ROMs contain many subroutines that

Example 5-12. Display "?" Prompt Using CRTOUT (033AH).

Addr	Op-Code (Hex)	Label	Mnemonic/ Operand	Remarks
5000	CD C9 01	CLS	CALL 01C9H	;clear screen
5003	3E 3F		LD A,3FH	;ASCII "?" into A
5005	CD 3A 03	CRTOUT	CALL 033AH	;display "?"
5008	3E 20		LD A,20H	;ASCII "b̸" into A
500A	CD 3A 03	CRTOUT	CALL 033AH	;display "b̸"
500D	2A A7 40		LD HL,(40A7H)	;get address of input buffer
5010	06 06		LD B,06H	;number of characters (n)
5012	CD D9 05	BUFFIN	CALL 05D9H	;input to n-characters
5015	C3 A0 43		JP 43A0H	;return to T-BUG

can be used to perform data conversions, but we will limit our discussion to only those ROM subroutines that are the most useful and easy to use. The use of existing subroutines to perform data conversions, instead of writing your own routines, will greatly reduce the task of writing assembly-language programs that must handle data in more than one format.

The Level II BASIC ROMs contain subroutines that enable you to convert from one data type to another, to convert between binary and ASCII representations, and to convert from ASCII to numeric representation. The data conversions that will be discussed are:

- Floating Point to Integer.
- Integer or Double Precision to Single Precision.
- Integer or Single Precision to Double Precision.
- ASCII String to Numeric.
- Numeric to Unformatted-ASCII String.
- Numeric to Formatted-ASCII String.

Some of these data conversions are performed by the Level II BASIC ROM subroutines that implement BASIC functions, others are performed by subroutines within the Level II BASIC's arithmetic and mathematic functions. One conversion, numeric-to-formatted ASCII string, is performed by the subroutine that is used by Level II BASIC PRINT USING statement.

Number Type Conversions

To convert a variable from one number type to another, such as from integer to single precision, you simply call the subroutine that implements the appropriate BASIC function. For instance, in BASIC you used the CINT function to convert a number to an integer. In assembly language you can use the same function by simply calling the subroutine that implements CINT! There are four ROM subroutines that you can use to perform number type conversions. Three of these subroutines are:

CALL 0A7FH CINT (FPA1-to-INT): converts the content of FPA1 to an integer, returns the result in the integer area of FPA1 (4121H-4122H), and updates the number type flag (NTF1, 40AFH) to 2; uses all registers. If a number greater than 32767 is generated, the "0V"-error message is displayed and control is returned to BASIC.

CALL 0AB1H CSNG (FPA1-to-SGL): converts the content of FPA1 to single-precision format, returns the result in the single-precision area of FPA1 (4121H-4124H), and updates NTF1 to 4; uses all registers.

CALL 0ADBH CDBL (FPA1-to-DBL): converts the content of FPA1 to double-precision format, returns the result in the double-precision area of FPA1 (411DH-4124H), and updates NTF1 to 8; uses all registers.

The fourth data conversion that often proves useful is the Level II BASIC FIX function which yields a "truncated" whole number result instead of a "largest" whole number as the CINT function does. For example, INT(−1.5) "rounds" the result to the next largest whole number and returns −2, while FIX(−1.5) "chops" the number at the decimal point and returns −1. To access this subroutine you use:

CALL 0B26H FIX (FPA1-to-"truncated" INT): truncates the floating-point content of FPA1 and returns the result in the appropriate source area of FPA1; NTF1 is not changed.

ASCII to Numeric Conversions

The Level II ROMs contain three subroutines that you can use to perform ASCII-to-numeric conversions. These subroutines permit you to perform these conversions: ASCII string-to-binary representation, ASCII string-to-integer format, and ASCII string-to-double precision format. You have already seen one of these subroutines, ASCBIN (0E6CH). That ROM subroutine was used earlier to automatically convert an ASCII string to its lowest possible binary number type (integer, single precision, or double precision). The three ASCII-to-numeric conversion subroutines are:

CALL 0E6CH ASCBIN (ASCII-to-binary): converts the ASCII string pointed to by the HL register pair to the lowest possible binary number type: integer if less than 32767 and no decimal point or "E" or "D" scientific-notation exponent descriptor; otherwise converts to single precision or double precision as appropriate (automatically converts to double precision if input exceeds 7 digits); result returned in appropriate area of FPA1; NTF1 updated to match result.

CALL 0E65H ASCDBL (ASCII-to-DBL): converts the ASCII string pointed to by the HL register pair to double-precision format; result returned in FPA1 (411DH-4124H). The ASCII string must be terminated with either a colon (:) or a zero byte (00H); uses all registers.

CALL 1E5AH ASCINT (ASCII-to-INT): converts the ASCII string pointed to by the HL register pair to an integer and returns the result in the DE register pair; terminates on the first nonnumeric character.

The use of these subroutines proves very handy when data must be input from the keyboard and then later processed by either arithmetic or mathematic routines. For example, the subroutine ASCBIN (0E6CH) enables you to interface the ASCII string output from the Level II BASIC's keyboard and display subroutines with your assembly-language programs, which require numeric data inputs. To interface the numeric output from your programs with the Level II BASIC ROM CRT video display subroutines, you can use the ROM subroutine BINASC (0FBDH).

Numeric to ASCII Conversions

The Level II BASIC ROMs contain two subroutines that perform numeric-to-ASCII conversions. One subroutine produces an *unformatted* output which contains *only* the ASCII values representing

Table 5-9. Format Specifiers for BINFOR (0FBEH)

A Register: contains formatting specifiers: 00H = Binary to ASCII without formatting. 80H + XXH = Binary to ASCII with formatting, where XXH equals: 01H = Exponential format: "###.#!!!!" 02H = RESERVED (not used) 04H = Sign follows number: "###.#-" 08H = Sign precedes number: "+###.#" 10H = Print $ before number: "$###.#" 20H = Print * before number: "*###.#" 40H = Print comma (,) every 3rd number: "#,###.#"
B Register: specifies number of digits to LEFT of decimal point, **less two.**
C Register: specifies number of digits to RIGHT of decimal point, **plus one.**

Note: A register contents may be intermixed, i.e., A = 91H means **print $** before number in **exponential format** (80 + 10 + 1).

the numeric input. The other subroutine produces a *formatted* output which may also contain such descriptor characters as "+", "–", "$", "*", or the comma (,). The two ROM subroutines that enable you to perform numeric-to-ASCII conversions are:

CALL 0FBDH BINASC (binary-to-unformatted ASCII): converts the content of FPA1 (integer, single precision, or double precision) to its corresponding, unformatted ASCII string and returns the result in memory locations 4130H-4151H; input must be terminated with a zero byte (00H).

CALL 0FBEH BINFOR (binary-to-formatted ASCII): converts the floating-point content of FPA1 to its corresponding, formatted ASCII string using the Level II BASIC PRINT USING statement formats, and stores the result in memory beginning at the address pointed to by the HL register pair. The contents of the A, B, and C registers specify the formatting to be used, as shown in Table 5-9.

This last ROM subroutine, BINFOR (0FBEH), proves very useful when writing assembly-language programs that require formatted output, such as financial reports, ledgers, and inventories, but it also has a problem. It *rounds up* the decimal portion of a formatted number, something you should remember when handling monetary figures where such rounding is undesirable.

An Example

The three routines shown in Example 5-13 illustrate how the Level II BASIC ROM subroutines may be used to convert keyboard input to ASCII string, ASCII string to binary, and binary to formatted ASCII numeric.

Example 5-13. Example of Formatted Data Conversion.

(A) *INPUT a String*

Addr	Op-Code (Hex)	Label	Mnemonic/ Operand	Remarks
5000	CD C9 01	INPUT	CALL 01C9H	;CLS, clear screen
5003	CD B3 1B		CALL 1BB3H	;QINPUT
5006	23		INC HL	;
5007	CD 6C 0E		CALL 0E6CH	;ASCBIN
500A	C3 A0 43		JP 43A0	;rtn T-BUG

(B) *CONVRT String to Lowest Binary Representation and Format*

Addr	Op-Code (Hex)	Label	Mnemonic/ Operand	Remarks
6000	21 EB 41	CONVRT	LD HL,41E8H	;string location/PRINT USING BUFF
6003	CD 6C 0E		CALL 0E6CH	;ASCBIN
6006	21 30 41		LD HL,4130H	;where store
6009	3E 90		LD A,90H	;A = 90H = $ prefix
600B	06 06		LD B,06H	;B = 06H = 8 spaces LEFT
600D	0E 03		LD C,03H	;C = 03H = 2 spaces RIGHT
600F	CD BE 0F		CALL 0FBEH	;BINFOR
6013	C3 A0 43		JP 43A0H	;rtn T-BUG

(C) *OUTPUT Formatted String to CRT Video Display*

Addr	Op-Code (Hex)	Label	Mnemonic/ Operand	Remarks
7000	21 30 41	OUTPUT	LD HL,4130H	;string location
7003	CD A7 28		CALL 28A7H	;display till zero byte
7006	C3 19 1A		JP 1A19H	;rtn BASIC

The first routine, called INPUT, is located at 5000H and accepts numeric input from the keyboard, stores the input string of ASCII values in the input buffer area of memory (41E8H-42E8H), converts the input to its lowest possible number type, and returns the result in the appropriate area of FPA1. The second routine, called CONVRT, is located at 6000H and converts the ASCII values stored in the input buffer area back into binary representation, formats the result as specified by the contents of the A, B, and C registers, and stores the formatted ASCII string in the PRINT USING buffer area (4130H-4151H) of memory. The third routine, called OUTPUT, is located at 7000H and displays the formatted contents of the PRINT USING buffer. Now that you know what each routine does, let's discuss how each accomplishes its respective tasks.

Key-in the three programs at the addresses indicated, and place FFH in each of the first 10 locations of the input buffer (41E8H-41F2H) and in each of the eight locations of FPA1 (411DH-4124H). Then, execute the first routine, INPUT. The screen will clear and the "?" prompt will appear. Type and enter the number, 123.456. The screen will again clear and the T-BUG prompt "#" will reappear, signalling a return to T-BUG. If you examine the contents of the PRINT USING buffer (41E8H-42E8H), you will find the hexadecimal values: 31 32 33 2E 34 35 36 00, which are the ASCII values representing the number that was just entered. QINPUT (1BB3H) stores the ASCII values representing the keyboard input in the PRINT USING buffer. But, ASCII values are not what you want; you want binary values.

To convert the ASCII string contained in the PRINT USING buffer to its corresponding binary representation (integer, single precision, or double precision), the ROM subroutine ASCBIN (0E6CH) is used. Normally when this ROM subroutine is used, the programmer must load the HL register pair with the starting address of the ASCII string to be converted; but this step is not necessary when ASCBIN follows QINPUT as we said earlier. This occurs because upon leaving QINPUT, the HL register pair contains the value 41E7H, which is *one less* than the starting address of the PRINT USING buffer (41E8H). The INC HL instruction adds 1 to the content of the HL register pair, producing 41E8H, the desired address.

The second routine, CONVRT, is located at 6000H and converts the ASCII string stored in the PRINT USING buffer (41E8H-42E8H) into numeric representation so that it can be formatted by the ROM subroutine BINFOR (0FBEH), which accepts only numeric values. Here, ASCBIN does not follow QINPUT, so the HL register pair must be loaded with the starting address of the ASCII string in memory that is to be converted to numeric representation. In this case, the address is 41E8H, the starting address of the PRINT USING buffer. The output of ASCBIN is returned in FPA1.

Before the ROM subroutine BINFOR (0FBEH) can be called,

certain conditions must first be established: (1) the HL register pair must point to the memory location where the formatted output ASCII string is to be stored, (2) the A register must contain the appropriate formatting value (see Table 5-9), (3) the B register must contain *two less* than the desired number of spaces to the LEFT of the decimal point, and (4) the C register must contain *one more* than the desired number of spaces to the RIGHT of the decimal point. The values given in Example 5-13 specify a formatting of: (1) store the result in memory beginning at address 4130H, (2) print "$" before the number (A = 90H), (3) allocate 8 spaces (8 − 2 = 6) to the left of the decimal point (B = 06H), and 4) assign 2 spaces (2 + 1 = 3) to the right of the decimal point (C = 03H).

Now, execute the second routine, CONVRT, and examine the contents of the *numeric work area* (4130H-4149H). There, you will find the ASCII values: 20 20 20 20 24 31 32 33 2E 34 36 00, which represent the characters: b̸ b̸ b̸ b̸ $ 1 2 3 . 4 6 NULL. As you can see, BINFOR has rounded up the original decimal value ".456" to ".46", again something that you must remember when dealing with monetary figures.

The last routine, OUTPUT, displays the formatted ASCII string stored in the numeric work area. This routine automatically outputs the ASCII string pointed to by the HL register pair to the CRT video display until a zero byte (00H) is encountered. Executing OUTPUT causes the number that was entered earlier, 123.456, to be displayed in the specified format: eight spaces from the left margin to the decimal point, a dollar sign ($) prefix, and two decimal places.

CHAPTER 6

Arithmetic and Mathematic Functions

In this chapter we will discuss the Level II BASIC ROM subroutines that will enable you to quickly and simply write assembly-language programs to perform arithmetic and mathematic operations upon data.

One of the computer's greatest assets is its ability to perform lengthy and repeated arithmetic and mathematic operations (called "number crunching") with both speed and accuracy. But, a computer alone can do very little, because it is actually the *programs* within the software that perform the arithmetic and mathematic operations that do the number crunching. The computer is simply the tool.

The Microsoft authors of Level II BASIC, Paul Allen and Bill Gates, went to great effort to write a BASIC interpreter that is both accurate and efficient. Many hours were spent writing the excellent subroutines that comprise Level II BASIC, but their greatest efforts consisted of compressing the BASIC interpreter to fit in the available memory without sacrificing features.

The result of their efforts is amply demonstrated by the power and flexibility of Level II BASIC and the fact that it requires only 12K of memory. With this in mind, we should think twice about trying to write our own subroutines, especially arithmetic and mathematic routines; we might be able to write something that was either better or faster, but it is rather doubtful that we could write anything that was *both* better *and* faster! So, instead of attempting to "re-invent" the wheel with each assembly-language program that we write, we will use the existing Level II BASIC ROM subroutines that perform arithmetic and mathematic functions whenever our programs require such operations to be performed upon data.

Before proceeding further, let's define the difference between an *arithmetic* function and a *mathematic* function. Strictly speaking, mathematics is the science of numbers, and arithmetic is a subset of mathematics. But we can describe their difference in somewhat less abstract terms: arithmetic functions deal with relationships between *two* numbers; mathematic functions deal with the attributes (characteristics) of a *single* number. For instance, the arithmetic function ADDITION requires two numbers (operands), an *augend* and an *addend;* but the mathematical function SINE(X) requires only the single operand, X.

ARITHMETIC FUNCTIONS

The Level II BASIC ROMs contain 15 subroutines that you can use in your programs to perform arithmetic functions. These subroutines allow you to perform addition, subtraction, multiplication, division, and comparison, with each of the three number types, integer, single precision, and double precision. Some of these subroutines use registers for input/output while others use the floating-point accumulators (FPAs).

The five arithmetic functions that we will be discussing in this chapter are:

- Addition (+).
- Subtraction (−).
- Multiplication (*).
- Division (/).
- Comparison (<, =, >).

We will examine these functions according to their applications to the three number types, integer, single precision, and double precision.

Integer

There are five ROM subroutines that you can use to perform integer arithmetic. All integer arithmetic operands, or input variables, are passed to the using subroutine via the DE and HL register pairs. The results of integer addition, subtraction, and multiplication are returned in the HL register pair, but the result of integer division is returned in FPA1. This occurs because with integer addition, subtraction, or multiplication only an integer result can occur. With *integer division,* however, an integer quotient, or result, *will only occur* when the divisor and dividend are even multiples of each other. If any of these integer arithmetic operations exceed integer capacity (2^{15}), either by overflow or underflow, the operation is automatcially redone using the equivalent single-precision subroutine and the result is returned in FPA1. No error is flagged when this occurs.

The results of *all* comparisons, regardless of number type (integer, single precision, or double precision), are flagged in the A register. When the first operand is "less-than" the second operand (A<B), the result returned in the A register is +1 (01H). When the first operand is "greater-than" the second operand (A>B), the result returned in the A register is −1 (FFH). And, when the two operands are "equal" (A=B), the A register will contain zero (00H).

The five Level II BASIC ROM subroutines that you can use to perform integer arithmetic are shown in Table 6-1. To use any of these subroutines, you must load the first operand into the DE register pair; load the second operand into the HL register pair; and then call the appropriate ROM subroutine. The result will be returned in the HL register pair, unless a division (INTDIV) or comparison (INTCMP) was performed, in which case the result will be, respectively, in either FPA1 or the A register.

Table 6-1. Integer Arithmetic ROM Subroutines

Function	Subroutine	Operation	Result In
(+) ADDITION	INTADD (0BD2H)	DE + HL	HL
(−) SUBTRACTION	INTSUB (0BC7H)	DE − HL	HL
(*) MULTIPLICATION	INTMUL (0BF2H)	DE * HL	HL
(/) DIVISION	INTDIV (2490H)	DE / HL	FPA1
(<,=,>) COMPARISON	INTCMP (0A39H)	DE < HL	A = +1 (01H)
		DE > HL	A = −1 ((FFH)
		DE = HL	A = 0 (00H)

Example 6-1 illustrates the use of the Level II BASIC ROM integer addition subroutine, INTADD (0BD2H), and introduces you to the programming technique called *nesting*. This is the technique of embedding one or more subroutines within another subroutine, and is used whenever a routine or sequence of instructions is to be used *more than once* within a program. In this example, instead of writing the subroutine INPUT twice, once to input augend operand and again to input the addend operand, it is written only *once*, at the end of the program, and is simply *called* whenever it is needed. The use of nested subroutines whenever possible greatly simplifies and shortens *any* program, assembly language, *or* BASIC.

Use T-BUG and enter the program, and then execute it. Type and enter the floating-point number, 12345.5, when the first "?" prompt appears, and then type and enter 12345.6 when the second "?"

Example 6-1. Program To Add Two Integer Numbers and Display the Sum.

Addr	Op-Code				Label	Mnemonic/ Operand	Remarks
5000	CD	18	50		ADDEND	CALL INPUT	;input addend
5003	ED	5B	21	41		LD DE,(4121H)	;move from FPA1 to DE
5007	D5					PUSH DE	;store on stack
5008	CD	1B	50		AUGEND	CALL INPUT	;input augend
500B	2A	21	41			LD HL,(4121H)	;move from FPA1 to HL
500E	D1					POP DE	;retrieve addend
500F	CD	D2	0B		ADD	CALL INTADD	;DE + HL → HL
5012	22	00	60			LD (6000H),HL	;store sum at 6000H
5015	C3	A0	43		END	JP T-BUG	;return to T-BUG
5018	CD	C9	01		INPUT	CALL CLS	;clear screen
501B	CD	B3	1B			CALL QINPUT	;kybd scan and display
501E	23					INC HL	;
501F	CD	6C	0E			CALL ASCBIN	;ASCII to binary
5022	C3	7F	0A			JP CINT	;convert to INT

prompt appears. If you examine the content of memory locations 6000H-6001H you will find the sum, 6072H or 24,690 (12345.5 + 12345.6 = 3039H + 3039H = 6072H). How did we eliminate the decimals? Simple, by calling CINT (0A7FH) within the subroutine INPUT.

The program functions in the following manner: The first operand, the augend, is input and converted to an integer using the ROM subroutines, QINPUT (1BB3H), ASCBIN (0E6CH), and CINT (0ACFH), and is then loaded from FPA1 into the DE register pair and pushed onto the stack for temporary storage. Then, the second operand, the addend, is input and converted to an integer and loaded from FPA1 into the HL register pair. At this point, the augend is popped off the stack into the DE register pair, and INTADD (0BD2H) is called to "add" the two integer operands. The result is stored in memory at 6000H-6001H.

Of course, the observant reader will realize that this subroutine *could* be replaced by a single-byte instruction, ADD HL,DE (19H), saving some time and a small amount of memory. This is all right, *if* you are *sure* that the sum of the two integer operands will never exceed 32767. If there is any doubt, use INTADD with its automatic conversion to single-precision should the sum exceed integer capacity. Testing NTF1 will tell you whether the result will be in the HL register (integer result) or in FPA1 (single-precision result).

Single Precision

The five ROM subroutines that you can use in your assembly-language programs to perform single-precision arithmetic are

Table 6-2. Single-Precision Arithmetic ROM Subroutines

Function		Subroutine	Operation	Result in
(+)	ADDITION	SGLADD (0716H)	BCDE + FPA1	FPA1
(—)	SUBTRACTION	SGLSUB (0713H)	BCDE — FPA1	FPA1
(*)	MULTIPLICATION	SGLMUL (0847H)	BCDE * FPA1	FPA1
(/)	DIVISION	SGLDIV (08A2H)	BCDE / FPA1	FPA1
(<,=,>)	COMPARISON	SGLCMP (0A0CH)	BCDE < FPA1	A = +1 (01H)
			BCDE > FPA1	A = −1 (FFH)
			BCDE = FPA1	A = 0 (00H)

shown in Table 6-2. Single-precision arithmetic operands are passed to the using subroutine via the BC and HL register pairs and FPA1. The result of single-precision arithmetic operation is returned in FPA1. The result of a single-precision comparison, like an integer comparison, is flagged in the. A register using the same format.

When using any of the single-precision arithmetic ROM subroutines, you must load the first operand into the BC and DE register pairs (using the single precision BCDE register format discussed in Chapter 5); load the second operand into the single-precision area of FPA1 (4121H-4124H); and then call the appropriate ROM subroutine. The result of single-precision addition, subtraction, multiplication, and division is returned in FPA1. The result of a single-precision comparison, like an integer comparison, is flagged in the A register.

The program shown in Example 6-2 illustrates the use of the ROM single-precision subtraction subroutine, SGLSUB (0713H).

Example 6-2. Program To Subtract Two Single-Precision Numbers and Display the Difference.

Addr	Op-Code	Label	Mnemonic/ Operand	Remarks
5000	CD 19 50	MINUND	CALL INPUT	;input minuend
5003	CD BF 09		CALL FPAREG	;FPA1 into BCDE
5006	C5		PUSH BC	;store on stack
5007	D5		PUSH DE	;store on stack
5008	CD 1C 50	SUBTRA	CALL INPUT	;input subtrahend
500B	D1		POP DE	;retrieve minuend
500C	C1		POP BC	;retrieve minuend
500D	CD 13 07	SUBT	CALL SGLSUB	;BCDE — FPA1 → FPA1
5010	21 00 60		LD HL,6000H	;set pointer
5013	CD CB 09		CALL FPA1HL	;store diff at 6000H
5016	C3 A0 43	END	JP T-BUG	;return to T-BUG
5019	CD C9 01	INPUT	CALL CLS	;clear screen
501C	CD B3 1B		CALL QINPUT	;kybd scan and display
501F	23		INC HL	;
5020	CD 6C 0E		CALL ASCBIN	;ASCII to binary
5023	C3 B1 0A		JP CSNG	;convert to SGL

It inputs the first operand, the minuend, using the ROM subroutines, QINPUT (1BB3H), ASCBIN (0E6CH) and CSNG (0AB1H). Upon returning to the main portion of the program from the INPUT subroutine, the single-precision minuend operand is moved from FPA1 into the BC and DE register pairs using the ROM subroutine FPAREG (09BFH), and then both register pairs are pushed onto the stack for temporary storage. Then, the second operand, the subtrahend (number to be subtracted from the minuend), is input via a call to the INPUT subroutine. The single-precision subtrahend operand is returned in the single-precision area of FPA1. The minuend is popped from the stack back into the BC and DE register pairs, and the ROM subroutine SGLSUB (0713H) is called to perform the subtraction. The result is returned in the single-precision area of FPA1 and moved into memory locations 6000H-6004H using the ROM subroutine FPA1HL (09CBH).

Double Precision

Table 6-3 lists the five Level II BASIC ROM subroutines that you can use in your assembly-language programs to perform double-precision arithmetic operations. These subroutines use the floating-point accumulators FPA1 and FPA2 for both operands and the result. For all double-precision arithmetic operations the first operand must be in FPA1 and the second operand must be in FPA2. The result of a double-precision addition, subtraction, multiplication, and division is returned in FPA1. However, the result of a double-precision comparison, like an integer or a single-precision comparison, is flagged in the A register.

Table 6-3. Double-Precision Arithmetic ROM Subroutines

Function	Subroutine	Operation	Result in
(+) ADDITION	DBLADD (0C77H)	FPA1 + FPA2	FPA1
(−) SUBTRACTION	DBLSUB (0C70H)	FPA1 − FPA2	FPA1
(∗) MULTIPLICATION	DBLMUL (0DA1H)	FPA1 ∗ FPA2	FPA1
(/) DIVISION	DBLDIV (0DE5H)	FPA1 / FPA2	FPA1
(<,=,>) COMPARISON	DBLCMP (0A78H)	FPA1 < FPA2	A = +1 (01H)
		FPA1 > FPA2	A = −1 (FFH)
		FPA1 = FPA2	A = 0 (00H)

Enter the program shown in Example 6-3 using T-BUG and execute it. Then enter the double-precision number 1234.56789 when the first "?" prompt appears. Enter 9876.54321 when the second "?" prompt appears. When the T-BUG prompt "#" reappears, use T-BUG's command and inspect the content of the A register, which contains the flag that indicates whether operand A is less-than, greater-than, or equal-to operand B. In this example, operand A is

Example 6-3. Program To Compare Two Double-Precision Numbers.

Addr	Op-Code	Label	Mnemonic/ Operand	Remarks
5000	CD 30 50	A	CALL INPUT	;input operand A
5003	CD EC 0A		CALL SETDBL	;NTF1=8=# bytes to move
5006	21 1D 41		LD HL,411DH	;from FPA1
5009	11 00 60		LD DE,6000H	;to 6000H
500C	CD D2 09		CALL HLTODE	;store A at 6000H
500F	CD 33 50	B	CALL INPUT	;input operand B
5012	CD EC 0A		CALL SETDBL	;NTF1=8=# bytes to move
5015	21 1D 41		LD HL,411DH	;from FPA1
5018	11 27 41		LD DE,4127H	;to FPA2
501B	CD D2 09		CALL HLTODE	;move B into FPA2
501E	CD EC 0A		CALL SETDBL	;NTF1=8=# bytes to move
5021	21 00 60		LD HL,6000H	;from 6000H
5024	11 1D 41		LD DE,411DH	;to FPA1
5027	CD D2 09		CALL HLTODE	;move A into FPA1
502A	CD 78 0A	COMPAR	CALL DBLCMP	;compare A and B
502D	C3 A0 43	END	JP T-BUG	;return to T-BUG
5030	CD C9 01	INPUT	CALL CLS	;clear screen
5033	CD B3 1B		CALL QINPUT	;kybd scan and display
5036	23		INC HL	;
5037	CD 6C 0E		CALL ASCBIN	;ASCII to binary
503A	C3 DB 0A		JP CDBL	;convert to DBL

1234.56789 and operand B is 9876.54321, or A< B, so the A register should contain the value 01H. To verify this, you simply press the R key and T-BUG will display the current contents of the registers; and the A register does indeed contain 01H, the "less-than" flag.

The 15 Level II BASIC ROM subroutines that you can use to perform integer, single-precision, or double-precision arithmetic operations in your assembly-language programs are summarized in Table 6-4. Integer arithmetic supports the numbers from −32,768 to +32,767; single-precision arithmetic handles numbers in the range −1.701411E±38 to +1.701411E±38; and, double-precision arithmetic handles numbers in the range −1.701411834544556D±38 to +1.701411834544556D±38.

MATHEMATIC FUNCTIONS

The Level II BASIC ROMs contain 14 subroutines that you can use in your programs to perform mathematic operations upon data. These subroutines allow you to calculate the transcendental value of a variable, determine its sign and magnitude, or raise it to some power. Transcendental functions include the *trigonometric* (SIN, COS, TAN, etc.), *logarithmic* ($\log_{10}$ and $\log_e$) and *exponen-*

Table 6-4. Summary of Level II BASIC Arithmetic ROM Subroutines

Function		Integer (INT)	Single Precision (SGL)	Double Precision (DBL)
(+)	ADDITION	INTADD (0BD2H)	SGLADD (0716H)	DBLADD (0C77H)
		DE + HL → HL	BCDE + FPA1 → FPA1	FPA1 + FPA2 → FPA1
(—)	SUBTRACTION	INTSUB (0BC7H)	SGLSUB (0713H)	DBLSUB (0C70H)
		DE — HL → HL	BCDE — FPA1 → FPA1	FPA1 — FPA2 → FPA1
(*)	MULTIPLICATION	INTMUL (0BF2H)	SGLMUL (0847H)	DBLMUL (0DA1H)
		DE * HL → HL	BCDE * FPA1 → FPA1	FPA1 * FPA2 → FPA1
(/)	DIVISION	INTDIV (2490H)	SGLDIV (08A2H)	DBLDIV (0DE5H)
		DE / HL → FPA1	BCDE / FPA1 → FPA1	FPA1 / FPA2 → FPA1
(<,=,>)	MULTIPLICATION	INTCMP (0A39H)	SGLCMP (0A0CH)	DBLCMP (0A78H)
		DE<HL → A = +1	BCDE<FPA1 → A = +1	FPA1<FPA2 → A = +1
		DE>HL → A = —1	BCDE>FPA1 → A = —1	FPA1>FPA2 → A = —1
		DE=HL → A = 0	BCDE=FPA1 → A = 0	FPA1=FPA2 → A = 0

tial (e^X and X^Y) functions. You can also determine whether a variable is negative, zero or positive, and its absolute value. A variable can also be raised to any positive or negative power less than 2^{127}.

The 14 Level II BASIC ROM subroutines that you can use to perform mathematic operations upon data are:

- ABS(X)—Absolute value of X, $|X|$.
- ATN(X)—Arc-tangent of X, angle in *radians,* TAN^{-1}.
- COS(X)—Cosine of X, angle in *radians.*
- EXP(X)—Natural (base e) antilog of X, e^X.
- FIX(X)—Truncate value of X to integer.
- INT(X)—Largest whole number value of X.
- LOG(X)—Natural (base e) logarithm of X, ln X.
- X↑Y—Raise X to the Y power, X^Y.
- RANDOM—Reseed (randomize) the RND(X) function.
- RND(X)—Return random number between 0 and X.
- SGN(X)—Return sign of X, positive, negative, or zero.
- SIN(X)—Sine of X, angle in *radians.*
- SQR(X)—Square root of X, $\sqrt{X}$.
- TAN(X)—Tangent of X, angle in *radians.*

All of these ROM subroutines use single-precision operands and return single-precision results, except RANDOM, which requires no operand and returns no result.

TRIGONOMETRIC FUNCTIONS

There are four trigonometric functions contained in the Level II BASIC ROMs that you can use in your programs: sine, cosine, tangent, and arc-tangent. Table 6-5 lists the ROM subroutines that you can use in your assembly-language programs to implement these trigonometric functions. Note that the operands for the sine, cosine, and tangent subroutines must be in *radians,* not degrees! One radian is equal to 57.29577951 degrees ($180°/\pi$), and one degree equals 0.0174532952 radians ($\pi/180°$). The output is returned in FPA1 in single-precision format. Conversely, the ATN(X) subroutine expects a single-precision operand and returns a single-precision angle in *radians.*

To use any of the trigonometric functions, you must load the operand, in single-precision format, into FPA1 and then call the appropriate subroutine. The result is returned in FPA1, overwriting the original operand content, something that you should consider if the operand might be used more than once.

Example 6-4 inputs an angle in degrees, converts it to radians, and displays the result on the CRT. It consists of 15 instructions,

Table 6-5. Level II BASIC Trigonometric ROM Subroutines

Function	Subroutine	Input in	Mathematic Operation*	Result in
SIN(X)	SIN(X) (1547H)	FPA1	Sine of angle X	FPA1
COS(X)	COS(X) (1541H)	FPA1	Cosine of angle X	FPA1
TAN(X)	TAN(X) (15A8H)	FPA1	Tangent of angle X	FPA1
ATN(X)	ATN(X) (15BDH)	FPA1	Arc-tangent to angle	FPA1

*Note: All angles in *radians*, not degrees! All inputs and outputs in single-precision format.

of which 10 are calls to ROM subroutines! This should give you some idea of how much can be done using the existing Level II BASIC ROM subroutines.

This program inputs a number, assumed to be in degrees, using the ROM subroutines QINPUT (1BB3H), ASCBIN (0E6CH) and CDBL (0ADBH), and divides the result by the "degrees-per-radian" constant, 57.29577951, using the mathematic ROM subroutine DBLDIV (0DE5H). Notice that double-precision was used during both the input (CDBL) and division (DBLDIV) operations to reduce round-off errors. The result is converted to single precision just prior to calling the binary-to-ASCII conversion subroutine, BINASC (0FBDH).

Example 6-4. Program To Convert Degrees to Radians and Display Result.

```
                                   Mnemonic/
Addr     Op-Code        Label      Operand          Remarks
5000     CD  C9  01     INPUT      CALL  CLS        ;clear screen
5003     CD  B3  1B                CALL  QINPUT     ;kybd scan and display
5006     23                        INC  HL          ;
5007     CD  6C  0E                CALL  ASCBIN     ;ASCII to binary
500A     CD  DB  0A                CALL  CDBL       ;convert to DBL
500D     CD  EC  0A                CALL  SETDBL     ;NTF1=8=# bytes to move
5010     21  2B  50                LD  HL,502BH     ;from constant
5013     11  27  41                LD  DE,4127H     ;to FPA2
5016     CD  D2  09                CALL  HLTODE     ;constant into FPA2
5019     CD  E5  0D     DIVIDE     CALL  DBLDIV     ;FPA1/FPA2 → FPA1
501C     CD  B1  0A                CALL  CSNG       ;convert to SGL
501F     CD  BD  0F                CALL  BINASC     ;binary to ASCII
5022     21  30  41                LD  HL,4130H     ;set pointer
5025     CD  A7  28                CALL  OUTLIN     ;display until zero byte
5028     C3  B2  02     END        JP  SYSTEM       ;return to SYSTEM
502B     8D             CONST                       ;57.29577951 in
502C     1B                                         ;double precision
502D     E9                                         ;format
502E     D2
502F     E0
5030     2E
5031     65
5032     86
```

The hexadecimal values from 502BH to 5032H represent the constant, 57.29577951, in double-precision format. This number is loaded into FPA2 by the four instructions at 500DH-5018H, and is used by DBLDIV (0DE5H) as the divisor operand. Table 6-6 lists some of the more useful mathematical constants in both single-precision and double-precision formats.

Example 6-5 illustrates the use of the Level II BASIC ROM subroutine, COS(X). This program is nothing more than Example 6-4 with one additional instruction, CALL COS(X). Any number input is first converted to double precision, divided by the double-precision constant 57.29577951, and converted into single precision. Then, the ROM subroutine COS(X) (1541H) is called to calculate the cosine function of the single-precision quotient that resulted when the input operand was divided by the "degrees-to-radians" constant. The resultant cosine value, in single-precision format, is returned in FPA1, converted to ASCII, and displayed on the CRT.

Example 6-5. Program To Calculate and Display the Cosine of an Input Angle in Degrees.

Addr	Op-Code			Label	Mnemonic/ Operand	Remarks
5000	CD	C9	01	INPUT	CALL CLS	;clear screen
5003	CD	B3	1B		CALL QINPUT	;kybd scan and display
5006	23				INC HL	;
5007	CD	6C	0E		CALL ASCBIN	;ASCII to binary
500A	CD	DB	0A		CALL CDBL	;convert to DBL
500D	CD	EC	0A		CALL SETDBL	;NRF1=8=# bytes to move
5010	21	2E	50		LD HL,502EH	from constant
5013	11	27	41		LD DE,4127H	;to FPA2
5016	CD	D2	09		CALL HLTODE	;move constant into FPA2
5019	CD	E5	0D	DIVIDE	CALL DBLDIV	;FPA1/FPA2 → FPA1
501C	CD	B1	0A		CALL CSNG	;convert to SGL
501F	CD	41	15	COSINE	CALL COS(X)	;calculate cosine, FPA1
5022	CD	BD	0F		CALL BINASC	;binary to ASCII
5025	21	30	41		LD HL,4130H	;set pointer
5028	CD	A7	28		CALL OUTLIN	;display until zero byte
502B	C3	B2	02	END	JP SYSTEM	;return to SYSTEM
502E	8D			CONST		;57.29577951 in
502F	1B					;double precision
5030	E9					;format
5031	D2					
5032	E0					
5033	2E					
5034	65					
5035	86					

LOGARITHMIC AND EXPONENTIAL FUNCTIONS

There are four logarithmic and exponential functions that you can use from Level II BASIC. These four functions and the ad-

Table 6-6. Some Useful Mathematic Constants

	Single Precision (SGL)				Double Precision (DBL)							
	(EXP	MSB	. . .	LSB)	(EXP	MSB	. . .	. . .	. . .	. . .	. . .	LSB)
π	82	49	0F	DB	82	49	0F	DA	A2	92	2A	7E
2π	83	49	0F	DB	83	49	0F	DA	A2	92	2A	7E
ϵ	82	2D	F8	54	82	2D	F8	54	58	24	8C	DA
$180°/\pi$	86	65	2E	E1	86	65	2E	E0	D2	E9	1B	8D
$\pi/180°$	7B	0E	FA	35	7B	0E	FA	35	12	94	CC	1A
10	84	20	00	00	84	20	00	00	00	00	00	00
ln10	82	13	5D	8E	82	13	5D	8D	DD	AC	4B	AB

Table 6-7. Level II BASIC Mathematics ROM Subroutines that Implement Logarithmic and Exponential Functions

Function	Subroutine	Input in	Mathematic Operation	Result in
LOG(X)	LOG(X) (0809H)	FPA1	Natural (base e) logarithm of X, ln X	FPA1
EXP(X)	EXP(X) (1439H)	FPA1	Natural anti-logarithm of X, e^X	FPA1
X↑Y	X↑Y(13F7H)	X→BCDE Y→FPA1	Raise X to the Y power, X^Y	FPA1
SQR(X)	SQR(X) (13E7H)	FPA1	Square root of X, $\sqrt{X}$	FPA1

Note: All inputs and outputs in single-precision format.

dresses of the ROM subroutines are listed in Table 6-7. They allow you to find the *natural* (base e) logarithm (LOG(X)), *natural* anti-logarithm (EXP(X)), square root (SQR(X)), and exponential/power function (X↑Y) of a single-precision variable. Although Level II BASIC does not support the use of *common* (base-10) logarithms, they can be easily implemented in assembly language, as you will soon discover.

To use any of these logarithmic or exponential ROM subroutines, except X↑Y, you must load the operand, in single-precision format, into FPA1 and then call the desired subroutine. The result is returned in FPA1 in single-precision format, overwriting the original operand. For instance, Example 6-6 calculates and displays the natural logarithm ($\log_e$ X) of any positive number entered (logarithms of negative numbers are undefined).

Example 6-6. Program To Calculate and Display the Natural Logarithm of a Number Less-Than 1.701411835D + 38 (2^{127}).

Addr	Op-Code	Label	Mnemonic/ Operand	Remarks
5000	CD C9 01	INPUT	CALL CLS	;clear screen
5003	CD B3 1B		CALL QINPUT	;kybd scan and display
5006	23		INC HL	;
5007	CD 6C 0E		CALL ASCBIN	;ASCII to binary
500A	CD 77 09		CALL ABS(X)	;no negatives allowed
500D	CD B1 0A		CALL CSNG	;convert to SGL
5010	CD 09 08	LOG	CALL LOG(X)	;find ln X
5013	CD BD 0F		CALL BINASC	;binary to ASCII
5016	21 30 41		LD HL 4130H	;set pointer
5019	CD A7 28	DISPLA	CALL OUTLIN	;display until zero byte
501C	C3 B2 02	END	JP SYSTEM	;return to SYSTEM

To use the X↑Y subroutine, load X (the *base*) into the BC and DE register pairs, in single-precision format, and load Y (the *exponent*) into FPA1 in single-precision format. The single-precision result is returned in FPA1. Note that a fatal error back to Level II BASIC occurs when: (1) the base is negative and the exponent is not a whole number, (2) the absolute value of the result exceeds single-precision capacity ($2^{127} \simeq 10^{38}$), or (3) the base is zero and the exponent is negative.

The ROM subroutine that implements the exponential function, X↑Y, deserves special attention. Not only does it allow you to raise a number (base) to a power (exponent), it also enables you to calculate the *common anti-logarithm* of a number! This is possible because the anti-logarithm of any number is simply the base (10 for common logarithms) raised to the logarithmic-power ($10^{\log_{10} X} = X$)! This means that if you substitute the number 10 as a constant for the base (X) and enter a common logarithm as the variable for the exponent (Y) in the function X↑Y, the common anti-logarithm may be found. But, what good is a common anti-logarithm without first having a common logarithm? Let's see . . . .

The two most used bases for logarithms are base-10 (common) and base e (natural), although *any* base *could* be used just as easily. The Level II BASIC ROMs contain the necessary subroutines to calculate the natural logarithm of a number, but not the common logarithm, so we must find some way to express a common logarithm as a function of a natural logarithm. Luckily, just such a relationship exists:

$$\log_{10} X = \frac{\log_e X}{\log_e 10}$$

which states that the *ratio* of the natural logarithm of X to the natural logarithm of the constant 10 is the common logarithm of X! Or,

$$\log_{10} X = \frac{\ln X}{\ln 10} \text{ (NOTE: ln = natural logarithm)}$$

which can be simplified by substituting the value representing the natural logarithm of 10 ($\ln 10 = 2.302585093$) into the above equation. When this is done, we end up with exactly what we were after, the common logarithm of a number ($\log_{10} X$) expressed in terms of a natural logarithm ($\ln X$), divided by a constant:

$$\log_{10} X = \frac{\ln X}{2.302585093}$$

which is the basis for the program shown in Example 6-7. This program consists of the program given in Example 6-6 to find the natural logarithm of a number, plus instructions to divide by the constant 2.3025. . . . The result, in single-precision format, is returned in FPA1 as well as displayed on the CRT.

Example 6-7. Program To Calculate and Display the Common (Base 10) Logarithm of a Positive Number.

Addr	Op-Code			Label	Mnemonic/ Operand	Remarks
5000	CD	C9	01	INPUT	CALL CLS	;clear screen
5003	CD	B3	1B		CALL QINPUT	;kybd scan and display
5006	23				INC HL	;
5007	CD	6C	0E		CALL ASCBIN	;ASCII to binary
500A	CD	77	09		CALL ABS(X)	;no negatives allowed
500D	CD	B1	0A		CALL CSNG	;convert to SGL
5010	CD	09	08	LN X	CALL LOG(X)	;find ln X
5013	CD	EF	0A		CALL SETSGL	;NTF1=4=# bytes to move
5016	21	31	50	LN 10	LD HL,5031H	;from constant @ 5031H
5019	11	27	41		LD DE,4127H	;to FPA2
501C	CD	D2	09		CALL HLTODE	;constant into FPA2
501F	CD	BF	09		CALL FPAREG	;ln X into BCDE
5022	CD	A2	08	DIVIDE	CALL SGLDIV	;ln X/ln 10 – FPA1
5025	CD	BD	0F		CALL BINASC	;binary to ASCII
5028	21	30	41		LD HL,4130H	;set pointer
502B	CD	A7	28	DISPLA	CALL OUTLIN	;display until zero byte
502E	C3	B2	02	END	JP SYSTEM	;return to SYSTEM
5031	8E			CONST		;ln 10 (2.302585093)
5032	5D					;in single precision
5033	13					;format
5034	82					;

Using the ROM subroutine X↑Y (13F2H), you can also calculate the *power-* and *exponential* functions of a number. To find the "power" of a number, remember that the *base is the variable* and the *exponent is a constant* (X^C), where C is some constant. Conversely, to determine the "exponential" of a number, remember that the *exponent is the variable* and the base is a constant (C^X), where C is some constant. With this and the logarithmic relationship described above, you can determine *any base* logarithm and antilogarithm that you desire.

The square root function is implemented by loading a single-precision operand into FPA1 and calling the ROM subroutine SQR(X) (13E7H). The result is returned in FPA1 in single-precision format. Note that *only positive* operands are accepted, otherwise a fatal error back to Level II BASIC occurs. To eliminate this problem you can simply ensure that only positive operands reach the SQR(X) subroutine by placing the ROM subroutine ABS(X) (0977H) in your program between the input portion of your program and the call to SQR(X). This will convert all operands to positive numbers and eliminate the mistake of trying to take the square root of a negative number.

To find a "root," other than the square root ($\sqrt[2]{X}$), of a number, you can use the versatile X↑Y subroutine. Here, you let X be the number that you wish to find the root of, and let Y be the *reciprocal of the root* that you wish to extract. For instance, to find the cube root ($\sqrt[3]{X}$) of a number, X would equal the number you are trying to extract the cube root of, and Y would equal 1/3, or 0.3333333 ($\sqrt[3]{X} = X^{1/3} = X^{0.3333333}$). Similarly, you can extract noninteger roots in the same manner, just let Y equal the *reciprocal* of the root that you wish to extract.

SIGN AND MAGNITUDE FUNCTIONS

You have already seen three of the four sign and magnitude functions that you can use from the Level II BASIC ROM subroutines. They are: absolute value of a variable, ABS(X); truncate the decimal, FIX(X); and, largest whole number, INT(X). These have been discussed earlier because of their wide applicability. The only remaining function is the sign function, SGN(X), which returns the value −1, 0 or +1, representing, respectively, that the input operand is negative, zero or positive. These values are returned in the integer-area of FPA1 (and in the HL register pair). The four sign and magnitude ROM subroutines that you can use are listed in Table 6-8.

RANDOM FUNCTIONS

Level II BASIC contains two random number functions, RANDOM and RND(X). These functions perform, respectively, a reseeding or "randomization" of RND(X), and the generation of a pseudo-random *integer* number between one and X. The subroutine that implements RANDOM (01D3H) requires *no operand.* It simply copies the current contents of the R (memory refresh) register in the Z-80 CPU chip into memory locations 40ABH-40ACH, changing the value of the number used to "seed" the subroutine that generates the random number. The ROM subroutine RND(X) (14CCH) requires an integer operand, X, which is used to establish the "range" of the pseudo-random integer number generated, from 1 through X. A fatal error will occur if a number greater than 32767 is used for X. Typically, the ROM subroutine CINT (0A7FH) is placed after RND(X) (14CCH) to convert the output to an integer. Table 6-9 shows these functions and their ROM subroutines.

To use RND(X) in your programs, you must load the HL register pair with the *non-zero integer* value of X, in the range 1 to 32767, and then call RND(X) (14CCH). Assuming CINT (0A7FH) follows RND(X), the integer result is returned in both the integer-area of FPA1 (4121H-4122H) and the HL register pair.

Table 6-8. Level II BASIC Mathematic ROM Subroutines that Implement Sign and Magnitude Functions

Function	Subroutine	Input Operand(s)		Mathematic Operation	Result(s) in
		NTF1 (40AFH)	Input in		
ABS(X)	ABS(X) (0977H)	2, 4, 8	FPA1	Absolute value of X, $\|X\|$	FPA1*
FIX(X)	FIX(X) (0B26H)	4, 8	FPA1	Truncate value of X to integer	FPA1*
INT(X)	INT(X) (0B37H)	4, 8	FPA1	Largest whole number value of X	FPA1†
SGN(X)	SGN(X) (098AH)	2, 4, 8	FPA1	Sign of X, +, − or zero	FPA1‡

Note: *Results returned to respective areas of FPA1, i.e., integer to integer, etc.
†Results returned in integer area of FPA1 if less than 32767, otherwise in single-precision area of FPA1.
‡Result returned in integer-area of FPA1.

Table 6-9. Level II BASIC ROM Subroutines that Implement Random Number Generation

Function	Subroutine	Input in	Operation	Result in
RANDOM	RANDOM (01D3H)	(none)	Reseed RND(X)	(none)
RND(X)	RND(X) (14CCH)	*HL	Random # 1-X	FPA1†

Note: *Input operand must be non-zero integer.
†Result returned is single-precision; must be converted to integer before using.

Although the actual procedures and programming are beyond the scope of this book, you can modify any of these ROM subroutines to yield precisions greater than are now produced, such as double-precision trigonometric and logarithmic functions, etc. To do this you will need to disassemble and study the ROM subroutine(s) that actually perform the function that you wish to extend the precision of. Use the address listed for the subroutine as a starting place to begin your disassembly. It won't be easy, but it *can* be done!

In most cases, the single-precision results produced by the Level II BASIC arithmetic and mathematic ROM subroutines are more than adequate. However, to ensure the highest accuracy possible, you should perform all computations prior to the limiting arithmetic or mathematic function subroutine in double precision, and then convert to single precision just before calling the function.

REVIEW EXERCISES

1. **Write a program to multiply two integer numbers and store the product at 6000H.**
2. **What must be done to Example 6-2 to add, instead of subtract, the two single-precision numbers?**
3. **Write a program to calculate and display the tangent of an angle in radians.**
4. **Modify the program in Exercise 3 to accept angles in degrees.**
5. **Write a program to simulate the conditional three-way branch (+,0,−) used in FORTRAN and BASIC using the SIGN(X) function.**

CHAPTER 7

Cassette, Printer, and Port I/O

A computer without data is useless. Without some means of accepting and returning information to the outside world, a computer would serve no useful purpose, it would simply be a do-nothing box of microelectronics, because the very purpose of a computer *is* data handling. In fact, by definition, a microcomputer must contain a central processing unit, memory, *and input/output*, or it is not a computer. The function of input and output (I/O) is to interface the computer to the programmer and the outside world. It allows us to communicate with the computer in the form of control, programs, and data, and allows the computer to return results to us in some way that we can understand and use. In this chapter we will discuss three of the devices that the TRS-80 uses to perform I/O and some of the Level II BASIC ROM subroutines that can be used to control these devices.

MEMORY-MAPPED VERSUS PORT-ADDRESSED

The TRS-80 supports two types of I/O, *memory-mapped* and *port-addressed.* Memory-mapped I/O utilizes a specific memory address for the input and output of data. Examples of memory-mapped I/O devices that use memory addresses are: the keyboard, the CRT video display, the disks, and the printer. Port-addressed I/O use one (or more) of the Z-80's 256 input and 256 output port addresses. Examples of port-addressed devices are the cassette and part of the video display logic. In this chapter we will discuss the printer, the cassette, and general-purpose I/O ports.

You have already met two of the TRS-80's four memory-mapped IO devices, the keyboard and the CRT video display. These are examples of specialized I/O devices that perform specific I/O functions. The keyboard is an *input-only* device which accepts information from the programmer and passes it to the computer. The CRT video display is an *output-only* device which returns information from the computer to the programmer.

The two remaining memory-mapped devices supported by the TRS-80 are the disks and the printer. Unlike the keyboard and CRT video display which are unidirectional I/O devices, the disks and printer are bidirectional I/O devices which pass data both to and from the computer. The disks are beyond the scope of this book and will not be covered. The cassette is also a bidirectional I/O device. Thus, in this chapter we will be discussing three of the TRS-80's four bidirectional I/O devices: the cassette, the printer, and general-purpose I/O ports.

CASSETTE

Up to now, we have discussed only memory-mapped devices, such as the keyboard and the CRT video display. The cassette, however, is not a memory-mapped device. It is a port-addressed device that is accessed through port 255 (FFH). This port also controls the 32-/64-character mode of the CRT video display.

The Level II BASIC ROMs contain subroutines for writing (SAVE) and reading (LOAD) four different types of cassette tapes. These four types of tapes are: the BASIC *program* format created using the CSAVE statement, the BASIC *data* format created using the PRINT#-1 statement, the SOURCE code format created using the editor/assembler, and the OBJECT (binary) code format created using T-BUG's PUNCH command or the editor/assembler's ASSEMBLE command.

Because we are discussing how to do assembly-language programming using a monitor/debugging program, such as T-BUG, instead of using an editor/assembler, we will limit our discussion to the SYSTEM cassette tape format.

SYSTEM FORMAT

The SYSTEM cassette tape format used in creating object code (binary) tapes is shown in Table 7-1. The SYSTEM cassette tape format consists of six identifiers: the *leader* and *sync byte,* the SYSTEM *format header byte,* the *filename,* the *data block(s),* the *end-of-file* marker byte, and the *entry address.*

The *leader* consists of a string of 256 zeros followed by the *sync byte* consisting of the symmetrical bit pattern, 10100101 (A5H). The string of 256 zeros is used to "synchronize" the tape-reading subroutine with the output from the cassette, and thus compensate for small fluctuations in tape speed. The A5H sync byte signals the tape-reading subroutine that the leader has ended and data follows.

Table 7-1. TRS-80 SYSTEM Cassette Tape Format

```
LEADER (256 zeros) = SYNC BYTE (A5H)
55H—SYSTEM FORMAT HEADER BYTE
XX XX XX XX XX XX—6 character FILENAME
     3CH—Data Block Header Byte
     XX—Data Block Length (00H = 256 bytes)
      LSB\
          }Loading Address
     MSB/
     XX. . .XX—Data bytes
     XX—Checksum (load address = data)
78H—END-OF-FILE (EOF)
 LSB\
     }ENTRY ADDRESS
MSB/
```

Following the sync byte is the SYSTEM *format header byte* (55H). This format header byte tells the tape-reading subroutine that the data was recorded using the SYSTEM format (the other tape formats have their own format header byte codes). Next, comes the *filename* (XX XX XX XX XX XX), consisting of a six-character string of ASCII values, used to "name" the file. *ALL* six characters *must* be filled, either with a valid character or with *blanks* (20H).

After the filename comes the *data block header* (3CH) that serves as a "marker" to indicate *the beginning of each block of data.* It is followed by the *data length byte* (XX) which indicates the number of bytes of data contained in this particular block of data (00H = 256 bytes). This byte is usually set to 00H for all but the last data block, so that the maximum number of data bytes (256) will be recorded per data block, although *any* number from 1 to 256 may be used. Then comes the two-byte *loading address* (LSB/MSB) that specifies the starting address in memory where *this* block of data is to begin loading. This is followed by the *data block* (XX . . . XX) that consists of the actual data bytes stored in consecutive, ascending order (referenced to the loading address).

The *checksum* marks the "end" of a data block, and is the "sum," without carry, of the two load address bytes (LSB/MSB) *plus* each of the data bytes in that data block. For example, if the load address is 5000H and the data bytes are 00, 01, 02, 03, 04, and FF, then the checksum will be 59H. You can easily verify this by adding all of the bytes like this: 50 + 00 + 00 + 01 + 02 + 03 + 04 + FF = (01)59H. But, remember, the carry IS NOT used.

The sequence of "data header/data length/loading address/data block/checksum" is repeated as many times as necessary until the complete program has been recorded. To mark the "end" of the SYSTEM tape format, an *end-of-file* (EOF) byte (78H) is recorded, followed by the *entry address* (LSB/MSB) of the program being recorded.

Cassette Subroutines

The Level II BASIC ROMs contain seven subroutines that you can use to control the cassette. Using these subroutines allows you to write your own programs to read or write SYSTEM format tapes. Let's look at these seven cassette subroutines in closer detail.

CALL 0212H DEFCAS: defines the drive (cassette) and turns motor ON. Content of A register specifies *which* cassette: A = 0 for cassette #1, or A = 1 for cassette #2; uses all registers, all saved.

CALL 01F8H CASOFF: turns cassette in operation OFF; uses A register, contents not saved.

CALL 0287H WRLDR: writes leader and A5H sync byte to cassette in operation; uses all registers, contents of A register not saved.

CALL 0296H RDLDR: reads leader and A5H sync byte and displays the two asterisks (**) in the upper-right-hand corner of the CRT video display upon completion; readies tape-reading subroutine for data input; uses all registers, saves all contents.

CALL 0264H WRBYTE: writes a byte of data contained in the A register to the cassette in operation; uses HL, BC, and DE register pairs in addition to the A register, all saved, except A register.

CALL 0235H RDBYTE: reads a byte of data from cassette into the A register; uses and saves all registers.

CALL 0314H RDADDR: reads two *consecutive* bytes from cassette and places them into the HL register pair in LSB/MSB order; uses HL and A registers only.

There is one other subroutine that you might find useful, BLSTAR (022CH). Although this subroutine does not control cassette operation, it provides a means for "blinking" the asterisks (stars) to indicate when reading or writing is occurring:

CALL 022CH BLSTAR: alternately "blinks" the right asterisk of the two asterisks displayed by RDLDR (0296H); uses A register only, not saved.

Timing

Normally, you do not have to worry about timing when using any of these cassette read or write subroutines, because the timing is automatic. All that you must do is ensure that they are called often enough to keep up with the cassette's 500-baud data rate.

How often is often enough? Well, if you call a cassette read or write subroutine too soon, nothing happens, because the subroutine simply *waits* until the timing is correct before performing any additional operations. But, if you call a cassette read or write subroutine too late, you'll end up with "scrambled" data, because the timing will be out-of-sync. Calling a cassette read subroutine too late results in missed data, because the data on the tape will have already passed the recorder's playback head by the time the subroutine is ready to accept data. This generally produces a "checksum error." Calling a cassette write subroutine too late results in a loss of synchronization, from which there is no recovery. When this occurs, your only recourse is to shorten the time between calls and do the recording over.

To gain some idea of how late is too late, you can divide the time available between data pulses by the time required to execute a typical instruction. The cassette's 500-baud data rate means that there are 2000 microseconds between *sync pulses,* but only 1000 microseconds between a *sync* pulse and a *data pulse.* And, as you will recall, the typical Z-80 instruction takes about 4 microseconds, so *approximately* 250 individual instructions can be executed between a *sync* pulse and a data pulse. Remember to *include* the number of instructions within the called cassette read or write ROM subroutines!

Unless you are processing data in real-time, timing is usually not a problem; it takes very little time to transfer data between the cassette read or write subroutines and the memory locations. However, when you are handling data in real-time and are attempting to perform lengthy calculations between reading and writing, you can run into problems. Usually this occurs when performing arithmetic or mathematic operations since they take quite a bit of time to execute. When this occurs, you must either simplify and shorten the processing, or *postpone* it until later.

Cassette Read (CDUMP) Example

The program shown in Example 7-1 makes use of three of the Level II BASIC's cassette ROM subroutines: DEFCAS (0211H), RDLDR (0296H) and RDBYTE (0235H); to define the cassette and turn the motor ON, read the leader and sync byte, and read a byte of data.

This program will read-in *any* cassette tape (BASIC program, BASIC data, SOURCE, or SYSTEM) and dump the tape contents, byte for byte, into memory beginning at address 6000H. Using this program, you can examine the actual format of a SYSTEM tape, such as T-BUG. To do this, first enter the example program into memory, and then clear memory locations 6000H-600AH by entering

Example 7-1. CDUMP Program.

Addr	Op-Code	Label	Mnemonic/ Operand	Remarks
5000	CD 12 02	CDUMP	CALL DEFCAS	;CASS#1 ON
5003	CD 96 02		CALL RDLDR	;LEADER & SYNC BYTE
5006	21 00 60		LD HL,6000	;DUMP ADDRESS
5009	CD 35 02	BYTE	CALL RDBYTE	;READ A BYTE
500C	77		LD (HL),A	;STORE IT
500D	23		INC HL	;NEXT ADDRESS
500E	C3 09 50		JP BYTE	;ANOTHER BYTE

zeros. Insert the T-BUG copy tape into the recorder and press the PLAY button; nothing should happen. Now, execute the program by jumping to its starting address. The cassette will start running. The appearance of the two asterisks (**) in the upper-right-hand corner of the display indicates that the leader and sync byte have been read. Wait about 20-25 seconds after the "stars" (asterisks) appear and then press the RESET button. Because the length of a cassette tape program is not always known, this simple program is designed to read "forever." Thus, you must use the RESET button to regain control after the program has been read-in. The cassette will now stop and control will be returned to BASIC.

To get back to T-BUG, type and enter SYSTEM and /17312. Now, let's examine the contents of memory locations 6000H-64C7H. At location 6000H you will find 5H, the SYSTEM format header byte. It is followed by the six ASCII values 54 42 55 47 20 20, which represent the filename T-BUG$\not{b}\not{b}$ ($\not{b}$ = blank, 20H). Next, you will see 3CH, the data header byte that marks the start of each data block. Then you will see the data length byte, 00H, indicating a data block length of 256 bytes. At addresses 6009H-600AH you will find the loading address, 4380H (first address in T-BUG), for *this* data block. At address 600BH you see the first byte of data, EDH, which is the first byte of the T-BUG program. To verify this, use the T-BUG M command and inspect the content of memory location 4380H. You will find that it does indeed contain EDH.

To find the "end" of the first data block, add 100H to the address of the first byte of data (600BH + 100 = 610BH). There you will find the last byte of data (B9H) in the first data block. It is followed by another data header byte (3CH), which signals the beginning of another data block. This sequence repeats every 261 bytes (256 bytes of data plus 6 bytes of format) until the program is complete. Note that the *last* data block can be *any* length from 1 to 256 bytes. This is done automatically by the program that creates the SYSTEM tape.

Skipping ahead to memory location 64C4H, you will find the last byte of data (FDH) in the T-BUG program. It is followed by the end-of-file (EOF) byte (78H) and the entry address bytes (4380H). CDUMP is a very useful program that you can use with any format tape. Try it with a short BASIC program tape and see if you can determine the format used by BASIC program cassette tapes.

Cassette Write (CWRITE) Example

The program shown in Example 7-2 illustrates how you can use the cassette ROM subroutines to write data onto a cassette tape. This example program, called CWRITE, performs a simple memory dump to a cassette tape, of the content of all memory locations

Example 7-2. CWRITE Program.

Addr	Op-Code			Label	Mnemonic/ Operand	Remarks
5000	CD	C9	01		CALL CLS	;CLEAR SCREEN
5003	CD	39	50	START	CALL ADDR	;GET STARTING ADDRESS
5006	E5				PUSH HL	;START TO STACK
5007	CD	39	50	END	CALL ADDR	;GET ENDING ADDRESS
500A	D1				POP DE	;START INTO DE
500B	ED	52		LENGTH	S3C HL,DE	;LENGTH=HL-DE
500D	23				INC HL	;LENGTH+1
500E	23				INC HL	;LENGTH+1
500F	D5				PUSH DE	;START TO STACK
5010	E5				PUSH HL	;LENGTH TO STACK
5011	CD	12	02	CASSON	CALL DEFCAS	;CASS#1 ON
5014	CD	87	02		CALL WRLDR	;WRITE LEADER & SYNC
5017	D1				POP DE	;LENGTH INTO DE
5018	7B				LD A,E	;LSB INTO A-REGISTER
5019	CD	64	02		CALL WRBYTE	;WRITE IT
501C	7A				LD A,D	;MSB INTO A-REGISTER
501D	CD	64	02		CALL WRBYTE	;WRITE IT
5020	E1				POP HL	;START INTO HL
5021	7D				LD A,L	;LSB INTO A-REGISTER
5022	CD	64	02		CALL WRBYTE	;WRITE IT
5025	7C				LD A,H	;MSB INTO A-REGISTER
5026	CD	64	02		CALL WRBYTE	;WRITE IT
5029	7E			DATA	LD A,(HL)	;DATA INTO A-REGISTER
502A	CD	64	02		CALL WRBYTE	;WRITE DATA
502D	23				INC HL	;NEXT ADDRESS
502E	1B				DEC DE	;LENGTH-1
502F	7B				LD A,E	;E INTO A-REGISTER
5030	B2				OR A,D	;E-OR-D
5031	20	F6			JR NZ,DATA	;NZ=ANOTHER BYTE
5033	CD	F8	01		CALL CASOFF	;CASSETTE OFF
5036	C3	A0	43	FINIS	JP T-BUG	;RETURN TO T-BUG
5039	CD	B3	1B	ADDR	CALL QINPUT	;GET ADDRESS
503C	D7				RST 10H	;
503D	CD	6C	0E		CALL ASCINT	;CONVERT TO INT
5040	2A	21	41		LD HL,4121H	;FPA1 INTO HL
5043	C9				RET	;RETURN

Table 7-2. CWRITE Cassette Tape Format

LEADER (256 zeros) & SYNC BYTE (A5H)
LSB } FILELENGTH
MSB }
LSB } STARTING ADDRESS
MSB }
XX...XX DATA BYTES

between a starting address and an ending address. The contents of these memory locations are written onto the cassette as a single, continuous file. CWRITE is NOT campatible with the SYSTEM format.

The format of CWRITE is shown in Table 7-2 and consists of the normal SYSTEM tape header (256 zeros) and sync byte (A5H), followed by a *two-byte* filelength (LSB/MSB), a load address (LSB/MSB), and the actual data file. No other format data, such as filename, checksum, or end-of-file, are used. The two-byte filelenght permits up to 65535 bytes to be recorded at one time *vs* the maximum number of 256 bytes used with the SYSTEM format.

CWRITE allows you to write onto cassette tape any number of bytes (up to 65535) from any portion of memory. To use CWRITE, set the cassette recorder to RECORD, execute CWRITE by jumping to its starting address (5000H) and enter the STARTING address followed by the ENDING address (both in decimal).

Upon execution, CWRITE clears the CRT video display and displays the "?" prompt, indicating that it is ready to accept the STARTING address. Then a second "?" prompt is displayed below the first, indicating that CWRITE is ready to accept the ENDING address. The cassette recorder will then start and the contents of memory from the starting address through the ending address are written to the cassette tape.

CWRITE functions in the following manner: First, the CRT is cleared by calling the ROM subroutine CLS (01C9H). Then subroutine ADDR is called which accepts the starting address input from the keyboard using the ROM subroutine QINPUT (1BB3H). RST 10H sets the C flag. ASCINT (0E6CH) converts the ASCII input from the keyboard to integer and stores the result in FPA1 (4121H-4122H) which is then loaded into the HL register pair. Upon return, HL is pushed onto the stack. This sequence is repeated for the ending address. The starting address is then retrieved from the stack and subtracted from the ending address, and 2 is added to the result to obtain the actual filelength. Then, both the starting address and the filelength are pushed onto the stack. The cassette drive is then specified and the motor is turned ON using the ROM subroutine DEFCAS (0212H), followed by the leader and sync bytes being written onto the tape using WRLDR (0287H). The filelength (followed by the starting address) is then retrieved from the stack and written (LSB first, MSB second) onto the tape. Next, the HL register pair, which contains the starting address, is used as a pointer to load the first byte of data from memory into the A register. Subroutine WRBYTE (0264H) is called to write the data byte onto the tape. The HL register pair is then incremented to the next memory location, and the filelength (DE register pair) is decremented by one. The A register is then loaded with the content of the E register, which is then ORed with the content of the D register. If the result *is not* zero, another byte of data is fetched from memory and recorded, otherwise subroutine CASOFF (01F8H) is called to turn the cassette OFF, and control is returned to T-BUG.

CWRITE allows you to write programs, data and contents of ROM to tape, but it's not much use without some means of getting the previously recorded information back again. So, let's investigate the use of the ROM subroutines to read tapes written by CWRITE.

CREAD Example

The program shown in Example 7-3, called CREAD, is the complement of CWRITE; it reads the tapes written by CWRITE.

Example 7-3. CREAD Program.

Addr	Op-Code			Label	Mnemonic/ Operand	Remarks
5000	CD	12	02		CALL DEFCAS	;CASS#1 ON
5003	CD	96	02		CALL RDLDR	;LEADER & SYNC BYTE
5006	CD	14	03		CALL RDADDR	;GET LENGTH IN HL
5009	E5				PUSH HL	;STORE ON STACK
500A	CD	14	03		CALL RDADDR	;GET START IN HL
500D	D1				POP DE	;LENGTH IN DE
500E	CD	35	02	DATA	CALL RDBYTE	;READ A BYTE
5012	77				LD (HL),A	;STORE IT
5013	1B				DEC DE	;LENGTH-1
5014	23				INC HL	;NEXT ADDRESS
5015	7B				LD A,E	;E INTO A-REG
5016	B2				OR A,D	;E-OR-D
5017	20	F6			JR NZ,DATA	;NZ=NOTHER DATA
5019	CD	F8	01		CALL CASOFF	;CASSETTE OFF
501C	C3	A0	43	END	JP T-BUG	;RETURN TO T-BUG

It uses the cassette ROM subroutines, DEFCAS (0212H), RDLDR (0296H), RDADDR (0314H), and RDBYTE (0235H), and functions as follows: The ROM subroutine DEFCAS (0212H) defines the cassette drive and turns the motor ON, and RDLDR (0296H) reads the leader and sync bytes, and displays the two stars on the CRT. Then, RDADDR (0314H) reads the two consecutive bytes that comprise the filelength from the tape and loads them into the HL register pair, from which they are pushed onto the stack for temporary storage. RDADDR (0314H) is called again to read the two consecutive bytes that comprise the starting address from the tape and loads them into the HL register pair. The filelength is popped from the stack into the DE register pair, and RDBYTE (0235H) reads the first byte of data from the tape into the A register. This is then stored in memory using the HL register pair (starting address) as a pointer. The DE register pair is then decremented by one and the HL register pair is incremented by one to point to the next memory location. Finally, a test is made to see if the contents of the DE register pair (filelength) is zero using the same technique described in CWRITE.

PRINTER

Unlike the cassette which is port-addressed, the printer is a memory-mapped I/O device. That is, it receives and transmits data by using a *16-bit memory address*. In the TRS-80, this address, called LPADDR (37E8H), is located above the BASIC ROMs, but below the keyboard, CRT video display memory, and read/write memory (RAM) addresses. Data are passed *both ways* through this address. The printer *outputs* the ASCII value 3FH ("?") *to* the TRS-80 when it is ready to accept another character. When the computer detects this "?" the content of the A register is output *to* the printer *through* the memory address, LPADDR (37E8H). This is called "handshaking."

The Level II BASIC ROMs contain three subroutines that can be used to control the printer. They are the *printer status* subroutine LPSTAT (05D1H), the *send byte* to printer subroutine LPBYTE (033BH), and the *send byte and update line position* subroutine LPNCHR (039CH). Let's look at each of these subroutines:

CALL 003BH LPBYTE: sends the content of the A register to the printer via the C register; maintains a *line count* (number of *lines* printed) at address 4029H; content of DE register pair destroyed.

CALL 039CH LPNCHR: sends the content of the A register to the printer; maintains a *line position* (number of *characters* printed so far) at address 409BH; content of DE register pair saved.

CALL 05D1H LPSTAT: tests the printer status at LPADDR (37E8H) and returns the result in the F register: printer is "ready" if the Z flag is set (Z = 1), or "busy" if reset (Z = 0).

The use of these subroutines will greatly simplify the task of writing assembly-language programs that utilize the printer for I/O. However, you do not always have to use these subroutines as you will see in the following example.

JKL LPRINT Printer Example

The program shown in Example 7-4 is called JKL LPRINT and illustrates how data can be read from the CRT video display and sent to the printer. It was written by Robert Richardson (author, *Disassembled Handbook for TRS-80*) and Bryan Mumford (co-author, *Inside Level II*) and provides the nondisk user with the ability to print out the content of the video display to the printer by simultaneously pressing the J, K, and L keys. This program makes use of many of the points that we have discussed; such as the multiple-key entry from the keyboard discussed in Chapter 4, and the exchanging of the working and complement registers to preserve their contents when interrupting normal program operation.

Enter the program using T-BUG, but DO NOT execute it! In order for the JKL program to function, we have to "link" it to some other operation or function that the TRS-80 performs frequently. Thus, the JKL program must be linked to the video software that updates the video display. Since the address of the video display subroutine is stored in memory locations 401EH and 401FH, the starting address of JKL must be stored in these memory locations. At the end of the JKL program, the Z-80 has to jump to the normal video display subroutine, so that the video display operations are performed normally. The actual linking of the JKL program to the video subroutine is done by using the M command and changing the contents of 401EH-401FH from 0458H to 7D00H, the beginning address of JKL.

That's all there is to it! JKL is now operational. It resides quietly in memory until you call it into action by simultaneously pressing the J, K, and L keys. When this is done, it directs the contents of the video memory to the printer to produce a hardcopy of whatever is on the screen (no graphics, however). You can terminate the printing at any time by simply pressing the SPACEBAR. Let's see how the JKL program operates.

First, the AF and AF′ and the working and complement registers are swapped to preserve the contents of the interrupted program. Then the address of the 'H I J K L M N O' keyboard row is tested for an input value of 28 (J + K + L = 4 + 8 + 16 = 28). If it IS NOT 28, then the registers are all swapped back, and control is passed back to the *video driver routine* (0458H). If the input value IS 28, program control continues as follows: The HL register pair is loaded with 3C00H, the first address of the video display memory. The DE register pair is loaded with 10H (16 decimal), the number of rows in the video display, and the BC register pair is loaded

Example 7-4. JKL LPRINT Program.

Addr	Op-Code			Label	Mnemonic/ Operand	Remarks
7D00	08				EX AF,AF'	;SWAP ALTERNATE REGISTER
7D01	D9				EXX	;SWAP ALTERNATE REGISTERS
7D02	3A	02	38		LD A,3802	;JKL KEYBOARD ROW
7D05	FE	1C			CP 1C	;JKL PRESSED=28 DECIMAL
7D07	20	38			JR NZ,RETURN	;RETURN NORM VIDEO NOT 0
7D09	21	00	3C		LD HL,3000	;1ST VIDEO CHARACTER MEM
7D0C	11	10	00		LD DE,0010	;NUMBER OF VIDEO LINES
7D0F	01	40	00	LOOP1	LD BC,0040	;VIDEO CHARACTERS/LINE
7D12	CD	31	7D	LOOP2	CALL TEST	;CHECK FOR PRINTER READY?
7D15	7E				LD A,(HL)	;1ST VIDEO CHARACTER TO A
7D16	32	E8	37		LD (37E8),A	;OUTPUT CHAR TO PRINTER
7D19	3A	40	38		LD A,(3840)	;KYBD LINE WITH SPACEBAR
7D1C	FE	80			CP 80	;SPACEBAR PRESSED = 128
7D1E	28	19			JR Z,OUT	;GOTO 'OUT' IF ZERO
7D20	23				INC HL	;ADD +1 TO VIDEO LOCATION
7D21	0D				DEC C	;MINUS 1 TO CHAR COUNTER
7D22	20	EE			JR NZ,LOOP2	;GOTO NEXT CHAR NOT ZERO
7D24	CD	31	7D		CALL TEST	;CHECK FOR PRINTER READY?
7D27	3E	0D			LD A,0D	;0DH = CARRIAGE RETURN
7D29	32	E8	37		LD (37E8),A	;DO IT!
7D2C	1D				DEC E	;MINUS 1 TO LINE COUNTER
7D2D	20	E0			JR NZ,LOOP1	;START ON NEXT LINE NOT 0
7D2F	18	08			JR OUT	;QUICK EXIT IF DONE
7D31	3A	E8	37	TEST	LD A,(37E8)	;PRINTER READY = 3FH = ?
7D34	FE	3F			CP 3F	;IS IT 3F?
7D36	20	F9			JR NZ,TEST	;LOOP TILL PRINTER READY
7D38	C9				RET	;RETURN — LINE AFTER CALL
7D39	CD	31	7D	OUT	CALL TEST	;IS PRINTER READY ?
7D3C	3E	0D			LD A,0D	;0DH = CARRIAGE RETURN
7D3E	32	E8	37		LD (37E8),A	;DO IT!
7D41	08			RETURN	EX AF,AF'	;RETURN ORIG REGISTER
7D42	D9				EXX	;RETURN ORIG REGISTERS
7D43	C3	48	04		JP 0458	;GOTO STD VIDEO ROUTINE

Courtesy Richcraft Engineering Ltd.

with 40H (64 decimal), the number of characters per line in the video display.

At this point, a call is made to the TEST subroutine within the

JKL program to check the status of the printer. If the printer is "ready" it outputs a "?" character (3FH) through the printer address, 37E8H, so program execution continues. However, if the printer is not ready, a loop is executed until it IS ready, and then program execution continues (hence a printer MUST be connected to the TRS-80 or "lock-up" will occur).

Program execution continues with a byte of data from the video display memory being sent to the printer, followed by the keyboard (address 3840H) being tested for an input value of 128 (spacebar). If this value is found, program control branches to the OUT subroutine within the JKL program where a *carriage return* (CR, 0DH) is sent to the printer to terminate the current line in print, and an exit is made back to the video driver routine after all of the registers have been swapped back. If the spacebar has NOT been pressed, another byte of data is copied from the video display memory into the A register and sent to the printer. This sequence continues until one of two conditions are met: (1) all of the video display memory contents have been sent to the printer, or (2) the spacebar is pressed and the printing is terminated.

As you can see, this program does not use any of the ROM subroutines mentioned earlier. Also, the manner in which the status of the printer is continually tested until a "ready" is received is worth noting. This technique will be necessary for just about *all* printer output programs that you may write. Using JKL lets you make a hardcopy of your assembly-language programs for both debugging purposes and for documentation—by simply pressing the JKL keys.

PORT I/O

There are no Level II BASIC ROM subroutines that directly support the input and output of data through the ports (except the cassette) because port I/O is *very* simple. However, the Z-80 instruction set does contain 24 instructions that perform port I/O —12 input port instructions and 12 output port instructions. These instructions control the passage of data between the ports and the Z-80's internal registers.

Although there are only 256 port *addresses* (00H-FFH), you really have 512 ports available, because each port can be addressed as either an input or as an output. Thus, each port may be addressed separately to provide 256 *input-only* ports and 256 *output-only* ports, or in combination to provide 256 *input/output* ports. The first port is port 0 (00H) and the last port is port 255 (FFH). In the TRS-80, only port 255 is used (for the cassette and video), leaving the remaining 255 unused port addresses for you to use as you wish.

To use the Z-80's ports, you will need additional hardware and interfacing to decode the digital address and control signals from the computer; however, the design and construction of this hardware and interfacing is beyond the scope of this book and will not be covered. For specific information on this subject, you are referred to *TRS-80 Interfacing, Books 1 and 2* (Howard W. Sams & Co., Inc., Indianapolis, IN 46268).

INPUT Instructions

The Z-80 instruction set contains 12 instructions that control the *input* of data from input ports. These instructions allow you to specify the movement of data using one of three addressing modes: immediate, register-indirect, and indirect. The Z-80's 12 input port instructions are listed in Table 7-3A; an explanation of each follows.

IMMEDIATE–IN A,*n*. In the immediate addressing mode, data are input from the port specified by the immediate byte, *n*, and placed in the A register. Only the A register can be addressed in this manner.

REGISTER-INDIRECT–IN *X*,(C). In the register-indirect addressing mode, data are input from the port specified by the content

Table 7-3. A) Z-80 Port Input and Output Instructions

A. Port INPUT Instruction ADDRESSING MODE:	MNEMONIC/OPERAND	REMARKS
IMMEDIATE	IN A,*n*	*n* = source port
REGISTER-INDIRECT	IN X,(C)	(C) = source port X = destination register (A, B, C, D, E, H, or L)
INDIRECT	INI (HL),(C)	input & inc HL, dec B
	INIR (HL),(C)	input & inc HL, dec B, repeat until B = 0
	IND (HL),(C)	input & dec HL, dec B
	INDR (HL),(C)	input & dec HL, dec B, repeat until B = 0
B. Port OUTPUT Instructions ADDRESSING MODE:	**MNEMONIC/OPERAND**	**REMARKS**
IMMEDIATE	OUT *n*,A	*n* = destination port
REGISTER-INDIRECT	OUT (C),X	X = source register (A, B, C, D, E, H, or L) (C) = destination port
INDIRECT	OUTI (C),(HL)	output & inc HL, dec B
	OTIR (C),(HL)	output & inc HL, dec B, repeat until B = 0
	OUTD (C),(HL)	output & dec HL, dec B
	OTDR (C),(HL)	output & dec HL, dec B, repeat until B = 0

of the C register and placed into the working register specified by *X*, where *X* may be either the A, B, C, D, E, H, or L register.

INDIRECT–IN*X* (HL),(C). In the *indirect addressing mode*, data are input from the port specified by the content of the C register pair. In *indirect port input addressing*, the HL register pair specifies *where* the data are to be stored, the B register specifies the *number* of bytes to be input, and the C register specifies the *source port*. Indirect addressing is used to load blocks of data from a port directly into memory. There are four different indirect port input instructions. These four instructions are specified by the *X* character as follows:

*I*ncrement (*X* = I) – INI (HL),(C). A byte of data is input from the port specified by the content of the C register and loaded into the memory location pointed to by the HL register pair; the HL register pair is incremented by one, and the B register is decremented by one.

*I*ncrement and *R*epeat (*X* = IR) – INIR (HL),(C). Data are automatically input from the port specified by the content of the C register and loaded into the memory locations pointed to by the HL register pair until the content of the B register reaches zero. After each data value is input, the HL register is incremented by one and the B register is decremented by one. The process is then repeated until the content of the B register is decremented to zero.

*D*ecrement (*X* = D) – IND (HL),(C). A byte of data is input from the port specified by the content of the C register and loaded into the memory location pointed to by the HL register pair; the HL register pair is then decremented by one, and the Be register is also decremented by one.

*D*ecrement and *R*epeat (*X* = DR) – INDR (HL),(C). Data are automatically input from the port specified by the content of the C register and loaded into the memory locations pointed to by the HL register pair until the content of the B register reaches zero. The HL register pair and the B register are each decremented by one, and the process is automatically repeated until the B register is decremented to zero.

OUTPUT Instructions

The Z-80 instruction set contains 12 output port instructions that complement the 12 input port instructions and control the output of data from the Z-80 to any one of the 256 possible output ports. Just as with the input port instructions, there are three addressing modes: immediate, register-indirect, and indirect. These instructions are listed in Table 7-3B; an explanation of each follows.

IMMEDIATE–OUT *n*,A. In the immediate addressing mode, the content of the A register is output to the port specified by the immediate byte, *n*.

REGISTER-INDIRECT–OUT (C),*X*. In the register-indirect addressing mode, the content of the working register specified by *X* (A, B, C, D, E, H, or L) is output to the port specified by the content of the C register.

INDIRECT–OUT*X* (C),(HL) and OT*XX* (C),(HL). In the *indirect addressing mode,* data are output from the memory location pointed to by the HL register pair to the port specified by the content of the C register. In *indirect port output addressing,* the HL register pair specifies the memory location where the data are to *come from,* the B register specifies the *number* of bytes to be output, and the C register specifies the *destination port.* The four indirect output port instructions are specified by the *X* and *XX* characters as follows:

> *I*ncrement (*X* = I) – OUTI (C),(HL). A byte of data is output from the memory location pointed to by the HL register pair to the port specified by the content of the C register, the HL register pair is incremented by one and the B register is decremented by one.
>
> *I*ncrement and *R*epeat (*XX* = IR) – OTIR (C),(HL). Data are automatically output from the memory locations pointed to by the HL register pair to the port specified by the content of the C register until the content of the B register reaches zero. The HL register is incremented by one, the B register is decremented by one, and the process automatically repeats until the B register is decremented to zero.
>
> *D*ecrement (*X* = D) – OUTD (C),(HL). A byte of data is output from the memory location pointed to by the HL register pair to the port specified by the content of the C register, the HL register pair and the B register are each decremented by one.
>
> *D*ecrement and *R*epeat (*XX* = DR) – OTDR (C),(HL). Data are automatically output from the memory locations pointed to by the HL register pair to the port specified by the content of the C register until the content of the B register reaches zero. After each output, the HL register pair and B register are each decremented by one, and the process is automatically repeated until the B register is decremented to zero.

Hypothetical Example

Because we do not have the necessary hardware to implement an example which uses the I/O ports, we must assume a hypothetical situation where such a "black box" exists. For example, our black box will be a temperature-sensing device which generates an 8-bit digital value in degrees (°C). Our task is to input and convert the data to degrees Fahrenheit (°F) and display the result on the CRT.

Example 7-5 shows a program that will input a byte of data from our hypothetical black box Celsius thermometer, convert that input to degrees Fahrenheit, and then display the result using many of the Level II BASIC ROM subroutines that you have studied.

Example 7-5. Hypothetical Port I/O Example.

```
INPUT    IN   A,00          ;GET TEMP FROM PORT 0
         LD   L,A           ;LSB=TEMP
         LD   H,00          ;MSB=00
         LD   DE,(XXXX)     ;GET 1.8 CONSTANT
         CALL INTMUL        ;TEMP*1.8 INTO FPA1
         LD   DE,(YYYY)     ;GET 32 CONSTANT
         CALL CINT          ;TEMP*1.8 TO INT
         LD   HL,(4121)     ;MOVE TO HL
         CALL INTADD        ;(TEMP*1.8)+32
         LD   A,L           ;MOVE TO A-REG
         CALL CS            ;CLEAR SCREEN
         CALL CRTBYT        ;DISPLAY IT
         JR   INPUT         ;DO IT AGAIN
```

Although only a hypothetical example, this program illustrates what you can do using the Z-80 port I/O instructions and some of the Level II BASIC ROM subroutines. The mathematical relationship between temperature measured in °C and °F is:

$$°C = .555(°F - 32) \text{ or } °F = 1.8(°C) + 32$$

REVIEW QUESTIONS

1. **Describe the difference between a memory-mapped I/O and a port-addressed I/O.**
2. **How many different ports can you address?**
3. **Theoretically, how many memory-mapped I/O devices can the Z-80 address?**
4. **What is the purpose of the 3CH byte in the SYSTEM cassette tape format?**
5. **Which cassette will be turned ON if the content of the A register is 01H when ROM subroutine DEFCAS (0212H) is called?**
6. **What is the difference between ROM subroutines 0235H and 0314H?**
7. **What happens if a cassette read or write ROM subroutine is called too soon?**
8. **What is the function of the printer's output of the value 3FH?**
9. **What occurs if the printer is sent data, but there is no printer connected?**
10. **What is the function of the B, C, and HL registers in the Z-80 port I/O instructions INIR/INDR and OTIR/OTDR?**

CHAPTER 8

Putting It All Together

Now that you have an understanding of the TRS-80's Z-80 microprocessor and its instruction set, of how to use T-BUG to do assembly-language programming, of the different areas of the memory map, and of how to use some of the Level II BASIC ROM subroutines—it is time that we discussed how to bring everything together and actually write assembly-language programs.

In this chapter we will discuss some of the tips, tricks, and techniques of writing assembly-language programs using the Level II BASIC ROM subroutines. At the end of this chapter, you will have covered everything that is needed to be able to write your own assembly-language programs on the Model I TRS-80 microcomputer.

THINK IN BASIC, WRITE IN ASSEMBLY . . .

Typically, the first stumbling block that you encounter when sitting down to write an assembly-language program for the first time is deciding where to begin. Obviously, you should start at the beginning, but what comes first? Well, you begin an assembly-language program just as you do a BASIC program. First, you *define* the problem. Second, you define the goal (are you looking for apples or for oranges?). And, *last,* you do the actual coding, or writing, of the program. Why? Because, if you don't understand the problem well enough to define it, you probably don't understand it well enough to solve it. Defining the problem gives you a starting point to work *from* and lets you inventory what you have to work with (and against). Defining the goal gives you an ending point to work *towards,* because often an "exact" answer is not possible or practical, and you need to know when "close enough" is sufficient.

Also, when there is NO answer, you need to decide when to "give up." All of these things must be considered before you sit down and actually do the program coding, because they will greatly influence how the program is written. Think of the program coding that you do as the "path" that connects the problem with the goal. Without a clear definition of both the problem and the goal, your program, like a meandering path, will have no defined starting point nor ending point and will just wander along aimlessly. So, you begin your assembly-language programming by *planning* what you want to accomplish and how you are to accomplish it.

OK, you've done your planning. You have the problem and the goal defined and now you are ready to do the coding. Now what? How do you translate your plans into the appropriate Z-80 instruction codes? Simple, you THINK IN BASIC and WRITE IN ASSEMBLY LANGUAGE! This is possible because the thought-processes that you developed while learning to program in BASIC are equally valid in assembly language. This is especially true when you consider that many of the ROM subroutines that you will be using are the same subroutines that implement the BASIC function!

But, what about the "other" stuff, the coding that isn't related to a BASIC subroutine? Which instructions do you use to do what? Again, rely upon your BASIC programming experience and you can't go wrong. For instance, earlier we compared a BASIC FOR-NEXT statement with its equivalent assembly-language coding. We said that the BASIC statement contained a *single*, multi-purpose instruction to the computer, while the equivalent assembly language coding consisted of *multiple*, special-purpose instructions to the computer. Thus, you can think out and draft your program in BASIC, and then break the BASIC up into its singular functions for converting to assembly language. Let's see how this works.

In the BASIC FOR-NEXT example, you supplied a starting number, an ending number, and a step size (if other than 1); and the Level II BASIC interpreter took it from there. BASIC takes your starting address, adds the step size to it, and compares the result with your ending number. When the result is equal to, or greater-than, the ending number, the computer exits from the loop and normal program execution continues. So, basically, what you have is a starting number, a means of incrementing (or decrementing) this number, a comparison, and a branch back to the instructions that are to be repeated.

Thus, for your assembly language program you would need: some convenient place to store the starting number (a register pair); an increment instruction; a way to compare the sum created in step 2 with the ending number; and a conditional branch (jump) back to whatever instructions that you want to be repeated.

Armed with this information you can look up the appropriate Z-80 instructions and op-codes using the information given in Chapter 2. For example, in Fig. 2-7, the 16-bit load instructions, you find that LD BC,nn (op-code 01 nn) will load an immediate two-byte value nn (the starting address) into the BC register pair. Then, in Fig. 2-12, the 16-bit arithmetic instructions, you find that INC BC (03H) will increment the content of the BC register pair. Next, you must look in Fig. 2-11, the 8-bit arithmetic and logic instructions, for instructions to perform the comparison, because there are NO 16-bit comparison instructions. Hence, you must use *two* 8-bit comparisons, one for the most-significant byte and one for the least-significant byte of the ending number. However, as you look through the 8-bit arithmetic and logic instructions you find that there are NO instructions that test the B or C register contents against an immediate byte of data. Instead, you must first load the LSB of the ending number into the A register, and then *compare the content of the C register with the content of the A register.* This process is then repeated using the MSB of the ending number and the B register contents. Finally, you must look in the jump instructions (Fig. 2-18) for an instruction to perform a conditional jump when the comparisons are nonzero. Such an instruction is JP NZ,nn (C2 nn). Now, you match the op-codes and hexadecimal operands for each instruction with the memory locations where you want the program to reside, and you've just written an assembly-language program. Later in this chapter we will discuss one of the Z-80's instructions that will enable you to perform this whole procedure using just two instructions.

RELATIVE VERSUS ABSOLUTE ADDRESSING

There are two ways to specify an address, *relative* and *absolute.* A relative address is one that is *specified by the number of memory locations that it is away from a reference memory location,* and thus is position independent. An example of relative addressing is when you refer to your neighbor's house as being "three houses down" from your house. The reference address is your house and the relative address is "three down" The number of spaces (addresses) away from the reference address is called the *displacement* and is denoted by the symbol e^{-2} to indicate that it is a signed, two's complement number. Displacements can be "positive" (forward) or "negative" (backward), and can be up to 127 spaces forward (e^{-2} = 7FH) or up to 128 spaces backward (e^{-2} = 80H). Table 8-1 lists the positive (forward) and negative (backward) displacements and their hexadecimal codes that are used with relative (and "indexed") addressing.

To use Table 8-1, you must know how the program counter (PC) operates. As you will recall, the PC always contains the address of the first byte of the *next* instruction to be executed. Because the jump-relative instructions are two bytes in length, the PC will automatically be advanced two bytes, and point to the first byte of the next instruction. Thus, you must begin your forward or backward counting *from the first byte of the NEXT instruction,* NOT from the current jump-relative instruction! This means that the *minimum forward jump* is *two,* not zero, because although the displacement may be zero (e^{-2} = 00H), the PC is already pointing to the next instruction ($0 + 2 = 2$). Conversely, the *minimum backward jump* again is *two,* not one, because jumps must always be made to the first byte of an *instruction,* NOT to data or operands. So, just to get back to the current jump-relative instruction you need a negative displacement of two (e^{-2} = FEH; $-2+2 = 0$). Thus, the *maximum forward jump* is 129 ($+127 + 2 = 129$) and the *maximum backward jump* is 126 ($-128 + 2 = 126$).

An *absolute address* is one that is specified by a 16-bit memory address within the memory map. Absolute addressing, as the name implies, is absolute or "fixed," such as your home address and the addresses of the Level II BASIC ROM subroutines. It is a simple and easily understood method of addressing, because the address

Table 8-1. Relative Displacements and Their Hexadecimal Values

Forward (00H-7FH)																	
↓MSB	0	1	2	3	4	5	6	7	8	9	A	B	C	D	E	F	←LSB
0	0	1	2	3	4	5	6	7	8	9	10	11	12	13	14	15	
1	16	17	18	19	20	21	22	23	24	25	26	27	28	29	30	31	
2	32	33	34	35	36	37	38	39	40	41	42	43	44	45	46	47	
3	48	49	50	51	52	53	54	55	56	57	58	59	60	61	62	63	
4	64	65	66	67	68	69	70	71	72	73	74	75	76	77	78	79	
5	80	81	82	83	84	85	86	87	88	89	90	91	92	93	94	95	
6	96	97	98	99	100	101	102	103	104	105	106	107	108	109	110	111	
7	112	113	114	115	116	117	118	119	120	121	122	123	124	125	126	127	

Backward (80H-FFH)																	
↓MSB	0	1	2	3	4	5	6	7	8	9	A	B	C	D	E	F	←LSB
8	128	127	126	125	124	123	122	121	120	119	118	117	116	115	114	113	
9	112	111	110	109	108	107	106	105	104	103	102	101	100	99	98	97	
A	96	95	94	93	92	91	90	89	88	87	86	85	84	83	82	81	
B	80	79	78	77	76	75	74	73	72	71	70	69	68	67	66	65	
C	64	63	62	61	60	59	58	57	56	55	54	53	52	51	50	49	
D	48	47	46	45	44	43	42	41	40	39	38	37	36	35	34	33	
E	32	31	30	29	28	27	26	25	24	23	22	21	20	19	18	17	
F	16	15	14	13	12	11	10	9	8	7	6	5	4	3	2	1	

is always the same no matter where you are in memory. However, as you will soon see, this is not always a desirable feature.

Relocatable Code

One of the greatest benefits of using relative addressing is the ability to write *relocatable code,* that is, programs that you can move anywhere in memory and still have operate properly without having to modify them first. T-BUG is NOT a relocatable program.

What makes a program "relocatable?" It is not the actual use of relative *vs* absolute addressing that determines whether or not a program is relocatable, but rather HOW the relative and absolute addressing are used. Relocatable code is made by using relative addressing for all addressing *within* the program, and using absolute addressing for all addressing *outside* the program. Thus, if your program needs to jump to the last byte *in* the program, you would use relative addressing. But, if it needs to jump to some memory address *outside* your program, such as to one of the ROM subroutines, you would use absolute addressing.

A shortcoming of using relative addressing is that normally you are limited to jumps of less than 129 bytes forward or 126 bytes backward. This limitation can be bypassed by using *relay jumps* within your programs. They will enable you to extend indefinitely the number of memory locations that you can relatively address. These relay jumps are simply unconditional jump relative (JR e^{-2}) instructions imbedded in your program that are accessed only by another jump relative instruction. This is accomplished by placing an unconditional jump relative instruction *immediately in front* of the relay jump relative instruction which directs "normal" program control "around" the relay jump relative instruction. Using this technique, you are no longer limited to jumps of only 129 spaces forward or 126 spaces backwards. Figure 8-1 illustrates this technique.

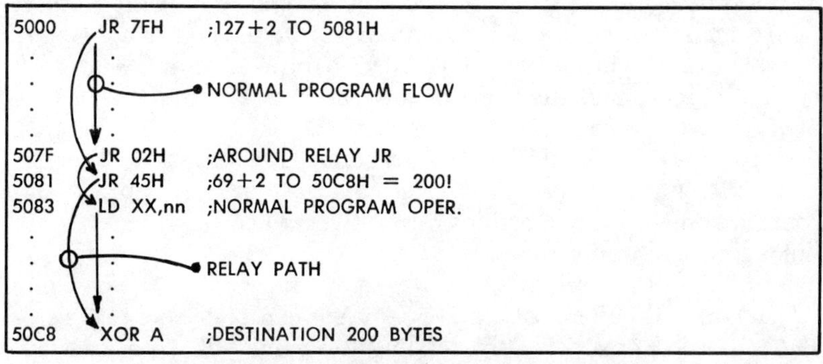

Fig. 8-1. Relay relative jump 200 bytes in a program.

Relocating Code

Now that you've mastered relocatable code, how do you actually move a program to take advantage of its relocatability? It's much easier than you expect. In fact, you need only four instructions!

To move a block of code (programs or data) from one location to another you need one instruction to load the HL register pair with the "source" address of the code to be moved. You need a second instruction to load the DE register pair with the "destination" address of memory (where the code is to be moved to). The third instruction must load the BC register pair with the "length" (number of bytes to be moved). The fourth instruction that you need is the most important. It is the LDIR (ED B0) instruction which automatically moves a block of data from memory pointed to by the HL register pair, to memory pointed to by the DE register until the BC register pair contents are decremented to zero. Example 8-1 illustrates how you might copy T-BUG from its location in low memory into high memory (although you must remember that T-BUG will NOT operate properly when relocated).

Example 8-1. Program to Move T-BUG from Low Memory to High Memory Using LDIR.

Addr	Op-Code	Label	Mnemonic/Operand	Remarks
5000	21 80 43	SOURCE	LD HL,4380H	;START OF T-BUG
5003	11 00 60	DESTIN	LD DE,6000H	;HIGH MEMORY
5006	01 FF 05	LENGTH	LD BC,05FFH	;HOW MANY BYTES
5009	ED B0		LDIR	;DO IT
500B	C3 A0 43		JP 43A0H	;BACK TO T-BUG LOW

LDIR produces a *forward block move,* where the destination address is always greater than the last address of the source address. But, if the destination address is NOT greater than the last address of the source program, you must use a different instruction; otherwise the first-moved instructions will overwrite the end of the source program, destroying a part of it. When you need to move a block of data only a short distance, or any distance *less* that the length of the source program, you use a *backward block move.* For this, you use the LDDR (ED B8) instruction. Here, you load the HL and DE register pairs with the *last address* of the "source" and "destination" memory locations, respectively. The BC register again holds the "length," or byte count.

You can also use these block move instructions (especially LDIR) to "fill" blocks of memory with a constant, such as "zeroing" a portion of memory by loading the value 00H into each address. Or, you can "paint" the CRT screen white by loading the graphic character BFH into each of the CRT video memory addresses as shown in Example 8-2. You can also use these instructions to write your own memory test program, using LDIR to fill each

Example 8-2. Program to "Paint" CRT Video Display White Using LDIR and BFH Graphics Character.

Addr	Op-Code	Label	Mnemonic/Operand	Remarks
5000	21 00 3C	SOURCE	LD HL,3C00H	;START OF VIDEO MEM.
5003	11 01 3C	DESTIN	LD DE,3C01H	;NEXT LOCATION
5006	01 FF 03	LENGTH	LD BC,03FFH	;VIDEO MEMORY LENGTH
5009	36 BF		LD (HL),BFH	;GRAPHICS CHARACTER
500B	ED B0		LDIR	;DO IT
500D	C3 A0 43		JP 43A0H	;BACK TO T-BUG

memory location and LDDR to move backward checking/verifying the contents.

TIPS, TRICKS, AND TECHNIQUES
(. . . things I wish they'd told me before . . .)

The second area of assembly-language programming that will probably cause you problems has to do with the idiosyncrasies of both the Z-80 microprocessor and the TRS-80 hardware. Some things they just don't tell you, you have to find them out for yourself the hard way, usually by trial-and-error. The purpose of this section is to (hopefully) save you from having to repeat the same errors and problems that have plagued others. Unfortunately, not every stumbling block that you might encounter can be covered, but Chart 8-1 lists some of the more useful bits of information that you will find helpful. The chart lists some of the problems that you might encounter with the Z-80 as well as some of the problems due to the TRS-80 hardware, such as the "hardwiring" of the HALT (76H) instruction to the RESET pin on the CPU. Referring to this chart when you run into a programming problem can save you a lot of frustration and irritation.

THE STACK

The majority of the problems that you are likely to encounter will probably be related in some way or another to the improper use of the PUSH and POP instructions, especially when they are used within subroutines. The trick here is to treat these instructions as you would the parentheses "( )" in BASIC and *always* match a PUSH instruction with a POP instruction, and *vice versa!* If you don't, you end up with "dangling" information on the stack which can cause no end of trouble.

Chart 8-1. Tips, Tricks and Techniques (. . . things I wish they'd told me before . . .)

- (Z-80) INC and DEC instructions DO NOT affect the CARRY (C) flag! Only the ADD, ADC, SUB, and SBC instructions affect the status of the C flag.
- (Z-80) You CANNOT decrement a register pair (BC, DE, HL, SP, IX, or IY) to zero in a loop using JP NZ,nn, because this operation does not affect any of the status flags! Instead, use the technique of loading one byte into the A register and ORing the other byte with it to determine if the content of the register pair is zero.
- (Z-80) The AND, OR, and XOR instructions always reset the C flag, performing a complement to the SCF instruction.
- (Z-80) The result of SBC HL,rr is returned in HL (HL-rr→HL). Use the OR A instruction before SBC HL,rr to reset the C flag if necessary (rr = BC, DE, HL, or SP).
- (Z-80) The result of ADD IX,rr and ADD IY,rr is returned in IX and IY, respectively (rr = BC, DE, IX, IY, or SP). Note, the HL register pair is NOT included.
- (Z-80) To move data between index registers IX and IY and one of the register pairs (BC, DE, HL, or SP) use the PUSH and POP instructions:

```
PUSH   IX (or IY)
POP    rr (where rr = any register pair)
```

- (Z-80) DJNZ e^{-2} functions like an assembly-language version of the BASIC FOR-NEXT statement. The B register holds the number of loops to be executed. It is a jump relative instruction.
- (Z-80) The PUSH and POP instructions should always be matched (like BASIC's parentheses "( )"). There are exceptions to this, but you *must* know what you're doing to do so.
- (TRS-80) The HALT (76H) instruction no longer suspends CPU operation, because it has been "hardwired" to the RESET pin of the Z-80 CPU. It now causes a complete system reset!
- (TRS-80) FFH is the op-code for RST 56 at memory location 0038H and is the entry point for interrupts. It causes a jump to 4012H to occur (non-DOS) where an EI instruction enables the interrupts and a RET instruction returns control to the point of interruption.
- (TRS-80) Level II BASIC does not use the alternate (complement) register set except within a subroutine as temporary storage.
- (TRS-80) Level II BASIC uses the IX register only 21 times, and does not use the IY register at all.
- (TRS-80) Level II BASIC uses the register pairs in the following manner: HL as a pointer to characters in BASIC text and input strings, DE as a pointer to line numbers, and BC as byte storage or byte counter.
- (TRS-80) There are *at least* four different Level II BASIC ROMs. Use the following BASIC program to determine which one you have:

```
10  FOR I =11264 TO 12287:V=PEEK(I):S=S+V:NEXTI:X=S/16
20  A=(X-FIX(X))*16:Y=FIX(X)/16:B=(Y-FIX(Y))*256
30  PRINT (A+B)
```

  If the result is 176, it is ROM 1.0; 142 = ROM 1.1; 10 = ROM 1.2; 162 = ROM 1.3.
- (Z-80) XOR A will "zero" the content of A, but XOR B, XOR C, etc., WILL NOT zero the B or C registers! They are being XORed with the content of the A register, not with themselves (as in the case of XOR A).
- (Z-80) (1234H) is NOT the same as 1234H! (1234H) means use the "content of" 1234H; 1234H alone is only an address!

Passing Data to a Subroutine

One of the times when stack operations can become a problem is when you attempt to pass data *to* a subroutine using the stack. To understand why this is so, you must recall how the SP is used when a call is made to a subroutine from the main program. When a call instruction is encountered, the PC is already pointing to the first byte of the next instruction to be executed *in the main program.* Thus, as the call is executed, the content of the PC register is pushed onto the stack for storage and the call address is loaded into the PC. Thus, if you had pushed a data variable onto the stack, it is no longer at the top of the stack but rather one down from the top. The address where the main program will "resume" operation upon returning from the called subroutine is on the top of the stack!

So, how do you get the *data* off of the stack without losing the "return" address for the PC? This can be accomplished by using the Z-80 instruction that exchanges the content of HL and the top of the stack: EX (SP),HL (E3H). Instead of simply popping the data from the stack twice (once gets you the PC, second gets the data), you pop the PC content from the top of the stack into the HL register pair first. This brings the data you are really after to the top of the stack. Then, you use the EX (SP),HL instruction to swap the content of HL (the PC "resume" address) with the top of the stack (the data).

```
        PUSH  DE       ;DATA ONTO STACK
        CALL  DIVIDE
         .     .
         .     .
         .     .
DIVIDE  CALL  XYZ
        POP   HL       ;PC INTO HL
        EX    (SP),HL  ;DATA INTO HL, PC BACK TO STACK
         .     .
         .     .
         .     .
        RET
```

This way, you never lose the PC "resume" address from its correct position *at the top of the stack!* And, this technique is not limited to being used just once, it can be used as often as necessary in the subroutine.

Returning Data from a Subroutine

If passing data *to* a subroutine can cause problems, then it stands to reason that passing data *from* a subroutine will cause you problems too. As before, the problem lies with keeping the PC "resume" address at the top of the stack so that when control passes back to the main program from the subroutine, the correct address will be retrieved from the stack and loaded back into the PC. And, again, you can use the EX (SP),HL instruction to solve this problem. Instead of just pushing the data onto the stack (and "burying" the PC "resume" address in the process), you first load the data to be returned into the HL register pair and then use the EX (SP),HL instruction to exchange the content of HL and the top of the stack. This is then followed by a PUSH HL instruction.

```
        CALL   DIVIDE
        POP    DE       ;RETRIEVE DATA
         .      .
         .      .
         .      .
DIVIDE  CALL   XYZ
         .      .
         .      .
         .      .
        LD     HL,DATA  ;DATA INTO HL
        EX     (SP),HL  ;DATA ONTO STACK, PC INTO HL
        PUSH   HL       ;PC BACK TO TOP OF STACK
         .      .
         .      .
         .      .
        RET
```

What this does is load your data into the HL register pair, then exchange HL and the top of the stack (PC "resume" address). This leaves your data at the top of the stack and the PC "resume" address in HL, which is taken care of by the PUSH HL instruction so that it is returned to its correct position at the top of the stack.

Doesn't that tend to "bury" your data below the PC "resume" address? Not really, because as soon as the RET instruction in the called subroutine is encountered, the PC "resume" address is popped from the stack and loaded back into the PC register so that the main program can continue from the point where the call to the subroutine was made. This then brings the *last* data that you pushed onto the stack from within the subroutine to the top of the stack (remember the LIFO operation of the stack). You can use this technique as often as necessary within a subroutine to transfer more than one variable from the subroutine to the stack.

FOUR MORE REGISTERS

Another problem you will undoubtedly face is not having enough registers. That's right, not enough! This problem results from the possibility of conflict of use when using the Level II BASIC ROM subroutines. You have to be careful that you use a register in your program that won't interfere with, or be overwritten by, the subroutine that you are calling. Needless to say, this usually doesn't leave you with many registers to use. But, there is a solution to this problem, simply use the IX and IY registers.

As noted in Chart 8-1, Level II BASIC only uses the IX register a few times, and *does not use the IY register at all!* The IX register is only used 21 times (5 times at 03C3H-03DEH, 9 times at 0458H-04BCH and 7 times at 059AH-05D0H), so the chances of a register-use conflict are very small, except when calling the cassette and video display driver subroutines.

What does this mean to you? It means that there are *two more* 16-bit registers that you can use. But, you say that you would rather have a couple of 8-bit registers instead? No problem, simply use the proper instructions and you can use the IX and IY registers as *four separate one-byte registers!* There are no instructions to access the high and low bytes of the IX and IY registers, but they do exist! There are undocumented Z-80 instructions that enable you to both load and retrieve 8-bit data into either the "high" or "low" bytes of both the IX and IY registers. Using these undocumented instructions will give you *four more registers!*

To use these undocumented instructions you must "derive" the proper instructions from the existing instructions. These derived, undocumented instructions will always have two bytes. The first byte will always be either DD (IX register) or FD (IY register). The second byte will always be one of the 8-bit register-to-register instructions. When using these undocumented instructions, the H

Table 8-2. Undocumented IX and IY Index Register Instructions

	Source Register:						
Destination:	**A**	**B**	**C**	**D**	**E**	**H**	**L**
IX "high" (XXXXXXXX - - - - - - - -) 15 0	DD 67	DD 60	DD 61	DD 62	DD 63		DD 65
IX "low" (- - - - - - - - XXXXXXXX) 15 0	DD 6F	DD 68	DD 69	DD 6A	DD 6B	DD 6C	
IY "high" (XXXXXXXX - - - - - - - -) 15 0	FD 67	FD 60	FD 61	FD 62	FD 63		FD 65
IY "low" (- - - - - - - - XXXXXXXX) 15 0	FD 6E	FD 68	FD 69	FD 6A	FD 6B	FD 6C	

Note: DD 65 = load IX "low" into IX "high", or LD **IXH,IXL.**
DD 6C = load IX "high" into IX "low", or LD **IXL,IXH.**
FD 65 = load IY "low" into IY "high", or LD **IYH,IYL.**
FD 6C = load IY "high" into IY "low", or LD **IYL,IYH.**

and L registers become the passages that enable you to separately address the "high" or "low" byte of the IX and IY registers. Thus, to load an 8-bit value from the C register into the "low" byte of the IY register, you would select the LD L,C instruction (69H). The first byte of this undocumented instruction would be FD (IY register) and the second byte would be 69H (LD L,C), or FD 69. Table 8-2 lists some of the more useful undocumented IX and IY instructions. As you see, you can even load the content of the "low" byte into the "high" of the same register, and *vice versa*. However, you cannot directly move an 8-bit value from one index register to another, this transfer can only be done using all 16 bits. Also, you cannot move an immediate byte of data into one of these 8-bit IX or IY registers. To do this, you must first load it into one of the general-purpose registers, and then move it into the desired IX or IY register. You will probably find these "hidden" registers most useful as additional internal data storage; they don't have to be swapped back and forth with each subroutine.

REAL TIME

If you are just bringing data into the TRS-80 and then sending it directly to the cassette in a "data logging" mode, you will probably never have any timing problems. However, if the data must be manipulated before being recorded (such as from °C to °F), there is a good possibility that you will run into timing problems. The reason for this lies in the amount of time available between sync pulses and data pulses (1000 microseconds) using the cassette read/write subroutines. Unless you are prepared to *write your own* timing loops and delays, you are going to have to use the standard TRS-80 500 baud cassette data rate (unless you have a Model III which accepts both 500 and 1500 baud data rates). This isn't too bad, unless your application is one that requires a large amount of arithmetic or mathematical calculations. As you can see from Table 8-3 which lists typical execution times for various arithmetic and mathematic functions, some of these functions CANNOT be used in real-time processing because they take too long to execute.

If, however, your application does require arithmetic or mathematical calculations before the data can be used, you are then faced with two possibilities. The first, and easiest, approach is to simply record the *raw*, unprocessed data in real time and then perform the necessary calculations later, when you are not under a time limit. This is called "post processing."

The second, and more complicated, approach is to input the data for a period of time (called the "sample time") and store it in memory. Then, for another period of time (called the "process time") each datum is retrieved from memory and processed as necessary with the result being stored in its original memory location. Finally, when all the processing is done, the conditioned data are recorded from memory directly to the cassette. This is called "batch" or "sample processing." Each approach has its own merits and shortcomings. Let your specific application determine which one

Table 8-3. Arithmetic and Mathematic Function Execution Times

Arithmetic			
Function	**INT**	**SGL**	**DBL**
(+) ADDITION	130 μs	630 μs	1300 μs
(−) SUBTRACTION	210 μs	1300 μs	1300 μs
(*) MULTIPLICATION	900 μs	2200 μs	2200 μs
(/) DIVISION	5100 μs	4800 μs	42 ms!
Mathematic			
TRIGONOMETRIC	SIN(X)	25 ms	
	COS(X)	25 ms	
	ATN(X)	27 ms	
	TAN(X)	54 ms	
LOGARITHMIC/EXPONENTIAL	LOG(X)	19 ms	
	EXP(X)	28 ms	
	SQR(X)	48 ms	
	X↑Y	50 ms	

that you use, but remember that raw data can always be "reprocessed" if the results aren't what you expected. Processed data can be in error due to one of two sources, the data itself, or from faulty (improper) processing. Trying to determine which one is the source of the error can get very frustrating! So, as a rule-of-thumb, "keep it simple" and use post-processing whenever possible. It is simpler to use and much easier to debug.

LINKING BASIC WITH ASSEMBLY

Now that you know how to write your own assembly-language programs, how do you connect them with your BASIC programs? This is done using the USR(N) function in Level II BASIC, and is covered on pages 8/8 through 8/12 of the *Level II BASIC Reference Manual, 2nd Edition.*

As you know, the USR (N) function permits the passing of a two-byte, signed integer variable between BASIC and a machine-language program resident in memory. To use this function, you must first load the starting address of your assembly-language program object code into memory locations 408EH-408FH (LSB/MSB). This can be done either from BASIC using the POKE statement, or in assembly-language using an instruction such as LD (408E),HL, where HL was previously loaded with the starting address of your program.

To access the assembly-language program from BASIC, you now simply place the statement X=USR(N) in your BASIC program. To return control from the assembly-language program back to BASIC, terminate the assembly-language program with RET (C9H).

Passing Data From BASIC To USR

To pass a variable from BASIC to an assembly-language subroutine using the USR(N) function, the variable (N) must be in the range −32768 through +32767 inclusive, or an error will occur. To receive this variable in assembly language, your assembly-language subroutine must have the instruction CALL 0A7FH at or very near its beginning. The variable will be in the HL register pair in integer (INT) format.

Passing Data From USR To BASIC

To pass a variable back to BASIC from the assembly-language subroutine using the USR(N) function, you place the variable in the HL register pair and execute a JP 0A9AH instruction. The signed integer will be passed to BASIC through USR(N) to the BASIC variable X like this:

```
X = USR(N)  HL
```

Although only one variable can be passed at a time, any number of variables can be handled in this manner.

You are not restricted to using only one assembly-language program if you use the POKE command to load memory location 408EH-408FH with each new program's starting address *before* invoking USR(N), such as:

```
100  IF A<B THEN LSB=XX1: MSB=YY1:GOTO 130
110  IF A=B THEN LSB=XX2: MSB=YY2:GOTO 130
120  LSB=XX3:MSB=YY3        'REM  A>B
130  POKE 16526,LSB:POKE 16527,MSB
 .   .
 .   .
 .   .
```

where XX1 and YY1 are the decimal equivalents of the LSB and MSB of the starting address of the assembly-language program to be called. Remember that if you invoke the USR(N) function but do not plan on passing (or receiving) a variable, you still must put some value in for N, called a "dummy argument."

Keeping Machine Language Programs in "Low" Memory

Although the Radio Shack books tell you that in order to work correctly your machine-language programs must reside in "high" memory, above BASIC, this is not really true. There is a way to keep programs that aren't relocatable and load into low memory (T-BUG!), and have the Level II BASIC interpreter begin loading the BASIC program *after* the assembly-language program.

To "protect" an assembly-language program (or series of programs) already residing in low memory, you just load memory locations 40A4H-40A5H with an address *one greater* than the ending address of the assembly-language program(s), and terminate the last program with 00H. There are two reasons why this is possible. First, BASIC programs are inherently relocatable. And, second, BASIC programs are loaded into memory beginning at the address held in memory locations 40A4H-40A5H. Upon initialization, Level II BASIC loads these locations with 42E9H (higher with disks). The only "setup" that is necessary is that the address immediately preceding the first byte of the BASIC program be 00H. That's why you end the assembly-language program with 00H. Now, when you load your BASIC program from cassette into memory, it will load *after* your resident assembly-language program!

Let's see how this works with T-BUG. First, use the M command and change the content of 40A4H-40A5H from 42E9H to 4981H, an address one more than the 00H byte that must be placed at the end of T-BUG. Now, load in any short BASIC program that you have using the normal CLOAD procedure, but do not RUN the program yet. After the BASIC program is loaded, return to T-BUG by typing SYSTEM and then /17312. Now, look at the contents of memory beginning at 4980H on. You will see the BASIC program! And, T-BUG works fine. Now you know how to keep T-BUG in memory at the same time that you are writing BASIC programs which use USR(N) and assembly-language programs! T-BUG is then available to debug the assembly-language object code(s) and lets you use T-BUG to write SYSTEM *and* BASIC programs to cassette!

Yes, you CAN save BASIC programs on cassette using the SYSTEM format. However, to do so, you must know both the *starting address* and the *ending address* of the BASIC program. The starting address is the address that you earlier placed in memory locations 40A4H-40A5H. The ending address is automatically calculated during the CLOAD process and is stored at 40F9H-40FAH. Thus, to use T-BUG's PUNCH command to write a BASIC program to cassette in SYSTEM format, you can find the starting address at 40A4H-40A5H and the ending address at 40F9H-40FAH. This is illustrated in Table 8-4.

Table 8-4. Addresses Used to Save a BASIC Program Using SYSTEM Format

Beginning address, *aaaa*:	(40A4H-40A5H)
Ending address, *bbbb*:	(40F9H-40FAH)
Autostart address, cccc:	43A0H (assuming T-BUG + BASIC)
Filename, XXXXXX;	------

You can also record *both* the assembly-language program *and* the BASIC program together as a single file by using the beginning of the assembly-language program as the starting address (*aaaa*) and the end of the BASIC program as the ending address (*bbbb*). But, when this is done, you must manually load the starting and ending address into memory location 40A4H-40A5H and 40F9H-40FAH, respectively, before the BASIC program can be RUN.

A PROGRAM TO WRITE A SYSTEM TAPE

Level II BASIC contains a subroutine to *read* SYSTEM tapes (02B2H), but there are NO subroutines to *write* a SYSTEM tape. For this, you must use either T-BUG's PUNCH command or the Editor/Assembler's ASSEMBLE command. Example 8-3 is a program to write a SYSTEM tape that you can use alone, or within your own assembly-language programs. Although it is NOT relocatable "as is," this program can be used anywhere in memory with only a few changes. These changes will be noted as we discuss how the program works.

The program shown in Example 8-3 is called SYSWR. It loads into memory at 5000H-5088H and uses four external areas of memory, one to hold the filename, one to hold the starting address, one to hold the ending address and one to hold the entry address. The filename is stored in memory locations 6000H-6005H, but can be relocated to any location by changing the source-operands in the instructions at addresses 5000H and 500AH. The starting address is stored at memory locations 4FFAH-4FFBH, the ending address

Example 8-3. SYSWR, a Program to Write SYSTEM Format Cassette Tapes.

Addr	Op-Code	Label	Mnemonic/Operand		Remarks
5000	21 00 60		LD	HL,6000H	;FILENAME BUFFER
5003	06 06		LD	B,06H	;6 CHARACTERS
5005	36 20	FILL	LD	(HL),20H	;FILL W/BLANK SPACES
5007	23		INC	HL	;NEXT ADDRESS
5008	10 FB		DJNZ	FILL	;DO 6 TIMES
500A	FD 21 00 60		LD	IY,6000H	;IY=FILENAME POINTER
500E	AF		XOR	A	;CASSETTE #1
500F	CD 12 02		CALL	DEFCAS	;DEFCAS & MOTOR ON

```
5012  2A FC 4F       END     LD    HL,(4FFCH)   ;HL=ENDING ADDRESS
5015  ED 5B FA 4F    START   LD    DE,(4FFAH)   ;DE=STARTING ADDRESS
5019  AF                     XOR   A            ;CLEAR A REGISTER
501A  ED 52          LENGTH  SBC   HL,DE        ;LENGTH=HL-DE
501C  23                     INC   HL           ;LENGTH+1
501D  CD 87 02       LDRSYN  CALL  WRLDR        ;WR LEADER & SYNC BYTE
5020  3E 55                  LD    A,55H        ;SYSTEM FORMAT HEADER
5022  CD 64 02       SYSFOR  CALL  WRBYTE       ;WRITE "55H"
5025  06 06                  LD    B,06H        ;6 CHARACTERS
5027  FD 7E 00       FILNAM  LD    A,(IY+00H)   ;IY=FILENAME
502A  CD 64 02               CALL  WRBYTE       ;WRITE A CHARACTER
502D  FD 23                  INC   IY           ;NEXT CHARACTER
502F  10 F6                  DJNZ  FILNAM       ;DO 6 TIMES
5031  25             LOOP    DEC   H            ;DATA BLOCK LOOP
5032  FA 43 50*              JP    M,CLEARA     ;LESS THAN 256 BYTES?
5035  3E 3C                  LD    A,3CH        ;DATA BLOCK HEADER
5037  CD 64 02               CALL  WRBYTE       ;WRITE "3CH"
503A  AF                     XOR   A            ;DATA BLOCK LENGTH=00H
503B  CD 64 02               CALL  WRBYTE       ;WR "00H" (256 BYTES)
503E  CD 70 50*              CALL  DATBLK       ;DATA BLOCK SUBROUTINE
5041  18 EE                  JR    LOOP         ;DO IT AGAIN
5043  AF             CLEARA  XOR   A            ;CLEAR A REGISTER
5044  BD                     CP    L            ;LENGTH=0?
5045  28 0C                  JR    Z,EOF        ;IF YES THEN EOF
5047  3E 3C                  LD    A,3CH        ;DATA BLOCK HEADER
5049  CD 64 02               CALL  WRBYTE       ;WRITE "3CH"
504C  7D                     LD    A,L          ;DATA<256 BYTES?
504D  CD 64 02               CALL  WRBYTE       ;WR DATA LENGTH
5050  CD 70 50*      EOF     CALL  DATBLK       ;DATA BLK & CHECKSUM
5053  3E 78          EOF     LD    A,78H        ;EOF=78H
5055  CD 64 02               CALL  WRBYTE       ;WRITE "78H"
5058  3A FE 4F       ENTRYL  LD    A,(4FFEH)    ;LSB ENTRY ADDRESS
505B  CD 64 02               CALL  WRBYTE       ;WRITE LSB
505E  3A FF 4F       ENTRYH  LD    A,(4FFFH)    :MSB ENTRY ADDRESS
5061  CD 64 02               CALL  WRBYTE       ;WRITE MSB
5064  CD F8 01               CALL  CASOFF       ;CASSETTE OFF
5067  C9                     RET
5070  47             DATBLK  LD    B,A          ;NUMBER DATA BYTES
5071  7B                     LD    A,E          ;LSB LOAD ADDRESS
5072  CD 64 02               CALL  WRBYTE       ;WRITE LSB LOAD ADDR.
5075  7A                     LD    A,D          ;MSB LOAD ADDRESS
5076  CD 64 02               CALL  WRBYTE       ;WRITE MSB LOAD ADDR.
5079  83                     ADD   A,E          ;A=D+E OF LOAD AD-
                                                 DRESS
507A  4F                     LD    C,A          ;A INTO C=CHECKSUM
507B  1A             GETBYT  LD    A,(DE)       ;GET A BYTE OF DATA
507C  CD 64 02               CALL  WRBYTE       ;WRITE DATA
507F  81                     ADD   A,C          ;ADD TO CHECKSUM
5080  4F                     LD    C,A          ;UPDATE CHECKSUM
5081  13                     INC   DE           ;NEXT DATA
5082  10 F7                  DJNZ  GETBYT       ;DO 'TIL B REG=0
5084  79             CHKSUM  LD    A,C          ;CHECKSUM INTO A REG.
5085  CD 64 02               CALL  WRBYTE       ;WRITE CHECKSUM
5088  C9                     RET                ;RETURN
```

Note: *Denotes what must be changed to operate properly if relocated.

is stored at memory locations 4FFCH-4FFDH and the entry address is stored at memory locations 4FFEH-4FFFH. You can change these to whatever locations you wish by changing the source-operands in the instructions at memory locations 5012H (ending address), 5015H (starting address) and 5058H and 505EH (entry address). SYSWR functions in the following manner.

First, the buffer to hold the filename is defined (6000H-6005H) and the B register is loaded with the number of characters (6) in the filename, and this buffer is filled with blank spaces (20H). Then, the IY register is loaded with the address (6000H) of the buffer holding the filename. The A register is cleared and cassette #1 is defined using DEFCAS (0212H) and the motor turned ON. The ending address is loaded from 4FFCH-4FFDH into the HL register pair and the starting address is loaded from 4FFAH-4FFBH into the DE register pair. Then, the program "length" is determined by subtracting the starting address (DE) from the ending address (HL). One is added to the result to establish the actual program length.

At this point, the leader and sync byte are written to the cassette using WRLDR (0287H). The SYSTEM tape format header byte (55H) is loaded into the A register and written to the cassette using WRBYTE (0264H). The B register is loaded with the number of characters (6) that are to be written to the cassette as the filename and the IY register is pointed to the buffer at 6000H containing the filename. The DJNZ instruction executes the loop which fetches the six filename characters and writes them to the cassette using WRBYTE.

After the filename has been written, a short subroutine is entered which writes the data block header (3CH) and block length (00H) for all of the data blocks, except the last one. The actual fetching of data from memory, calculation of the checksum, and the writing of data to the cassette are performed in the subroutine DATBLK (5070H-5088H).

When the number of bytes of data remaining to be recorded is less than 256, control jumps to CLEARA (5043H) and the actual number of bytes is recorded as the data block length instead of 00H. The last data block is then recorded to the cassette and the end-of-file (78H) byte and entry address (LSB/MSB) are recorded. Then, CASOFF (01F8H) turns the cassette OFF and control is returned to the calling program.

SYSWR has been included so that you will have a means of writing data and programs to cassette without having to rely upon T-BUG. You can use SYSWR as a subroutine within your assembly-language programs and no longer need to load T-BUG each time that you wish to save a program or (especially) output data. Although SYSWR is NOT a relocatable program as given, it CAN be easily relocated by making appropriate changes to the three instructions at addresses 5032H (JP M,*5043H*), 503EH (CALL *5070H*) and 5050H (CALL *5070H*). To determine the proper source operand for 5032H, *add 43H* to the starting address of SYSWR that you intend to use. Likewise, you add 70H to the starting address to determine the starting address of the subroutine DATBLK.

You have now covered what you need to be able to plan, write, and execute your own assembly-language programs on the Model I TRS-80 microcomputer. As you become more proficient and comfortable at writing assembly language programs, you will find Appendix D and the Z-80 instruction tables found in Chapter 2 to be very handy. They will provide you with the information that will be needed most often to do assembly-language programming using the Level II BASIC ROM subroutines. Appendix D summarizes the Level II BASIC ROM subroutines discussed in this book, and the tables in Chapter 2 list the Z-80 instruction set in easy-to-use groupings.

When the challenge has gone from writing assembly language and the same search for new knowledge that prompted you to become interested in assembly-language programming in the first place returns, what do you do? Have you thought about Pascal or FORTH?

APPENDIX A

Recommended Reading List

Barden, Jr., William, *The Z-80 Microcomputer Handbook,* Howard W. Sams & Co,. Inc., Indianapolis IN 46268, 1978.

Barden, Jr., William, *TRS-80 Assembly/Language Programming,* Radio Shack Catalog No. 62-2006, 1979.

Barden, Jr., William, *Z-80 Microcomputer Design Projects,* Howard W. Sams & Co., Inc., Indianapolis, IN 46268, 1980.

Barden, Jr., William, *Programming Techniques for Level II BASIC,* Radio Shack Catalog No. 62-2062, 1980.

Blattner, John and Bryan Mumford, *Inside Level II,* Mumford Micro Systems, Summerland, CA 93067, 1980.

Daly, Raymond, et.al., *The BOOK, Vol. 1: Math,* Insiders Software Consultants, Inc., Springfield, VA 22152, 1980.

Farvour, James, *Microsoft BASIC Decoded & Other Mysteries,* IJG Computer Services, Upland, CA 91786, 1981.

Fuller, Roger, *Supermap+, Fuller Software,* Grand Prairie, TX 75051, 1980.

Howe, Jr., Hubert, *TRS-80 Assembly Language,* Prentice-Hall, Inc., Englewood Cliffs, NJ 07632, 1981.

Inman, Don and Kurt, *Introduction to T-BUG,* dilithium Press, Portland, OR 97116, 1979.

Miller, Alan, *8080/Z80 Assembly Language,* John Wiley & Sons, Inc., New York, NY 10016, 1981.

Mostek, *Z-80 Microcomputer System Micro-Reference Manual,* Mostek Corporation, Carrollton, TX 75006, Publication No. MK78516, 1978.

Mostek, *1979 Microcomputer Data Book,* Mostek Corporation, Carrollton, TX 75006, Publication No. MK7907, pp. 97-137, 1979.

Nichols, Nichols, and Rony, *Z-80 Microprocessor Programming & Interfacing, Books 1 and 2,* Howard W. Sams & Co., Inc., Indianapolis, IN 46268, 1979.

Osborne, Adam, et al., *Z-80 Programming for Logic Design,* McGraw-Hill Book Co., New York, NY 10036, 1979.

Radio Shack, *T-BUG Z-80 Monitor and Debugging Aid,* Catalog No. 26-2001, 1978.

Radio Shack, TRS-80 Microcomputer Technical Reference Handbook, Catalog No. 26-2103, 1978.

Radio Shack, *TRS-80 Model III Operation and BASIC Language Reference Manual,* Catalog No. 26-2112, 1980.

Richardson, Robert, *TRS-80 Disassembled Handbook, Vols. 1, 2, and 3,* Richcraft Engineering Ltd., Chautauqua, NY 14722, 1980.

Spracken, Kathe, *Z-80 and 8080 Assembly-Language Programming,* Hayden Book Co., Inc., Rochelle Park, NJ 07662, 1979.

Titus, Jonathan, *TRS-80 Interfacing,* Book 1, Howard W. Sams & Co., Inc., Indianapolis, IN 46268, 1979.

Titus, Titus, and Larsen, *TRS-80 Interfacing, Book 2,* Howard W. Sams & Co., Inc., Indianapolis, IN 46268, 1980.

Wadsworth, Nat, *Z-80 Instruction Handbook,* Scelbi Computer Consulting, Inc., Elmwood, CT 06110, 1978.

Wilkes, Richard and Hill, *The BOOK, Vol. 2: Input/Output,* Insiders Software Consultants, Inc., Springfield, VA 22152, 1980.

Zaks, Rodnay, *How to Program the Z-80, 2nd Edition,* Sybex, Inc., Berkeley, CA 94710, 1980.

APPENDIX B

Z-80 Op-Codes by Hex

The complete Z-80 Instruction set is given in the following tables. Table B-1 lists the Z-80 op-codes by hex. The remaining tables contain the op-codes for extended (direct) addressing.

Table B-1. Z-80 Op-Codes by Hex

Op-Code	Mnemonic	Op-Code	Mnemonic	Op-Code	Mnemonic
00	NOP	10 e	DJNZ e	20 e	JR NZ,e
01 n	LD BC,n	11 n	LD DE,n	21 n	LD HL,n
02	LD (BC),A	12	LD (DE),A	22 nn	LD (nn),HL
03	INC BC	13	INC DE	23	INC HL
04	INC B	14	INC D	24	INC H
05	DEC B	15	DEC D	25	DEC H
06 n	LD B,n	16 n	LD D,n	26 n	LD H,n
07	RLCA	17	RLA	27	DAA
08	EX AF,AF'	18 e	JR e	28 e	JR Z,e
09	ADD HL,BC	19	ADD HL,DE	29	ADD HL,HL
0A	LD A,(BC)	1A	LD A,(DE)	2A nn	LD HL,(nn)
0B	DEC BC	1B	DEC DE	2B	DEC HL
0C	INC C	1C	INC E	2C	INC L
0D	DEC C	1D	DEC E	2D	DEC L
0E n	LD C,n	1E n	LD E,n	2E n	LD L,n
0F	RRCA	1F	RRA	2F	CPL

Op-Code	Mnemonic	Op-Code	Mnemonic	Op-Code	Mnemonic
30 e	JR NC,e	40	LD B,B	50	LD D,B
31 n	LD SP,n	41	LD B,C	51	LD D,C
32 n	LD (nn),A	42	LD B,D	52	LD D,D
33	INC SP	43	LD B,E	53	LD D,E
34	INC (HL)	44	LD B,H	54	LD D,H
35	DEC (HL)	45	LD B,L	55	LD D,L
36 n	LD (HL),n	46	LD B,(HL)	56	LD D,(HL)
37	SCF	47	LD B,A	57	LD D,A
38 e	JR C,e	48	LD C,B	58	LD E,B
39	ADD HL,SP	49	LD C,C	59	LD E,C
3A nn	LD A,(nn)	4A	LD C,D	5A	LD E,D
3B	DEC SP	4B	LD C,E	5B	LD E,E
3C	INC A	4C	LD C,H	5C	LD E,H
3D	DEC A	4D	LD C,L	5D	LD E,L
3E n	LD A,n	4E	LD C,(HL)	5E	LD E,(HL)
3F	CCF	4F	LD C,A	5F	LD E,A

Op-Code	Mnemonic	Op-Code	Mnemonic	Op-Code	Mnemonic
60	LD H,B	70	LD (HL),B	80	ADD A,B
61	LD H,C	71	LD (HL),C	81	ADD A,C
62	LD H,D	72	LD (HL),D	82	ADD A,D
63	LD H,E	73	LD (HL),E	83	ADD A,E
64	LD H,H	74	LD (HL),H	84	ADD A,H
65	LD H,L	75	LD (HL),L	85	ADD A,L
66	LD H,(HL)	76	HALT	86	ADD A,(HL)
67	LD H,A	77	LD (HL),A	87	ADD A,A
68	LD L,B	78	LD A,B	88	ADC A,B
69	LD L,C	79	LD A,C	89	ADC A,C
6A	LD L,D	7A	LD A,D	8A	ADC A,D
6B	LD L,E	7B	LD A,E	8B	ADC A,E
6C	LD L,H	7C	LD A,H	8C	ADC A,H
6D	LD L,L	7D	LD A,L	8D	ADC A,L
6E	LD L,(HL)	7E	LD A,(HL)	8E	ADC A,(HL)
6F	LD L,A	7F	LD A,A	8F	ADC A,A

Op-Code	Mnemonic	Op-Code	Mnemonic	Op-Code	Mnemonic
90	SUB B	A0	AND B	B0	OR B
91	SUB C	A1	AND C	B1	OR C
92	SUB D	A2	AND D	B2	OR D
93	SUB E	A3	AND E	B3	OR E
94	SUB H	A4	AND H	B4	OR H
95	SUB L	A5	AND L	B5	OR L
96	SUB (HL)	A6	AND (HL)	B6	OR (HL)
97	SUB A	A7	AND A	B7	OR A
98	SBC A,B	A8	XOR B	B8	CP B
99	SBC A,C	A9	XOR C	B9	CP C
9A	SBC A,D	AA	XOR D	BA	CP D
9B	SBC A,E	AB	XOR E	BB	CP E
9C	SBC A,H	AC	XOR H	BC	CP H
9D	SBC A,L	AD	XOR L	BD	CP L
9E	SBC A,(HL)	AE	XOR (HL)	BE	CP (HL)
9F	SBC A,A	AF	XOR A	BF	CP A

Op-Code	Mnemonic	Op-Code	Mnemonic
C0	RET NZ	D0	RET NC
C1	POP BC	D1	POP DE
C2 nn	JP NZ,nn	D2 nn	JP NC,nn
C3 nn	JP nn	D3 n	OUT n,A
C4 nn	CALL NZ,nn	D4 nn	CALL NC,nn
C5	PUSH BC	D5	PUSH DE
C6 n	ADD A,n	D6 n	SUB n
C7	RST 0H	D7	RST 10H
C8	RET Z	D8	RET C
C9	RET	D9	EXX
CA nn	JP Z,nn	DA nn	JP C,nn
CB (SEE TABLE B2)		DB n	IN A,n
CC nn	CALL Z,nn	DC nn	CALL C,nn
CD nn	CALL nn	DD (SEE TABLE B4)	
CE n	ADC A,n	DE n	SBC A,n
CF	RST 8H	DF	RST 18H

Op-Code	Mnemonic	Op-Code	Mnemonic
E0	RET PO	F0	RET P
E1	POP HL	F1	POP AF
E2 nn	JP PO,nn	F2 nn	JP P,nn
E3	EX (SP),HL	F3	DI
E4 nn	CALL PO,nn	F4 nn	CALL P,nn
E5	PUSH HL	F5	PUSH AF
E6 n	AND n	F6 n	OR n
E7	RST 20H	F7	RST 30H
E8	RET PE	F8	RET M
E9	JP (HL)	F9	LD SP,HL
EA nn	JP PE,nn	FA nn	JP M,nn
EB	EX DE,HL	FB	EI
EC nn	CALL PE,nn	FC nn	CALL M,nn
ED (SEE TABLE B3)		FD (SEE TABLE B4)	
EE n	XOR n	FE n	CP n
EF	RST 28H	FF	RST 38H

Table B-2. Extended Instruction Set: CB XX, Where XX Is:

Op-Code	Mnemonic	Op-Code	Mnemonic	Op-Code	Mnemonic	Op-Code	Mnemonic
00	RLC B	10	RL B	20	SLA B	30	—
01	RLC C	11	RL C	21	SLA C	31	—
02	RLC D	12	RL D	22	SLA D	32	—
03	RLC E	13	RL E	23	SLA E	33	—
04	RLC H	14	RL H	24	SLA H	34	—
05	RLC L	15	RL L	25	SLA L	35	—
06	RLC (HL)	16	RL (HL)	26	SLA (HL)	36	—
07	RLC A	17	RL A	27	SLA A	37	—
08	RRC B	18	RR B	28	SRA B	38	SRL B
09	RRC C	19	RR C	29	SRA C	39	SRL C
0A	RRC D	1A	RR D	2A	SRA D	3A	SRL D
0B	RRC E	1B	RR E	2B	SRA E	3B	SRL E
0C	RRC H	1C	RR H	2C	SRA H	3C	SRL H
0D	RRC L	1D	RR L	2D	SRA L	3D	SRL L
0E	RRC (HL)	1E	RR (HL)	2E	SRA (HL)	3E	SRL (HL)
0F	RRC A	1F	RR A	2F	SRA A	3F	SRL A

Op-Code	Mnemonic	Op-Code	Mnemonic	Op-Code	Mnemonic	Op-Code	Mnemonic
40	BIT 0,B	50	BIT 2,B	60	BIT 4,B	70	BIT 6,B
41	BIT 0,C	51	BIT 2,C	61	BIT 4,C	71	BIT 6,C
42	BIT 0,D	52	BIT 2,D	62	BIT 4,D	72	BIT 6,D
42	BIT 0,E	53	BIT 2,E	63	BIT 4,E	73	BIT 6,E
44	BIT 0,H	54	BIT 2,H	64	BIT 4,H	74	BIT 6,H
45	BIT 0,L	55	BIT 2,L	65	BIT 4,L	75	BIT 6,L
46	BIT 0,(HL)	56	BIT 2,(HL)	66	BIT 4,(HL)	76	BIT 6,(HL)
47	BIT 0,A	57	BIT 2,A	67	BIT 4,A	77	BIT 6,A
48	BIT 1,B	58	BIT 3,B	68	BIT 5,B	78	BIT 7,B
49	BIT 1,C	59	BIT 3,C	69	BIT 5,C	79	BIT 7,C
4A	BIT 1,D	5A	BIT 3,D	6A	BIT 5,D	7A	BIT 7,D
4B	BIT 1,E	5B	BIT 3,E	6B	BIT 5,E	7B	BIT 7,E
4C	BIT 1,H	5C	BIT 3,H	6C	BIT 5,H	7C	BIT 7,H
4D	BIT 1,L	5D	BIT 3,L	6D	BIT 5,L	7D	BIT 7,L
4E	BIT 1,(HL)	5E	BIT 3,(HL)	6E	BIT 5,(HL)	7E	BIT 7,(HL)
4F	BIT 1,A	5F	BIT 3,A	6F	BIT 5,A	7F	BIT 7,A

Op-Code	Mnemonic	Op-Code	Mnemonic	Op-Code	Mnemonic	Op-Code	Mnemonic
80	RES 0,B	90	RES 2,B	A0	RES 4,B	B0	RES 6,B
81	RES 0,C	91	RES 2,C	A1	RES 4,C	B1	RES 6,C
82	RES 0,D	92	RES 2,D	A2	RES 4,D	B2	RES 6,D
83	RES 0,E	93	RES 2,E	A3	RES 4,E	B3	RES 6,E
84	RES 0,H	94	RES 2,H	A4	RES 4,H	B4	RES 6,H
85	RES 0,L	95	RES 2,L	A5	RES 4,L	B5	RES 6,L
86	RES 0,(HL)	96	RES 2,(HL)	A6	RES 4,(HL)	B6	RES 6,(HL)
87	RES 0,A	97	RES 2,A	A7	RES 4,A	B7	RES 6,A
88	RES 1,B	98	RES 3,B	A8	RES 5,B	B8	RES 7,B
89	RES 1,C	99	RES 3,C	A9	RES 5,C	B9	RES 7,C
8A	RES 1,D	9A	RES 3,D	AA	RES 5,D	BA	RES 7,D
8B	RES 1,E	9B	RES 3,E	AB	RES 5,E	BB	RES 7,E
8C	RES 1,H	9C	RES 3,H	AC	RES 5,H	BC	RES 7,H
8D	RES 1,L	9D	RES 3,L	AD	RES 5,L	BD	RES 7,L
8E	RES 1,(HL)	9E	RES 3,(HL)	AE	RES 5,(HL)	BE	RES 7,(HL)
8F	RES 1,A	9F	RES 3,A	AF	RES 5,A	BF	RES 7,A

Op-Code	Mnemonic	Op-Code	Mnemonic	Op-Code	Mnemonic	Op-Code	Mnemonic
C0	SET 0,B	D0	SET 2,B	E0	SET 4,B	F0	SET 6,B
C1	SET 0,C	D1	SET 2,C	E1	SET 4,C	F1	SET 6,C
C2	SET 0,D	D2	SET 2,D	E2	SET 4D	F2	SET 6,D
C3	SET 0,E	D3	SET 2,E	E3	SET 4,E	F3	SET 6,E
C4	SET 0,H	D4	SET 2,H	E4	SET 4,H	F4	SET 6,H
C5	SET 0,L	D5	SET 2,L	E5	SET 4,L	F5	SET 6,L
C6	SET 0,(HL)	D6	SET 2,(HL)	E6	SET 4,(HL)	F6	SET 6,(HL)
C7	SET 0,A	D7	SET 2,A	E7	SET 4,A	F7	SET 6,A
C8	SET 1,B	D8	SET 3,B	E8	SET 5,B	F8	SET 7,B
C9	SET 1,C	D9	SET 3,C	E9	SET 5,C	F9	SET 7,C
CA	SET 1,D	DA	SET 3,D	EA	SET 5,D	FA	SET 7,D
CB	SET 1,E	DB	SET 3,E	EB	SET 5,E	FB	SET 7,E
CC	SET 1,H	DC	SET 3,H	EC	SET 5,H	FC	SET 7,H
CD	SET 1,L	DD	SET 3,L	ED	SET 5,L	FD	SET 7,L
CE	SET 1,(HL)	DE	SET 3,(HL)	EE	SET 5,(HL)	FE	SET 7,(HL)
CF	SET 1,A	DF	SET 3,A	EF	SET 5,A	FF	SET 7,A

Table B-3. Extended Instruction Set: ED XX, Where XX Is:

Op-Code	Mnemonic	Op-Code	Mnemonic	Op-Code	Mnemonic
40	IN B,(C)	50	IN D,(C)	60	IN H,(C)
41	OUT (C),B	51	OUT (C),D	61	OUT (C),H
42	SBC HL,BC	52	SBC HL,DE	62	SBC HL,HL
43 nn	LD (nn),BC	53 nn	LD (nn),DE	63	—
44	NEG	54	—	64	—
45	RETN	55	—	65	—
46	IM 0	56	IM 1	66	—
47	LD I,A	57	LD A,I	67	RRD
48	IN C,(C)	58	IN E,(C)	68	IN L,(C)
49	OUT (C),C	59	OUT (C),E	69	OUT (C),L
4A	ADC HL,BC	5A	ADC HL,DE	6A	ADC HL,HL
4B nn	LD BC,(nn)	5B nn	LD DE,(nn)	6B	—
4C	—	5C	—	6C	—
4D	RETI	5D	—	6D	—
4E	—	5E	IM 2	6E	—
4F	—	5F	—	6F	RLD

Op-Code	Mnemonic	Op-Code	Mnemonic	Op-Code	Mnemonic
70	—	A0	LDI	B0	LDIR
71	—	A1	CPI	B1	CPIR
72	S3C HL,SP	A2	INI	B2	INIR
73 nn	LD (nn),SP	A3	OUTI	B3	OTIR
74	—	A4	—	B4	—
75	—	A5	—	B5	—
76	—	A6	—	B6	—
77	—	A7	—	B7	—
78	IN A,(C)	A8	LDD	B8	LDDR
79	OUT (C),A	A9	CPD	B9	CPDR
7A	ADC HL,SP	AA	IND	BA	INDR
7B nn	LD SP,(nn)	AB	OUTD	BB	OTDR
7C	—	AC	—	BC	—
7D	—	AD	—	BD	—
7E	—	AE	—	BE	—
7F	—	AF	—	BF	—

Table B-4. Extended Instruction Set: (For FD, Replace Each IX with IY)
(IX) = DD XX
(IY) = FD XX, Where XX Is:

Op-Code	Mnemonic	Op-Code	Mnemonic	Op-Code	Mnemonic
00	ADD IX,BC	10	—	20	—
01	—	11	—	21 nn	LD IX,nn
02	—	12	—	22 nn	LD (nn),IX
03	—	13	—	23	INC IX
04	—	14	—	24	—
05	—	15	—	25	—
06	—	16	—	26	—
07	—	17	—	27	—
08	—	18	—	28	—
09	ADD IX,BC	19	ADD IX,DE	29	ADD IX,IX
0A	—	1A	—	2A nn	LD IX,(nn)
0B	—	1B	—	2B	DEC IX
0C	—	1C	—	2C	—
0D	—	1D	—	2D	—
0E	—	1E	—	2E	—
0F	—	1F	—	2F	—

Op-Code	Mnemonic	Op-Code	Mnemonic	Op-Code	Mnemonic
30	—	40	—	50	—
31	—	41	—	51	—
32	—	42	—	52	—
33	—	43	—	53	—
34 d	INC (IX+d)	44	—	54	—
35 d	DEC (IX+d)	45	—	55	—
36 d n	LD (IX+d),n	46 d	LD B,(IX+d)	56 d	LD D,(IX+d)
37	—	47	—	57	—
38	—	48	—	58	—
39	ADD IX,SP	49	—	59	—
3A	—	4A	—	5A	—
3B	—	4B	—	5B	—
3C	—	4C	—	5C	—
3D	—	4D	—	5D	—
3E	—	4E d	LD C,(IX+d)	5E d	LD E,(IX+d)
3F	—	4F	—	5F	—

Op-Code	Mnemonic	Op-Code	Mnemonic	Op-Code	Mnemonic
60	—	70 d	LD (IX+d),B	80	—
61	—	71 d	LD (IX+d),C	81	—
62	—	72 d	LD (IX+d),D	82	—
63	—	73 d	LD (IX+d),E	83	—
64	—	74 d	LD (IX+d),H	84	—
65	—	75 d	LD (IX+d),I	85	—
66 d	LD H,(IX+d)	76	—	86 d	ADD A,(IX+d)
67	—	77 d	LD (IX+d),A	87	—
68	—	78	—	88	—
69	—	79	—	89	—
6A	—	7A	—	8A	—
6B	—	7B	—	8B	—
6C	—	7C	—	8C	—
6D	—	7D	—	8D	—
6E d	LD L,(IX+d)	7E d	LD A,(IX+d)	8E d	ADC A,(IX+d)
6F	—	7F	—	8F	—

Op-Code	Mnemonic	Op-Code	Mnemonic	Op-Code	Mnemonic
90	—	A0	—	B0	—
91	—	A1	—	B1	—
92	—	A2	—	B2	—
93	—	A3	—	B3	—
94	—	A4	—	B4	—
95	—	A5	—	B5	—
96 d	SUB (IX+d)	A6 d	AND (IX+d)	B6 d	OR (IX+d)
97	—	A7	—	B7	—
98	—	A8	—	B8	—
99	—	A9	—	B9	—
9A	—	AA	—	BA	—
9B	—	AB	—	BB	—
9C	—	AC	—	BC	—
9D	—	AD	—	BD	—
9E d	SBC A,(IX+d)	AE d	XOR (IX+d)	BE d	CP (IX+d)
9F	—	AF	—	BF	—

Op-Code	Mnemonic	Op-Code	Mnemonic
C0	—	D0	—
C1	—	D1	—
C2	—	D2	—
C3	—	D3	—
C4	—	D4	—
C5	—	D5	—
C6	—	D6	—
C7	—	D7	—
C8	—	D8	—
C9	—	D9	—
CA	—	DA	—
CB	(SEE TABLE B5)	DB	—
CC	—	DC	—
CD	—	DD	—
CE	—	DE	—
CF	—	DF	—

Op-Code	Mnemonic	Op-Code	Mnemonic
E0	—	F0	—
E1	POP IX	F1	—
E2	—	F2	—
E3	EX (SP),IX	F3	—
E4	—	F4	—
E5	PUSH IX	F5	—
E6	—	F6	—
E7	—	F7	—
E8	—	F8	—
E9	JP (IX)	F9	LD SP,IX
EA	—	FA	—
EB	—	FB	—
EC	—	FC	—
ED	—	FD	—
EE	—	FE	—
EF	—	FF	—

Table B-5. DD and FD Double-Extended Instructions: DD CB d XX FD CB d XX, Where XX Is:

Op-Code	Mnemonic	Op-Code	Mnemonic
CB d 06	RLC (IX+d)	CB d 46	BIT 0,(IX+d)
CB d 0E	RRC (IX+d)	CB d 4E	BIT 1,(IX+d)
CB d 16	RL (IX+d)	CB d 56	BIT 2,(IX+d)
CB d 1E	RR (IX+d)	CB d 5E	BIT 3,(IX+d)
CB d 26	SLA (IX+d)	CB d 66	BIT 4,(IX+d)
CB d 2E	SRA (IX+d)	CB d 6E	BIT 5,(IX+d)
CB d 3E	SRL (IX+d)	CB d 76	BIT 6,(IX+d)
		CB d 7E	BIT 7,(IX+d)

Op-Code	Mnemonic	Op-Code	Mnemonic
CB d 86	RES 0,(IX+d)	CB d C6	SET 0,(IX+d)
CB d 8E	RES 1,(IX+d)	CB d CE	SET 1,(IX+d)
CB d 96	RES 2,(IX+d)	CB d D6	SET 2,(IX+d)
CB d 9E	RES 3,(IX+d)	CB d DE	SET 3,(IX+d)
CB d A6	RES 4,(IX+d)	CB d E6	SET 4,(IX+d)
CB d AE	RES 5,(IX+d)	CB d EE	SET 5,(IX+d)
CB d B6	RES 6,(IX+d)	CB d F6	SET 6,(IX+d)
CB d BE	RES 7,(IX+d)	CB d FE	SET 7,(IX+d)

APPENDIX C

Summary of Flag Effects

Instruction	D7 S	Z		H		P/ V	N	D0 C	Comments
ADD A,s; ADC A,s	↕	↕	X	↕	X	V	0	↕	8-bit add or add with carry
SUB,s; SBCA,s; CP,s; NEG	↕	↕	X	↕	X	V	1	↕	8-bit subtract, subtract with carry, compare and negate accumulator
AND s	↕	↕	X	1	X	P	0	0	} Logical operations
OR s; XOR s	↕	↕	X	0	X	P	0	0	
INC s	↕	↕	X	↕	X	V	0	•	8-bit increment
DEC s	↕	↕	X	↕	X	V	1	•	8-bit decrement
ADD DD, SS	•	•	X	X	X	•	0	↕	16-bit add
ADC HL, SS	↕	↕	X	X	X	V	0	↕	16-bit add with carry
SBC HL, SS	↕	↕	X	X	X	V	1	↕	16-bit subtract with carry
RLA; RLCA; RRA; RRCA	•	•	X	0	X	•	0	↕	Rotate accumulator
RL s; RLC s; RR s; RRC s; SLA s; SRA s; SRL s	↕	↕	X	0	X	P	0	↕	Rotate and shift locations
RLD; RRD	↕	↕	X	0	X	P	0	•	Rotate digit left and right
DAA	↕	↕	X	↕	X	P	•	↕	Decimal adjust accumulator
CPL	•	•	X	1	X	•	1	•	Complement accumulator
SCF	•	•	X	0	X	•	0	1	Set carry
CCF	•	•	X	X	X	•	0	↕	Complement carry
IN r, (C)	↕	↕	X	0	X	P	0	•	Input register indirect
INI; IND; OUTI; OUTD	X	↕	X	X	X	X	1	X	} Block input and output
INIR; INDR; OTIR; OTDR	X	1	X	X	X	X	1	X	Z = 0 if B ≠ 0 otherwise Z = 1
LDI; LDD	X	X	X	0	X	↕	0	•	} Block transfer instructions
LDIR; LDDR	X	X	X	0	X	0	0	•	P/V = 1 if BC ≠ 0, otherwise P/V = 0
CPI; CPIR; CPD; CPDR	↕	↕	X	↕	X	↕	1	•	Block search instructions Z = 1 if A = (HL), otherwise Z = 0 P/V = 1 if BC ≠ 0, otherwise P/V = 0
LD A, I; LD A, R	↕	↕	X	0	X	IFF	0	•	The content of the interrupt enable flip-flop (IFF) is copied into the P/V flag
BIT b, s	X	↕	X	1	X	X	0	•	The state of bit b of location s is copied into the Z flag

The following notation is used in this table:

SYMBOL	OPERATION
C	Carry/link flag. C=1 if the operation produced a carry from the MSB of the operand or result.
Z	Zero flag. Z=1 if the result of the operation is zero.
S	Sign flag. S=1 if the MSB of the result is one.
P/V	Parity or overflow flag. Parity (P) and overflow (V) share the same flag. Logical operations affect this flag with the parity of the result while arithmetic operations affect this flag with the overflow of the result. If P/V holds parity, P/V=1 if the result of the operation is even, P/V=0 if result is odd. If P/V holds overflow, P/V=1 if the result of the operation produced an overflow.
H	Half-carry flag. H=1 if the add or subtract operation produced a carry into or borrow from bit 4 of the accumulator.
N	Add/Subtract flag. N=1 if the previous operation was a subtract.
	H and N flags are used in conjunction with the decimal adjust instruction (DAA) to properly correct the result into packed BCD format following addition or subtraction using operands with packed BCD format.
↕	The flag is affected according to the result of the operation.
●	The flag is unchanged by the operation.
0	The flag is reset by the operation.
1	The flag is set by the operation.
X	The flag is a "don't care".
V	P/V flag affected according to the overflow result of the operation.
P	P/V flag affected according to the parity result of the operation.
r	Any one of the CPU registers A, B, C, D, E, H, L.
s	Any 8-bit location for all the addressing modes allowed for the particular instruction.
ss	Any 16-bit location for all the addressing modes allowed for that instruction.
ii	Any one of the two index registers IX or IY.
R	Refresh counter.
n	8-bit value in range <0, 255>
nn	16-bit value in range <0, 65535>

Courtesy Mostek Corp.

APPENDIX D

Summary of Level II BASIC ROM Subroutines

- **FLOATING POINT ACCUMULATORS**

411DH-4124H	FPA1:	4121-4122 = INT (HL)
		4121-4124 = SGL (BCDE)
		411D-4124 = DBL
4127H-412EH	FPA2:	4127-4129 = INT (DE)
		4127-412A = SGL (BCDE)
		4127-412E = DBL
414AH-4151H	FPA3:	SGL-multiplication & DBL-division work area.
40AFH	NTF1:	Number Type Flag for FPA1: 2=INT, 3=STR, 4=SGL, 8=DBL.
40B0H	NTF2:	Number Type Flag for FPA2: 2=INT, 3=STR, 4=SGL, 8=DBL.
0A9DH	SETINT:	Set NTF1 = 2.
0AEFH	SETSGL:	Set NTF1 = 4.
0AECH	SETDBL:	Set NTF1 = 8.
25D9H	RST32:	Test content of FPA1, result in F:
		Z=1=STR
		S=1=INT
		P/V=1=SGL
		C=0=DBL

- **MOVING VARIABLES**

09B1H	HLFPA1:	MEM-to-FPA1 ((HL)-to-FPA1), SGL.
09CBH	FPA1HL:	FPA1-to-MEM (FPA1-to-(HL)), SGL.
09B4H	REGFPA:	REG-to-FPA1 (BCDE-to-FPA1), SGL.
09BFH	FPAREG:	FPA1-to-REG (FPA1-to-BCDE), SGL.
09C2H	HLBCDE:	MEM-to-REG ((HL)-to-BCDE), SGL.
09A4H	FPASTK:	FPA1-to-Stack, SGL.
09D2H	HLTODE:	MEM-to-MEM ((HL)-to-(DE)), DBL, NTF1 = # bytes moved.
09D3H	DETOHL:	MEM-to-MEM ((DE)-to-(HL)), DBL, NTF1 = # bytes moved.
09FCH	SGLDBL:	FPA1-to-FPA2, NTF1 must be 4 or 8.

• KEYBOARD INPUT

Address	Label	Description
002BH	KBSCAN:	Single keyboard scan; ASCII value returned in A.
035BH	KBDSCN:	Same as 002BH, except DE saved.
0049H	GETCHR:	KBSCAN plus "loop" instructions.
1BB3H	QINPUT:	Keyboard input & display "?"; up to 240 characters; typically followed by RST 10.
0E6CH	ASCBIN:	ASCII-to-binary, result in FPA1; NTF1 set to 3.
40A7H-40A8H	BUFPTR:	Location of Input Buffer Pointer.
41E8H-42E8H	INPBUF:	Input Buffer; up to 240 characters.

• CRT VIDEO DISPLAY

Address	Label	Description
0033H	CRTBYT:	Display ASCII value in A at current cursor position.
4020H-4021H	CCRPOS:	Location of Current Cursor Position.
032AH	DSPCHR:	Display ASCII value in A if Device Type Flag = 00H.
40A6H	CCPPTR:	Location of Current Cursor Position pointer.
409CH	DTF:	Device Type Flag, 01H = LP, 00H = CRT, FFH = CASS.
0FBDH	BINASC:	Binary-to-ASCII; FPA1 & NTF1 specify source.
28A7H	OUTLIN:	(HL)-to-CRT, automatically displays and updates cursor position until zero byte encountered; HL points to string location, NTF1 set to 3.
3C00H-3FFFH	VIDMEM:	CRT video memory addresses.
401EH	VIDDRA:	Video Driver address.
0458H	VIDDRR:	Video Driver routine.
01C9H	CLS:	Clear CRT video display & home cursor.
022CH	BLSTAR:	Alternately blink right ** on CRT.

• CASSETTE

Address	Label	Description
0212H	DEFCAS:	Define cassette & turn motor ON; content of A specifies which cassette: A=0=cass#1, A=1=cass#2.
01F8H	CASOFF:	Turn cassette OFF.
0287H	WRLDR:	Write LEADER & SYNC byte.
0296H	RDLDR:	READ LEADER & SYNC byte and display ** when done.
0264H	WRBYTE:	Write a byte of data in A to cassette.
0235H	RDBYTE:	Read a byte of data from cassette into A.
0314H	RDADDR:	Read two consecutive bytes from cassette into HL.

• LINE PRINTER

Address	Label	Description
37E8H	LPADDR:	Line printer memory-map address.
003BH	LPBYTE:	Send content of A to printer via C; update line counter.
4029H	LPCTRA:	LP Line Counter.
039CH	LPNCHR:	Send content of A to printer; update line position.
409BH	LPPOSC:	LP Line Position Counter.
05D1H	LPSTAT:	Test LP status, result in F: Z=1=READY, Z=0=BUSY.

• DATA CONVERSIONS

Address	Label	Description
0A7FH	CINT:	FPA1-to-INT; NTF1 set to 2; "OV" error if >32767.
0AB1H	CSNG:	FPA1-to-SGL; NTF1 set to 4.
0ADBH	CDBL:	FPA1-to-DBL; NTF1 set to 8.
0B26H	FIX:	FPA1-to-truncated FPA1; NTF not changed.
0E6CH	ASCBIN:	ASCII-to binary, automatically to lowest possible number type, DBL if more than 7 digits.
0E65H	ASCDBL:	ASCII-to-DBL;! source pointed to by HL; string must end with colon (:) or zero byte (00H).
1E5AH	ASCINT:	ASCII-to-INT; source pointed to by HL; result in DE; terminates on first non-numeric character.

0FBDH	BINASC:	Binary-to-ASCII (unformatted), result in FPA3 (4130-4151H), terminated with a zero byte.
0FBEH	BINFOR:	Binary-to-ASCII (formatted); PRINT USING format; regs A, B and C specify format: A=00H=no formatting. 81H=Exponential format. 84H=Sign follows number if negative. 88H=Sign precedes number if positive. 90H=Print $ before number. A0H=Print * before number. C0H=Print comma (,) every 3rd place. B=Number of digits to LEFT of decimal point. C=Number of digits to RIGHT of decimal point.

- **ARITHMETIC FUNCTIONS**

+	0BD2H	INTADD:	DE+HL	→HL†	†Automatically defaults to SGL if INT capacity exceeded.
	0716H	SGLADD:	BCDE+FPA1	→FPA1	
	0C77H	DBLADD:	FPA1+FPA2	→FPA1	
−	0BC7H	INTSUB:	DE−HL	→HL†	
	0713H	SGLSUB:	BCDE−FPA1	→FPA1	
	0C70H	DBLSUB:	FPA1−FPA2	→FPA1	
*	0BF2H	INTMUL:	DE*HL	→HL†	
	0847H	SGLMUL:	BCDE*FPA1	→FPA1	
	08A2H	DBLMUL:	FPA1*FPA2	→FPA1	
/	2490H	INTDIV:	DE / HL	→FPA1	
	08A2H	SGLDIV:	BCDE / FPA1	→FPA1	
	0DE5H	DBLDIV:	FPA1 / FPA2	→FPA1	
<=>	0A39H	INTCMP:	DE@HL	in A:	@ = < = +1 = 01H in A
	0A0CH	SGLCMP:	BCDE@FPA1		> = −1 = FFH
	0A78H	DBLCMP:	FPA1@FPA2		= = 0 = 00H

- **MATHEMATIC FUNCTIONS**

TRIG	1547H	SIN(X):	4 in FPA1 → 4 in FPA1		NOTE: operand → result
	1541H	COS(X):	4 in FPA1 → 4 in FPA1		2 = INT
	15A8H	TAN(X):	4 in FPA1 → 4 in FPA1		4 = SGL
	15BDH	ATN(X):	4 in FPA1 → 4 in FPA1		8 = DBL
LOG	0809H	LOG(X):	4 in FPA1 → 4 in FPA1	ln X	
	1439H	EXP(X):	4 in FPA1 → 4 in FPA1	e^X	ALL angles in radians
	1357H	X↑Y:	X in BCDE → 4 in FPA1 Y in FPA1	X^Y	
	13E7H	SQR(X):	4 in FPA1 → 4 in FPA1		
S & M	0977H	ABS(X):	2,4,8 in FPA1 → 2,4,8 in FPA1		
	0326H	FIX(X):	4,8 in FPA1 → 4,8 in FPA1		
	0B37H	INT(X):	4,8 in FPA1 → 2 in FPA1	(>32767 = 4 in FPA1)	
	098AH	SGN(X):	2,4,8 in FPA1 → 2 in FPA1		
RND	01D3H	RANDOM:			
	14CCH	RND(X):	2 in HL → 4 in FPA1 (must be converted to INT)		

- **BASIC PROGRAMS**

40A4H-40A5H Location of starting address of BASIC program.
40F9H-40FAH Location of ending address of BASIC program (after CLOAD).

• MISCELLANEOUS SUBROUTINES

02B2H	SYSTEM:	SYSTEM input entry.
27C9H	FREMEM:	Returns amount of free memory as SGL in FPA1.
213FH	CRTTAB:	Tab cursor to position n on display line; n must be integer 0-3FH in E register; HL register pair must point to address containing zero byte.
0553H	SCROLL:	Scroll CRT video display up one line.
057CH	CRTCLR:	Clear CRT video display from n to end of display; n must be integer 0-3FH; HL must contain 3C00H+n.
1A19H	BASIC2:	Entry point to Level II BASIC.

APPENDIX E

Decimal/Hex Conversion Table

00-0F Hex	Decimal		10-1F Hex	Decimal		20-2F Hex	Decimal		30-3F Hex	Decimal	
00	0	0	10	4096	16	20	8192	32	30	12288	48
01	256	1	11	4352	17	21	8448	33	31	12544	49
02	512	2	12	4608	18	22	8704	34	32	12800	50
03	768	3	13	4864	19	23	8960	35	33	13056	51
04	1024	4	14	5120	20	24	9216	36	34	13312	52
05	1280	5	15	5376	21	25	9472	37	35	13568	53
06	1536	6	16	5632	22	26	9728	38	36	13824	54
07	1792	7	17	5888	23	27	9984	39	37	14080	55
08	2048	8	18	6144	24	28	10240	40	38	14336	56
09	2304	9	19	6400	25	29	10496	41	39	14592	57
0A	2560	10	1A	6656	26	2A	10752	42	3A	14848	58
0B	2816	11	1B	6912	27	2B	11008	43	3B	15104	59
0C	3072	12	1C	7168	28	2C	11264	44	3C	15360	60
0D	3328	13	1D	7424	29	2D	11520	45	3D	15616	61
0E	3584	14	1E	7680	30	2E	11776	46	3E	15872	62
0F	3840	15	1F	7936	31	2F	12032	47	3F	16128	63

40-4F

Hex	Decimal	
40	16384	64
41	16640	65
42	16896	66
43	17152	67
44	17408	68
45	17664	69
46	17920	70
47	18176	71
48	18432	72
49	18688	73
4A	18944	74
4B	19200	75
4C	19456	76
4D	19712	77
4E	19968	78
4F	20224	79

50-5F

Hex	Decimal	
50	20480	80
51	20736	81
52	20992	82
53	21248	83
54	21504	84
55	21760	85
56	22016	86
57	22272	87
58	22528	88
59	22784	89
5A	23040	90
5B	23296	91
5C	23552	92
5D	23808	93
5E	24064	94
5F	24320	95

60-6F

Hex	Decimal	
60	24576	96
61	24832	97
62	25088	98
63	25344	99
64	25600	100
65	25856	101
66	26112	102
67	26368	103
68	26624	104
69	26880	105
6A	27136	106
6B	27392	107
6C	27648	108
6D	27904	109
6E	28160	110
6F	28416	111

70-7F

Hex	Decimal	
70	28672	112
71	28928	113
72	29184	114
73	29440	115
74	29696	116
75	29952	117
76	30208	118
77	30464	119
78	30720	120
79	30976	121
7A	31232	122
7B	31488	123
7C	31744	124
7D	32000	125
7E	32256	126
7F	32512	127

80-8F

Hex	Decimal	
80	32768	128
81	33024	129
82	33280	130
83	33536	131
84	33792	132
85	34048	133
86	34304	134
87	34560	135
88	34816	136
89	35072	137
8A	35328	138
8B	35584	139
8C	35840	140
8D	36096	141
8E	36352	142
8F	36608	143

90-9F

Hex	Decimal	
90	36864	144
91	37120	145
92	37376	146
93	37632	147
94	37888	148
95	38144	149
96	38400	150
97	38656	151
98	38912	152
99	39168	153
9A	39424	154
9B	39680	155
9C	39936	156
9D	40192	157
9E	40448	158
9F	40704	159

A0-AF

Hex	Decimal	
A0	40960	160
A1	41216	161
A2	41472	162
A3	41728	163
A4	41984	164
A5	42240	165
A6	42496	166
A7	42752	167
A8	43008	168
A9	43264	169
AA	43520	170
AB	43776	171
AC	44032	172
AD	44288	173
AE	44544	174
AF	44800	175

B0-BF

Hex	Decimal	
B0	45056	176
B1	45312	177
B2	45568	178
B3	45824	179
B4	46080	180
B5	46336	181
B6	46592	182
B7	46848	183
B8	47104	184
B9	47360	185
BA	47616	186
BB	47872	187
BC	48128	188
BD	48384	189
BE	48640	190
BF	48896	191

C0-CF Hex	Decimal		D0-DF Hex	Decimal		E0-EF Hex	Decimal		F0-FF Hex	Decimal	
C0	49152	192	D0	53248	208	E0	57344	224	F0	61440	240
C1	49408	193	D1	53504	209	E1	57600	225	F1	61696	241
C2	49664	194	D2	53760	210	E2	57856	226	F2	61952	242
C3	49920	195	D3	54016	211	E3	58112	227	F3	62208	243
C4	50176	196	D4	54272	212	E4	58368	228	F4	62464	244
C5	50432	197	D5	54528	213	E5	58624	229	F5	62720	245
C6	50688	198	D6	54784	214	E6	58880	230	F6	62976	246
C7	50944	199	D7	55040	215	E7	59136	231	F7	63232	247
C8	51200	200	D8	55296	216	E8	59392	232	F8	63488	248
C9	51456	201	D9	55552	217	E9	59648	233	F9	63744	249
CA	51712	202	DA	55808	218	EA	59904	234	FA	64000	250
CB	51968	203	DB	56064	219	EB	60160	235	FB	64256	251
CC	52224	204	DC	56320	220	EC	60416	236	FC	64512	252
CD	52480	205	DD	56576	221	ED	60672	237	FD	64768	253
CE	52736	206	DE	56832	222	EE	60928	238	FE	65024	254
CF	52992	207	DF	57088	223	EF	61184	239	FF	65280	255

APPENDIX F

ASCII Table

Control		Numbers Symbols		Upper Case		Lower Case	
0 NUL 00H	16 DLE 10H	32 SP 20H	48 0 30H	64 @ 40H	80 P 50H	96 \ 60H	112 p 70H
1 SOH BREAK 01H	17 DC1 11H	33 ! 21H	49 1 31H	65 A 41H	81 Q 51H	97 a 61H	113 q 71H
2 STX 02H	18 DC2 12H	34 " 22H	50 2 32H	66 B 42H	82 R 52H	98 b 62H	114 r 72H
3 ETX 03H	19 DC3 13H	35 # 23H	51 3 33H	67 C 43H	83 S 53H	99 c 63H	115 s 73H
4 EOT 04H	20 DC4 14H	36 $ 24H	52 4 34H	68 D 44H	84 T 54H	100 d 64H	116 t 74H
5 ENQ 05H	21 NAK 15H	37 % 25H	53 5 35H	69 E 45H	85 U 55H	101 e 65H	117 u 75H
6 ACK 06H	22 SYN 16H	38 & 26H	54 6 36H	70 F 46H	86 V 56H	102 f 66H	118 v 76H
7 BEL	23 ETB 32-CH	39 '	55 7	71 G	87 W	103 g	119 w

08H	18H	28H	38H	48H	58H	68H	x 78H
9 HT 09H	25 EM FORWARD → 19H	41) 29H	57 9 39H	73 I 49H	89 Y 59H	105 i 69H	121 y 79H
10 LF 0AH	26 SUB DOWN ↓ 1AH	42 * 2AH	58 : 3AH	74 J 4AH	90 Z 5AH	106 j 6AH	122 z 7AH
11 VT 0BH	27 ESC UP ↑ 1BH	43 + 2BH	59 ; 3BH	75 K 4BH	91 [5BH	107 k 6BH	123 { ↑ 7BH
12 FF 0CH	28 FS HOME CURSOR 64-CH 1CH	44 , 2CH	60 < 3CH	76 L 4CH	92 \ 5CH	108 l 6CH	124 ¦ ↓ 7CH
13 CR ENTER 0DH	29 GS CURSOR TO BEGINNING OF LINE 1DH	45 – 2DH	61 = 3DH	77 M 4DH	93] 5DH	109 m 6DH	125 } ← 7DH
14 SO CURSOR ON 0EH	30 RS CURSOR TO END OF LINE 1EH	46 . 2EH	62 > 3EH	78 N 4EH	94 ^ 5EH	110 n 6EH	126 ~ → 7EH
15 SI CURSOR OFF 0FH	31 US CLEAR TO END OF SCREEN 1FH	47 / 2FH	63 ? 3FH	79 O 4FH	95 _ CURSOR 5FH	111 o 6FH	127 delete 7FH

FORMAT:

DECIMAL	ASCII CHARACTER	TRS-80
	HEX	

APPENDIX G

Answers to Review Questions

CHAPTER 1

1. High-level, assembly-level, and machine-level programming.
2. Binary; i.e., ONEs and ZEROs.
3. Symbolic.
4. "English-like."
5. Mnemonics . . . labels.
6. (A) Machine-level. (B) High-level.
7. Source code.
8. Source . . . object.
9. Op-codes.
10. Mnemonics and op-codes represent microprocessor instructions; labels and operands represent addresses and data variables.
11. Assembly-language programming consists of selecting a sequence of microprocessor instructions which when executed produce the desired results.
12. Multi-purpose (BASIC) . . . specific (assembly language).
13. 7 clock cycles.
14. 4 microseconds.
15. Speed and memory conservation.

CHAPTER 2

1. CPU or microprocessor.
2. General-purpose, 8-bit, digital.
3. Dynamic.
4. Microprocessor + I/O + memory.
5. Data bus, address bus, and control bus.
6. 256 input and 256 output, or 512 total.
7. Two.

8. A, F, B, C, D, E, H, and L.
9. $2^{16} = 65{,}536 = 64K$ addresses.
10. Accumulator or A register.
11. Indicate status of an ALU operation via the condition of the flags.
12. Indirect addressing . . . the contents of the memory location addressed or pointed to by the register(s) enclosed in parentheses.
13. Indirect addressing.
14. $Z = 1$.
15. Permit conditional or decision-making instructions to exist.
16. C register is the source; B register is the destination: LD B C.
17. 19 1A . . . low-byte first (19H), then the high-byte (1AH).
18. Both use 2's complement numbers to compute their displacement.
19. No 16-bit logical instructions exist.
20. Jump does not save original contents of PC register; call does by pushing it onto the stack before loading a new address into the PC.

CHAPTER 3

1. Respectively, decimal and hex address for T-BUG autostart (entry).
2. Jump back into Level II BASIC.
3. Causes current contents of Z-80's registers to be displayed.
4. ONLY after a B(breakpoint) command has been executed.
5. Access address 482EH using M command, enter new contents; actual transfer occurs upon JUMP or GO command.
6. Autostart (entry) address for T-BUG.
7. >__.
8. #.
9. *?.
10. 3C00H.
11. As ASCII values.
12. On an un-modified Model I TRS-80, a "*" will be displayed, because no lowercase characters can be displayed. On a modified Model I or Model III TRS-80, a "j" will be displayed.
13. "Call" Level II BASIC's CLEAR SCREEN (CLS) subroutine at 01C9H, by using CD C9 01 in your program.
15. Add 30H to the number (30H + 1 = 31H) and store the result at address 3C00H.

CHAPTER 7

1. Memory-mapped I/O is addressed through a *16-bit memory address* and port-addressed I/O is addressed through an *8-bit port.*
2. There are 512 different ports, 256 inputs, and 256 outputs.
3. As many as there are memory addresses, $2^{16} = 65{,}536$.
4. Begins *each* new data block.
5. Cassette #2 (If Expansion/Interface is connected).
6. Subroutine 0235H reads ONE byte from tape into A register; but 0314H reads TWO consecutive bytes from tape into the HL register pair.
7. Nothing, it simply waits until the timing is correct.

8. Handshaking, it tells the computer that the printer is ready for another byte of data.
9. "Lockup" occurs, because the computer will look for the "?" character that does not exist.
10. The HL register pair specifies the *source/destination* memory address, the B register specifies the *number* of bytes (256 maximum) to be input/output, and the C register specifies the *destination/source* port.

Index

D

E

F

G

H

I

J

T

U

V

W

Z

READER SERVICE CARD

To better serve you, the reader, please take a moment to fill out this card, or a copy of it, for us. Not only will you be kept up to date on the Blacksburg Series books, but as an extra bonus, **we will randomly select five cards every month, from all of the cards sent to us during the previous month. The names that are drawn will win, absolutely free, a book from the Blacksburg Continuing Education Series.** Therefore, make sure to indicate your choice in the space provided below. For a complete listing of all the books to choose from, refer to the inside front cover of this book. Please, one card per person. Give everyone a chance.

In order to find out who has won a book in your area, call (703) 953-1861 anytime during the night or weekend. When you do call, an answering machine will let you know the monthly winners. Too good to be true? Just give us a call. Good luck.

If I win, please send me a copy of:

____

I understand that this book will be sent to me absolutely free, if my card is selected.

For our information, how about telling us a little about yourself. We are interested in your occupation, how and where you normally purchase books and the books that you would like to see in the Blacksburg Series. We are also interested in finding authors for the series, so if you have a book idea, write to The Blacksburg Group, Inc., P.O. Box 242, Blacksburg, VA 24060 and ask for an Author Packet. We are also interested in TRS-80, APPLE, OSI and PET BASIC programs.

My occupation is ____________________
I buy books through/from ____________________
Would you buy books through the mail? ____________________
I'd like to see a book about ____________________
Name ____________________
Address ____________________
City ____________________
State ____________________ Zip __________

MAIL TO: BOOKS, BOX 715, BLACKSBURG, VA 24060
!!!!!PLEASE PRINT!!!!!